MURDER ON THE MIDDLE PASSAGE

MURDER ON THE MIDDLE PASSAGE

The Trial of Captain Kimber

—◆—

Nicholas Rogers

THE BOYDELL PRESS

First published 2020
The Boydell Press, Woodbridge

ISBN 978-1-78327-482-6

The Boydell Press is an imprint of Boydell & Brewer Ltd
PO Box 9, Woodbridge, Suffolk IP12 3DF, UK
and of Boydell & Brewer Inc.
668 Mt Hope Avenue, Rochester, NY 14620–2731, USA
website: www.boydellandbrewer.com

A catalogue record of this publication is available
from the British Library

This publication is printed on acid-free paper

For Elaine.

Contents

Illustrations

Acknowledgements

———◆———

This is my first retirement project. The idea for this book emerged when I held a Benjamin Meaker visiting professorship at the University of Bristol in the summer of 2017. Two months in the Bristol archives convinced me there was more to be said about Captain Kimber and his trial for murdering an enslaved African, both in terms of its legal implications and its place in abolition history. I should like to thank the Institute of Advanced Studies at Bristol for sponsoring my visit, and Richard Sheldon and Ron Hutton of Bristol's history department for supporting it.

Friends in the field of eighteenth-century British history helped in various ways. Deborah Valenze put me in touch with Anna Haller, who kindly scanned two critical versions of the trial for me in New York. Madge Dresser, Jim Epstein, Jo Innes and Steve Poole read drafts of the book and gave me excellent feedback on how it read and important advice about how I might improve it. In particular, chapter 5 on Abolition and Revolution would have been the poorer without their input. I presented a talk on the Kimber trial to the Osgoode Society Legal History Seminar in Toronto, and in a more impromptu fashion, at my own retirement conference in Toronto. I thank both audiences for their helpful comments.

I am indebted to the trustees of the British Museum, the National Portrait Gallery, the British Library, the Bristol Museum and Art Gallery and the Library of Congress in Washington DC for permission to use illustrations from their collections. I should also like to thank the staff of the National Archives at Kew, the Huntington Library in San Marino, California, the British Library, the Bristol Archives, and the University of Toronto's Robarts Library for providing me with crucial sources. A lot can be done on the internet, but certainly not everything, especially for a microhistory of this kind.

It has been a pleasure to work with the Boydell Press once again. Michael Middeke and Megan Milan responded quickly and enthusiastically to the proposal and Megan steered me through the appropriate stages of production with the help of Rohais Landon, Nick Bingham and Elizabeth Nichols. I thank them all.

I owe a special debt to my daughter Kate who designed the cover, redrew the map, and photographed the final print for me. It is wonderful to have such a talented graphic artist in the family.

Elaine Stavro lived with this book from start to finish. It has been a special comfort and joy to share it with her, notwithstanding the brutal and disagreeable nature of the subject.

Abbreviations

AE	*Abolition and Emancipation,* an Adam Matthew microform collection
BA	Bristol Archives
BL	British Library
BMAG	Bristol Museum and Art Gallery
BRS	Bristol Record Society
ECSTC	Eighteenth-Century Short Title Catalogue
FFBJ	*Felix Farley's Bristol Journal*
HL	Huntington Library, San Marino, California
JHC	*Journals of the House of Commons*
LMA	London Metropolitan Archives
Lambert	Sheila Lambert, ed., *House of Commons Sessional Papers of the Eighteenth Century,* 175 vols (Wilmington, DE, 1975)
MMM	Merseyside Maritime Museum, Liverpool
SV	slave voyages database, www.slavevoyages.org
TNA	The National Archives, Kew, London
UCL	University College, London
www.ucl.ac.uk/lbs	University College, London, legacies of slave ownership

Preface

The villain of our tale, Captain Kimber, is an accessible yet elusive figure; accessible in that you can find him on the internet within seconds, as the leering master of one of Isaac Cruikshank's memorable prints.[1] There he is, whip in hand, ready to flog a female slave who is suspended from a pulley by only one leg. She is exposed to the gaze of sailors, helpless in her nakedness. The sailors themselves, a little nonplussed by the spectacle, seem reluctant voyeurs, and the one assigned the task of hoisting up the girl has a good mind to let her drop to the deck.

This print, ironically titled *The Abolition of the Slave Trade*, appeared a week after Wilberforce's exposure of the fatal flogging in the House of Commons on 2 April 1792. It is often used as an illustration in books on the transatlantic slave trade,[2] and yet little is known about the incident. Apart from two brief forays into the rhetoric and reception of the event,[3] we know little about it: about Kimber, about his slave ship, about the circumstances of the trial, the verdict, its legal implications and political ramifications. This micro-history aims to recover the story and its place in the first phase of the struggle to abolish the slave trade in Britain. It is a story of atrocity, of legal culpability, of a battle between abolitionists and pro-slave traders about the uses and abuses of evidence. It links the well-known figures of the abolition movement to the sailors who risked their lives and their livelihoods in exposing the brutal conditions of the slave trade and the horrors of the Middle Passage. It situates John Kimber, the captain of a Bristol ship, in the slipstream of local society and politics. It looks closely at the reasons why an abolition movement with such momentum in 1792 stalled in an era of revolutionary politics. In its last chapter it fans out to explain why Captain Kimber was criminally indicted for murdering an African girl during the Middle Passage when slaves were generally regarded as 'cargo'. It compares the punishment of slaves to that of other marginal groups, specifically soldiers and sailors. And it explores the manner in which literary scholars have used the Kimber case as a synecdoche of the trauma of the Middle Passage.

The Kimber trial was central to the abolition debate of the 1790s and deserves its own narrative. It should be more than a footnote or cameo of abolition history.

1. Isaac Cruikshank, *The Abolition of the Slave Trade*, 10 April 1792

1

Ship shape, Bristol fashion

———◆———

It is a dramatic, disconcerting image, so disconcerting that it threatens to overwhelm whatever narrative one might construct around it. A black female is hoisted by one leg, clad only in a striped cotton wrap. She is hoisted up for all to see. The captain, one John Kimber, leers at the viewer, whip in hand. He is looking forward to flogging this girl for her 'virjen modesty', an act that bewilders one of the sailors. 'My Eyes, Jack,' he exclaims, 'our Girles at Wapping are never flogged for their modesty.' To which his crew mate retorts, 'By G—d, that's too bad, if he had taken her to bed with him it would be well enough, Split me, I'm almost sick of this Black Business.'[1] The seamen take the sexual commerce of the ship for granted. The girl is fair game. She is a slave, a commodity. Has she refused the captain's advances? Is he into humiliation and bondage? Is this what turns him on? The seaman hoisting up the slave, dressed like the others in his portside best, is unhappy with the assignment. He has a 'good mind to let her go', although quite why is unclear. As for the three female slaves in the background, two of whom are chained by the hands, it is impossible to know how they are reacting to the spectacle. They are huddled together, whispering, involuntary witnesses to the torture.

Isaac Cruikshank produced this print on 10 April 1792, a week after the flogging and the subsequent death of the slave was disclosed by William Wilberforce in the House of Commons.[2] Wilberforce described the event in a sentimental mode, horrified that a fifteen-year-old girl should be subjected to such depravity. He didn't sexualise the punishment like Cruikshank, although the details he offered of the girl's suspension, by wrists and ankles, could lend itself to the artist's interpretation. Cruikshank certainly played with the ambiguity. The spectacle is both horrific and salacious. It could touch evangelical and louche taste in its degeneracy.

———◇———

I'll begin by noting that this story is in many respects a Bristol one, for the ship Kimber commanded was the *Recovery*, a 189-ton vessel registered in the port and owned by four Bristol merchants. When the *Recovery* sailed from Kingroad at the mouth of the Avon, Bristol was still a very important Atlantic port. With its population of roughly 60,000 inhabitants in 1790, Bristol served as an important service and distribution centre for the economy of the South-West and Wales, as well as trading with Europe, Ireland, Africa and the Americas. The bustle of trade and industry was very evident at its quays. They featured dense clusters of mastheads, 'the oddest and most surprising sight imaginable',[3] Alexander Pope once remarked; and further back cone-shaped sugar-houses, so full of smoke that on calm days the spires of the churches were obscured. Foundries and ropewalks were also scattered along the rivers Avon and Frome, adding to the smell and pollution of the city. Edward Clarke, who visited Bristol around the time the *Recovery* sailed, believed Bristol captured 'the throng and bustle of the metropolis'. Its 'busy faces, crowded streets, carts, coaches, smoke and noise, represent so exactly the hurry and confusion of London.'[4]

Bristol contributed and profited considerably from the expansion of empire in the eighteenth century and the emergence of Britain as a world power. The volume of overseas trade from Bristol grew from 15,500 tons in 1709, to 19,000 by 1751, to 43,000 by 1792. After the American War, it centred increasingly on the West Indies. This was its dynamic sector, and Bristol played an important role in

2. Nicholas Pocock, *Wapping and Gib Corner, Bristol harbour c 1790*

its national expansion. British exports to the West Indies rose six-fold in the first 75 years of the eighteenth century; in 1790, at £1.69 million, they constituted 11.8 per cent of Britain's total exports. Imports from the Caribbean were worth even more, some £4.045 million or 21.9 per cent of the total, the principal products being sugar, cotton, coffee and indigo.[5] The annual value of shipping and cargoes in the Bristolian trade to the West Indies was between £400,000 and 500,000 in 1790; the value of the imports was almost £775,000, over 19 per cent of the British total.

Sugar, cotton, coffee and indigo were slave-grown products, and Bristolians invested in slavery. Over the course of the long eighteenth century, from 1698 to 1807, Bristolians financed over 2,000 slaving ventures, about 19 per cent of the total from British ports. In the early years of that century, Bristol had been the leading slave port, taking command of the trade once the monopoly of the Royal African Company officially ended in 1698, and holding it until roughly 1745, when Liverpool came to the fore. In the years before 1730 Bristol had emerged as the most efficient carrier of slaves, more efficient than London or Nantes.[6] Between 1730 and 1745, Bristol was routinely the single most important port in the African trade, fitting out an average of 36 ventures per year and responsible for about 40 per cent of all British voyages to the Guinea coast. Liverpool consistently outpaced Bristol after 1745, but the West Country port's interest in the trade remained substantial, despite the fact its share of the total traffic fell from 43 per cent in the 1740s to 17 per cent in the 1760s. Indeed, the number of slaves exported from Africa to the Americas in Bristol ships actually doubled between 1750 and 1770 from around 20,000 per year to 40,000, a reflection of the overall expansion of the British trade and Bristol's ability to hold on to markets in Virginia, Antigua and St Kitts and to compete well in newly acquired islands like Dominica.[7] Although Bristol's elite moved away from direct involvement in the slave trade as the century wore on, the rise of new merchants responsible for both funding and fitting out vessels ensured that Bristol's participation in the trade would continue beyond the American War of Independence, albeit on a diminished scale. Bristol's merchants fitted out over 500 voyages in the period 1770–1807, when the trade was finally abolished. Within that time frame, there was a significant boost in ventures in the years prior to the French war of 1793. This was the moment, in the Indian summer of Bristol slaving, when Kimber captained the *Recovery* to purchase Africans in New Calabar, or Elem Kalabari, in the Lower Niger Delta.

The 1790s were also the period when the abolitionists were mobilising the public for a big push on parliament. From small beginnings in 1787, the abolition movement had begun to win sympathy beyond its original core of adherents among the Quakers and Dissenting sects. Between February and May 1788, over 100 petitions dealing with the slave trade were presented to parliament, many from the industrial

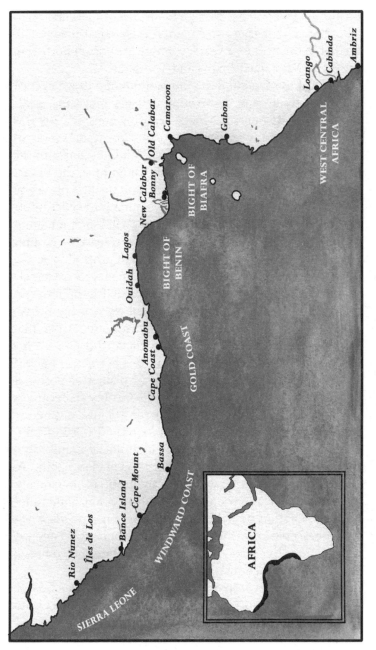

3. Map of West African slave ports

north. Over 10,000 people signed the one from Manchester. Abolitionists managed to broaden their constituency still further in the next four years, winning greater support from the South West, East Anglia and Scotland.

Crucial to sustaining the momentum of outrage against the slave trade was discovering reliable first-hand testimony about its operations and exposing abuses.[8] This was acknowledged early on, even before the slave traders thought it necessary to defend their position. Within months of the formation of the London Abolition Committee, the Reverend Thomas Clarkson was dispatched on the first of several fact-finding tours, scouring the slave ports for insider information about the trade and collecting vital data on ships' crews from the muster rolls.[9] These research ventures became imperative to the cause. Among other things, the slave trade lobby had argued that its seamen were extremely useful to the navy because they developed immunities to tropical diseases, a factor which boded well for the British naval presence in the Caribbean. It consistently carped that the well-meaning, evangelical Christians who pressed for abolition knew nothing about the trade's business, or about the labour supply necessary to cultivate plantation produce. What really went on in Africa and the Caribbean became a vitally contested subject, fought over in submissions before the Committee on Trade and Plantations of the Privy Council in 1788 and 1789. This was the first official inquiry into the slave trade and one in which Clarkson made a significant contribution, mustering witnesses and testifying personally. Tactically the Trade tried to slow down, if not blunt, abolitionist agitation by belittling its testimony, crowding out its witnesses before the Privy Council, and subsequently dragging out the subsequent inquiries before the House of Commons and the Lords.[10]

Clarkson's first stop on his fact-finding tour was Bristol. He arrived there in late June 1787 and made contact with key Quakers who had been actively distributing anti-slavery tracts at their Men's Monthly Meeting. These included Harry Gandy, a Bristol conveyancer[11] or property lawyer who had sailed on two slaving voyages in his youth. He introduced Clarkson to seven other Quaker families including the Harfords, who were well placed in civic politics. It was largely through their auspices and the help of Josiah Tucker, the Dean of Gloucester and Rector of St Stephen's, that Clarkson managed to get access to the muster rolls in Merchants' Hall, where he was able to gather information about the mortality of crews on slaving voyages and corroborate stories he had gathered about their mistreatment.

Clarkson found that while Bristolians were willing to talk openly about the trade, there was an ingrained fatalism about the prospects for change. 'There were facts … in everybody's mouth concerning it,' he remarked, 'and everybody seemed to execrate it, though no-one thought of its abolition.'[12] In part this may reflect the hegemonic character of Bristol's elite, which so dominated the city's trade and social landscape and continued to promote its slaving interests. Even within the local Quaker community, which had largely accommodated itself to slavery, it was only on the margins that the old reservations about slavery lingered.[13] Even so, Clarkson made some progress by virtue of events on the river. In July 1787, the *Brothers*, a 190-ton vessel owned by James Jones, bound for the Gold Coast and Grenada, was having great trouble raising a crew because of the alleged ill-treatment of sailors by Captain Jeffrey Howlett on the previous voyage. This abuse resulted in an extraordinary toll of deaths and the brutal punishment of a black seaman named John Dean, who, for a trifling offence, had been pinned to the deck and had hot pitch poured into incisions in his back. With the help of Truman Harford, Clarkson gained access to the muster roll of the ship, which confirmed the appalling mortality of the crew. Eighty per cent of the original members died on the voyage, forcing Howlett to enter extra men in Africa and St Vincent.[14] John Dean is listed very inconspicuously at

the very end of the roll; there is no evidence of his mistreatment in this formal entry. But Clarkson later corroborated
the tale of ill treatment with his surviving shipmates and
his landlord, who saw the scars on his back. John Dean had
unfortunately left for London, but not before he had secured
an attorney to sue Captain Howlett for damages. This didn't
deter the owners of the *Brothers*, the James Jones syndicate,
of employing Howlett on another voyage to the Gold Coast,
although 1787 was to prove his last.[15]

The *Brothers* voyage was exactly the kind of episode
by which Clarkson wanted to expose the iniquities of the
slave trade. He searched for more, 'agonized to think that
this trade should last another day'.[16] Henry Sulgar of the
Moravians steered Clarkson towards a notorious confron-
tation in the Bight of Biafra in which Bristol traders played
off two rival trading groups in Old Calabar in 1767 and
colluded in the massacre of one of them. Bristolians learnt
about this massacre because two Efik princes from Old
Town, Calabar, survived to tell the tale. They were part of
the trading party that had been betrayed by Captain James
Bivins [sometimes Bevan] of the Bristol ship, the *Duke of
York*. Bivins was part of a consortium of British slavers that
had initially offered to mediate between the two factions in
Old Calabar, only to betray the Old Town group to the New
or Duke Town faction.[17] The two princes, Old Town leaders, were captured and sent into slavery in St Vincent and
subsequently Virginia. They were lucky; their brother was
beheaded and many in their party slaughtered. Fortunately,
the brothers, Little Ephraim and Ancona Robin John, were
part of a select group of African leaders who were educated
in English and attuned to British ways, and they managed
to parley their way to freedom. Captain Terrence O'Neil of
the *Greyhound* had offered to buy them in Virginia when
their master died there and return them to Old Calabar via
Bristol. In reality he conspired to make a handsome profit
of these two hybridised, upper class Africans, who would

make excellent go-betweens in the slave trade. When the Robin Johns arrived in Bristol in 1774, they were imprisoned on the *Brickdale*, owned by the merchant and future MP Henry Lippincott and bound for Virginia. Thomas Jones, a Bristol merchant who knew and traded with their father, tried to secure their release by a writ of habeas corpus from Lord Mansfield, only to find Lippincott unwilling to hand them over without compensation. They were locked up for failing to pay their 'transportation costs' from Virginia, but even so, Little Ephraim Robin John and his brother wrote to Lord Mansfield in London and secured an audience with him. While the chief judge of King's Bench pondered their status – were they slaves or freemen illegally enslaved? – the case was settled to their advantage outside of court, with Captain Bivins agreeing to pay compensation for the princes' capture and enslavement. This settlement was recognised by King's Bench.[18]

The case raised, however, all sorts of issues that abolitionists might exploit: the anarchy of coastal trading; the lack of honour among British slavers; the legal status of African traders torn from the Guinea coast and enslaved. Clarkson was able to mobilise this case to the abolitionists' advantage, not only because he located a seaman in the British navy at Portsmouth who had been present at the massacre while crewing for the *Canterbury*, but because it resonated in public memory. While in Bristol, the Robin Johns had befriended John Wesley and converted to Methodism. Their story and that of Captain William Floyd, the chief mate of another Bristol boat involved in the massacre of 1767, eventually found their way into the *Arminian Magazine* and subsequently into the newspapers.[19] By the time Wilberforce mentioned the episode in April 1792, this time in conjunction with an attack upon New Calabar in which Captain Kimber was implicated, it was fairly common knowledge.

Clarkson pressed on with his inquiries at a feverish rate, working to the point of exhaustion. He boarded two sloops in the Avon that had carried slaves to the Caribbean and were now up for private sale as pleasure yachts. In one, 70 slaves were to be stowed in a hold 31 feet long, 10 feet wide and at best 5 feet high: about 22 cubic feet per slave, a confinement that astonished and enraged him. He also searched for suitable witnesses to present before the Commons select committee. Old captains gave him a wide berth and shunned him in the street. Some of them possibly had a small stake in a slave voyage or received a pension from the Society of Merchant Venturers, the elite group of Bristol merchants who ran Bristol docks and dominated the city's political institutions. They did not want to live out their days rocking the boat.

Clarkson had great difficulty getting captains to testify, but he had better success with other officers in the trade. Through the Quaker Walter Chandler, Clarkson won an audience with a surgeon named Gardiner who had entered the slave trade out of 'necessity'. Gardiner damned the trade but would not give evidence because his practice was too precarious to withstand the ostracism of merchant patrons, a predicament Clarkson encountered on more than one occasion.[20] Eventually he found a medical man who was willing to testify, one James Arnold, who had served two voyages as a surgeon's mate and one as a surgeon on the *Little Pearl* in 1786. He had several stories to tell: how the chief mate of the *Pearl* so mistreated the slaves that they nearly killed him in the hold; how two slaves who broke from their chains were scalded with hot fat, and then shot or beaten to death; how one boy slave was starved to death.[21] Arnold was about to go on a fourth voyage in the trade; he needed the money, he said, but he was prepared to swear an affidavit on the murder of the boy before George Daubeny, one of the few magistrates seemingly sympathetic to abolition. He also promised to keep a journal of his next voyage for the abolition committee, as did Gardiner; discreetly, because owners of slave ships resented the exposure.

Clarkson found the task of collecting evidence about the slave trade a daunting one. He secured the help of the landlord of the *Seven Stars*, located between St Thomas and Redcliff Street in Temple Parish. The landlord tipped him off about how seamen were inveigled into crewing for a slaver because of the debts they racked up in the disreputable pubs of Marsh Street. Clarkson visited these cheap lodgings and alehouses and was pretty appalled by the revelry he encountered there. 'Music, dancing, rioting, drunkenness and profane swearing were kept up from night to night.'[22] He found that people would talk but they wouldn't testify. As soon as he brought out pen and paper, they tightened up. Through his inquiries, Clarkson learnt that the captain of the *Alfred*, Edward Robe, had been a complete tyrant to his crew. Eleven of the original 27 of the crew died, and Robe so maltreated the surgeon's mate that he had tried to commit suicide by jumping over the side. Clarkson tracked down the mate, only to find him delirious and wrapped in bandages from his wounds. He needed some corroborative evidence if the captain was to be taken to court, and it seemed he might get it from Thomas Dixon, whose lip was split wide open by Captain Robe during a minor altercation off Lundy. Dixon had a grudge against Robe, but neither he nor Matthew Pike, who was flogged for insubordination and had his arm broken at Black River, Jamaica, seemed to Clarkson to be entirely reliable witnesses; and while further inquiries disclosed that Robe had beaten another seaman to death, one Charles Osler [Horseler], hard evidence eluded him.[23] Mr Daniel Burgess, the deputy town clerk, advised Clarkson that such suits took time to assemble and wound their way slowly through court, and that if he wanted to prosecute errant captains successfully, he had to support sailors on shore to assure their accessibility. Otherwise there was a good chance they would be at sea when they were needed.

Clarkson pursued only one case during his Bristol visit, and he came to it by way of another slave-trade surgeon,

Alexander Falconbridge, who was to serve the abolitionists in several capacities, including rehabilitating the early settlers in Sierra Leone, a colony established in 1787 to pursue peaceful trade with Africa and to provide a livelihood for ex-slaves destitute in London, and subsequently black loyalists from Nova Scotia.[24] Falconbridge had been on four voyages to Africa in the period 1780–1787, three under Captain James Fraser and one with James McTaggart of the *Alexander*. In his testimony to the Privy Council and in his own published account, Falconbridge offered invaluable information about the workings of the slave trade and its hazards. On the *Alexander*, he had witnessed the brutal treatment of the crew, who were persistently beaten by McTaggart and his chief mate, to a point where one black boy jumped through the gun-ports in an effort to drown or be eaten by sharks, declaring 'it would be much better for him to be killed at once than to be daily treated with so much cruelty.'[25] Falconbridge observed the disconsolate nature of slaves, who pined for their homeland and sometimes preferred death to survival. He also remarked on the resistance of others, noting that slaves sometimes went on hunger strike and occasionally rose up to free themselves from captivity and take over the boat. Barricades had to be built to prevent this eventuality. Long periods on the coast, he concluded, were bad for slaves and the crews, making them more susceptible to disease. Even small contingencies could create havoc on a crowded slave-ship, for the grounding of the *Alexander* on a sandbar at Bonny for six to seven days in pouring rain, with the airports shut, resulted in an outbreak of dysentery that swept through the hold, killing over a hundred slaves, some 28 per cent of those on board.

Falconbridge offered other observations that were to be helpful to the abolitionists in their exposure of the trade. He corroborated what Clarkson had asserted in his first essay on the slave trade: that many slaves were kidnapped from villages; they were not simply criminal outcasts, debtors or prisoners of war. This was a point disputed by the Trade, who wanted to suggest that transporting Africans across the ocean was little different from sending British convicts to Botany Bay. Indeed, given the anarchy and human sacrifice that proliferated in Africa, it alleged that captives were transported for their own benefit! Falconbridge also confirmed that families were sometimes separated when slaves were sold in scrambles, that is, in quick, informal auctions from the holds, repudiating arguments from planters that family solidarities were respected. In his capacity as a student at the Bristol Royal Infirmary, he observed that the hard treatment of seamen on slave voyages irreparably destroyed their health. Many who left the ships in the West Indies were in a 'weak, ulcerated and otherwise diseased state' to a point that they perished there, and those that came to the Infirmary suffered chronic illnesses, and sometimes blindness. Unlike other seamen who visited the Infirmary as outpatients, their illnesses were not the result of industrial accidents so much as rough treatment in tropical climes.

Falconbridge's disclosures pushed Clarkson to investigate the hazards of the slave trade for himself. He learnt that three seamen of the *Thomas* had just returned to Bristol after eight months in a 'crippled and deplorable state'. One had caught a fever on the African coast and lost his eyesight; the second was lame with badly ulcerated legs; and the third was a 'mere spectre'.[26] The seamen complained they had been badly treated by the captain, William Vicars, but they directed Clarkson's attention to the alleged murder of William Lines by the chief mate. Clarkson contacted Lines' mother in Bristol to learn more about the matter. She told him these three seamen were not witnesses to the crime; what they knew about Lines' death was hearsay, but she could provide him with the names of four others who were there. Clarkson examined them individually and became convinced of the murder. He urged Lines' mother to appear before the magistrates with her witnesses and demand an inquiry. Two or three slave-merchants were on the bench when Lines' mother lodged her complaint, and they gave Clarkson 'savage looks'. They muttered that 'scandalous reports' had been spread around the city concerning the slave trade, 'but sailors were not used worse in Guineamen than in other vessels'.[27] Clarkson was not intimidated by these comments and told the mayor if he did not do his duty he was 'amenable to a higher court'. On that note the examinations proceeded, with Captain Vicars responding to the allegation of murder by claiming Lines had died of dysentery. Despite this claim, the chief mate was taken up and sent to gaol to await trial by an admiralty court. As it happened the trial came on faster than anticipated. Harry Gandy alerted Clarkson to this fact as the abolitionist campaigner was returning from a tour of Liverpool and the Midlands. By the time the trial was called, two of the witnesses had been bribed by slave merchants and sent off to sea. The other two were working in the Welsh coalmines. Clarkson attempted to locate them, braving high winds at the Aust ferry, and he eventually discovered them near Neath. Despite this, he failed to get them to the London Old Bailey in time for the trial, with the result that the case against the chief mate was dismissed for lack of evidence.[28]

Thomas Clarkson was troubled by the result. He feared it might impugn his own reputation and prejudice his interviews with other potential supporters. Yet Clarkson's willingness to take on the slaving interest seems to have galvanised support for the cause, at least among seamen. Sailors came forward with tales of abuse seeking redress: from the *Alexander*, the *Fly*, the *Little Pearl* and the *Wasp*, a vessel that would feature in the Kimber affair. A few Anglican divines rallied to Clarkson, including John Camplin, a minor canon of the Cathedral and the vicar of St Nicholas, who often officiated at Bristol's church court. He protected Clarkson from mercantile calumny. Along with some prominent Dissenting ministers like Caleb Evans, Quaker merchants and liberal professionals like Dr Edward Long Fox, who would play an important role in the inquiry into the Bristol Bridge riots of 1793,[29] Camplin became part of the local committee who would organise the abolition petition to parliament in 1788.

Still, there were abolitionists who thought Clarkson's confrontational approach would needlessly alienate powerful interests. In Liverpool, Clarkson took down evidence at the *King's Arms*, where he encountered men who tried to provoke him, toasting 'Success to the Trade' and musing that 'they had heard of a person turned mad, who had conceived the thought of destroying Liverpool and all its glory'.[30] Dr James Currie thought Clarkson ruffled too many feathers among the Liverpudlian traders, many of who were 'men of general fair character'.[31] He was also troubled by Clarkson's preference for the testimony of the 'lowest class of seaman' rather than middling citizens and merchants, a comment that betrayed his belief that footloose, mobile seamen were inherently untrustworthy.

Clarkson was not interested in such stereotypes. He clearly believed that the men who directly experienced the squalor and brutality of the trade were the ones who could best expose it. The difficulty, as Clarkson clearly saw, was co-ordinating their testimony and ensuring it reached trial or public notice. The issue had plagued him in the Lines case, and it would do again with Peter Green, a seaman who was flogged to death when his ship, the *Vulture*, lay in the Bonny River. Alexander Falconbridge had picked up the story when he visited Bonny as a ship surgeon, and Clarkson pursued the inquiry when the *Vulture* was docked in Liverpool. Members of the crew confirmed Green's death, and one George Ormond, who had been discharged from the ship in Jamaica, filled in the details of what happened. According to Ormond, Peter Green was the steward of the ship who quarrelled with Rodney, the ship's black female translator, over access to the wine store of the captain, James

Brown.[32] Rodney claimed Ormond attacked her and the captain took her side. With the help of two mates he flogged Green for two and a half hours, stripping the flesh off his back with a cat o' nine tails and beating out his brains with a knotted rope. This was done in the presence of the captain of the *Alfred*, the notorious Edward Robe. The severity of the punishment is so extreme one can reasonably speculate that sexual proprietorship was involved. Green had allegedly assaulted the captain's girl. Green was barely alive when the officers cut him down and lowered him into an open boat. He was found dead the following morning by seaman Paul Berry and buried at Bonny Point.[33]

Ormond's account tallied with what Clarkson had learnt from Falconbridge and from the muster rolls, but he wanted some further corroboration. So Ormond arranged for Clarkson to eavesdrop on another seaman's testimony in a local pub. Clarkson recognised the voice of one of the men he had interviewed aboard the *Vulture*; he heard him say: 'If Peter Green was not murdered, no man ever was.'[34] With that evidence in hand, Clarkson decided to prosecute the three officers, although he was warned that 'many in the town were already incensed against' him, and there was a chance he 'should be torn to pieces'.[35] He received threatening letters; he hesitated to leave his lodgings in Williamson Square without the company of Falconbridge, who was armed for emergencies. On one occasion, eight or nine men, including one of Green's murderers, accosted Clarkson on the pier. Clarkson feared the gang would throw him off the pier head into the turbulent Mersey, but he luckily escaped with only 'blows' and 'imprecations'.[36] Ormond, meanwhile, was sent to London out of harm's way, as was another witness to the crime, Patrick Murray. Clarkson had their depositions taken at Bow Street before Sir Sampson Wright, who then requested the Liverpool magistrates to detain Captain James Brown and the two mates for further inquiries. But the officers had already sailed to Africa on the *Vulture*,[37] and

Clarkson could not afford to maintain his prosecuting witnesses until the ship returned a year or so later. As he noted
with some irritation, 'expenses of this kind' were beyond
those sanctioned by the London Abolition Committee, and
although he raised a little money by private subscription, it
was not enough.[38] Consequently, he launched a civil suit to
get some out-of-court settlement for Ormond and Murray.
In this he succeeded, only to find they were entrapped in
confidentiality agreements that prevented them taking any
further action at law against the captain and crew.[39] Clarkson came close to indicting the officers of the *Vulture* for
murder, but in the end, he was outmanoeuvred. In Liverpool
as in Bristol, he faced hostility and legal obstruction.

Clarkson was well aware he was operating 'behind
enemy lines' in these two Atlantic ports, but in Bristol at
least, the full power of the Trade did not show itself until
the spring of 1789, when its supporters launched petitions to
parliament against abolition. No less than six petitions were
tabled: from the African merchants, the West India planters and merchants, the shipbuilders, the merchants in the
Newfoundland cod trade, and the Bristol corporation.[40] The
committee set up to defend the trade included two current
and one future MPs, and a familiar cluster of Bristol bank-
ers and merchants, including representatives of the Bright,
Cave, Pinney, Protheroe and Vaughan families. This was not
a sectional protest at all, but one that mobilised the ramified
social and economic links between slavery and the Atlantic economy. It featured ship-owners, ship builders, former
masters, investors in the trade, plantation owners, import
and export merchants and manufacturers whose livelihood
depended on slave labour in the Caribbean. As the list of
Bristolians compensated for slavery would reveal, the town
elite benefited materially from slave assets even when they
were not directly involved in the trade. A significant number
were embedded in civic life, as aldermen, common coun-
cillors, members of the Merchant Venturers or officers of

the Colston societies. A noticeable minority intermarried to shore up their assets, consolidate their businesses and reduce the risk of bankruptcy.[41]

The Bristol committee contended that the abolition of the slave trade would undermine the labour supply so necessary to the plantation economy. It would ruin trades that provisioned the islands, trades that provided manufacturing wares to Africa and a huge range of luxury consumer goods to the Caribbean and serviced the shipping industry. The Trade also argued that it was a valuable nursery for the navy, particularly so because it provided men-of-war with seamen who could handle the pathogens of Africa and the Caribbean. Seamen new to the tropics often went down like ninepins, as did the vast majority of the soldiers who were sent to St Domingue in 1791 to try to contain the revolt there. On a national note, the petitioners stressed the repercussions of abandoning a trade from which France, Spain and other European powers might profit. Not to mention the local fallout. Forty per cent of all Bristolian trades were linked in some way to the traffic in slaves and disrupting that traffic spelt doom. The fact that the slave trade constituted about 12 per cent of Bristol's overseas commerce was not the issue. It was the synergy of slave-based economies that mattered.

The local power of these men can be illustrated by their civic affiliations. On the African and West Indian committees, at least five merchants served as mayor in their lifetime, seven as aldermen, seven as high officials among the Merchants Venturers, usually Master but sometimes as Warden. Two, Edward Brice and George Daubeny, were Governors of the Corporation of the Poor in the years 1788–92, and a further two, Philip Protheroe and John Fisher Weare, had recently been Presidents of the Anchor Society, one of the societies that distributed charity to the city's poorer inhabitants. These were men who could place or ostracise people. A seaman with a family, or with strong Bristolian roots, might

hesitate to flout their will. Many people were disgruntled
with the slave trade, but they were reluctant to speak out.
This explains why the abolitionists had such a hard time
finding witnesses to the brutalities of the trade and why it
was difficult to secure convictions against vicious captains.
It was an issue that would haunt the case of Captain Kimber.

Despite the strength and seeming durability of their
local affiliations, some of the traders were troubled by the
abolitionist agitation, which was gathering momentum.
When Clarkson visited Bristol, the local newspapers were
extremely coy about publishing material favourable to abolition. Abolitionist voices were more likely to be heard in
the pulpit or on the stage, a liminal space for parody, satire
and subversion. John Wesley preached a sermon against the
slave trade in March 1787 when lightning disrupted the congregation, an occurrence the aging preacher interpreted as
a supernatural event, as if Satan feared his kingdom would
be delivered up.[42] Six months later Bristolians were alerted
to a production of George Colman's *Inkle and Yarico* at London's Haymarket theatre, and the following year the play
was staged in Bristol itself. *Inkle and Yarico* is based on the
story of a slave-catcher, Thomas Inkle and his Amerindian
lover, Yarico, who travel to Barbados from America. It surfaced as a folk tale in Richard Ligon's *History of Barbados*,
was popularised by Richard Steele in the *Spectator* and was
subsequently adapted as a play by George Colman in 1755.
Although by no means hostile to the plantation regime
and set in an idyllic Caribbean island, it did revolve around
Inkle's betrayal and selling of Yarico into slavery in order to
marry the governor's daughter. In other words, amid the
songs and gaiety of a comic opera, it could remind audiences
of the ambitions that drove the slave trade at the expense of
human ties of friendship, love and family.[43]

Little of this surfaced in the local press. When Clarkson
wanted to publicise his essay on the slave trade, he had to
go to Bath to visit Richard Cruttwell of the *Bath Chronicle*.

He found little interest in criticising the slave trade in Bristol, despite the fact it fielded five newspapers. Yet by 1788 times were changing. The abolitionists organised a petition to parliament, donated money to the central committee in London, and in the late spring Bonner and Middleton's *Bristol Journal* published Falconbridge's *Account of the Slave Trade* in serial form. John Pinney, who owned a plantation in Nevis, was troubled by these developments. He wrote to his agent in a state of panic.

> The present alarming crisis, respecting the abolition of
> the African Trade, operated so strongly on my mind that
> I am resolved to contract with the utmost expedition all
> my concerns in the West Indies. Never again, upon my
> own private account, will I enter into a new engagemen-
> tin that part of the world.[44]

His partner, James Tobin, who had returned from Nevis in 1784 and had engaged the Reverend James Ramsay[45] in an extended debate over the nature of planter society in the Caribbean, was more sanguine. In April 1788, he thought 'much of the spirit of enthusiasm seems to have evaporated and the minds of the generality of the nation are much opened by the ample discussion this question has undergone'.[46] This was an unduly complacent view, because the Privy Council inquiry into the slave trade was about to begin, and within two months Sir William Dolben had successfully passed a motion to regulate the trade. His bill restricted the number of slaves that were packed into the vessels and offered bonuses to surgeons to minimise the deaths of the Middle Passage.[47]

The Bristol slaving interest opposed this bill; Matthew Brickdale, the Tory MP for the City, seconded a motion to postpone the debate, believing it required 'cool consideration' not hasty judgments as the parliamentary session closed.[48] Yet ultimately the Bristol traders swam with the tide. Regulation might be a way of fending off abolition. This was James Tobin's view. He admitted that the slave

trade was a form of 'unnatural traffic' that was morally inde-
fensible. It could only be defended on political grounds, in
terms of national policy. In reality, this was the thrust of
the Trade's earlier rationale, and it was reinforced when the
Bristol elite chose John Baker Holroyd, Lord Sheffield, as
one of its MPs in 1790.

In the run-up to the general election of 1790, Holroyd
published a pamphlet on the abolition issue.[49] A regular
writer on economic matters, he believed Wilberforce and
company were guilty of a false humanity, whipping up a
'popular phrenzy' of sentiment for enslaved Africans that
recklessly ignored matters of national policy and empire.
Immediate abolition would place intolerable burdens on
existing slaves in the Caribbean. It would likely be evaded
because planters and English capital would transfer the
importation of Africans to foreign vessels. If imposed, abolition would deprive 'our commercial edifice of one of its
main supports', for slave-based labour and products were
imbricated into the fabric of Britain's overseas trade and
empire. A more reasonable, humane and practical solution was to regulate the trade, to refine the regulations of
the Dolben Act regarding the traffic in slaves and, through
import duties and baby bonuses, gradually wean the West
Indies from its reliance on imported African labour to a
more self-sustaining plantation system. This would benefit
everyone: planters, the public, the slaves themselves, who
through disciplined labour could become 'civilised' contrib-
utors to Britain's capitalist empire. Holroyd thought far too
much sentimentality had been invested in the freedom of
the slaves. Many Africans were already enslaved on their
continent: 'their lives as much at the mercy of their unciv-
ilised owners as those of their cattle'. They would remain
slaves, 'but slaves to civilised masters'.[50] In fact, they would
enjoy better standards of living and security than the English
peasantry who were 'not free from the painful uncertainty,
the solicitous inquietude of providing for a family'. Indeed,

in practice the English poor had to trade off much of their
independence for deference, for a studded subservience to
'parish officers and considerable men in the neighbourhood'.
In discounting the allure of freedom for Africans, Holroyd
offered some frank observations on the plight of Britain's
working poor. The poor laws did not insulate the male
plebeian from the 'necessity of constant labour to provide
what he deems bare necessities for his family'.[51] Toil and
precarity were the hallmarks of eighteenth-century wage
labourers. On these matters, [freedom aside, of course] Holroyd thought slaves were better off.

Not all of Holroyd's ideas would have been sweetly
received by Bristol's commercial elite. His 'cargo' formula
was slightly more liberal than the Dolben Act; three slaves to
every two tons rather than five slaves every three. He would
have banned small slavers under 100 tons and set a limit of
250–300 slaves for any ship, whatever its size.[52] Yet Holroyd
offered a robust defence of Britain's economy of which slave-
based labour was an integral part; he cast the abolitionists
as irresponsible, zealous wreckers, blind to every social and
economic consequence of an immediate ban. He also suggested they were hypocritical in their claim that abolition
was their only goal. Their present object was 'an indirect
and future abolition of slavery and a direct and immediate
abolition of the slave trade', he declared.[53] This reinforced the
notion that abolitionists were really intent on an assault on
colonial property for which Britain had already paid a high
price in the American War of Independence. Their ultimate
goal raised the possibility that planters, and by implication
every mortgagee, annuitant and bondholder who had an
interest in the plantation system, would not necessarily be
compensated. It also raised the spectre of race war if expectations of freedom could not be quickly met.

Holroyd fitted the bill for Bristol. He removed the anxiety that the Atlantic port would be swept away in a tsunami
of abolition. There were men in parliament, he assured his

readers, who could confront the duo of Wilberforce and Pitt on the folly of immediate abolition, especially in the Lords. He was elected for Bristol without much of a contest. The party caucuses in the city shored up the two seats, much to the dismay of a few disgruntled Tories and independent freemen who were shut out of a vote; not for the first time in popular memory, either, for Bristol seemed to relapse into arranged elections every time the two clubs overspent, which they had seriously done in 1784.

Not a word about abolition was heard at the hustings.[54] The only slavery voiced there came from frustrated freemen, angry that Bristol's bigwigs had arrogated to themselves the right of choosing the MPs. They had turned the freemen into 'slaves', a familiar turn of phrase in the libertarian lexicon. Despite this rhetorical flourish the so-called Society of Independent Freemen proved to be a top-down caucus promising to deliver thousands of votes for the right price, or so David Lewis claimed.[55] Money mattered, and festive fare. As the *General Evening Post* tersely remarked, Bristol was 'settled without contest'.[56] This was not exactly the case, for the outsider David Lewis vied for some electoral space with the party nominees, Holroyd the Whig and the Tory Henry Somerset, the Marquis of Worcester. Lewis quickly conceded defeat, securing only twelve votes on the opening day of the election. With a dash of noblesse oblige, the victors offered him a moment of recognition for his efforts. According to the *Whitehall Evening Post*, the three men were 'drawn by the populace in open carriages in triumph through the streets of the city, where great riot and confusion prevail'.[57]

Bristol voters seem to have devoted a lot of energy breaking heads, and no doubt lamenting the loss of their freedom, which they had purportedly traded for a few gallons of beer.[58] Despite the emergence of an abolition committee and the promotion of a petition against the slave trade the year before, abolition was not voiced at the hustings. It scarcely surfaced in Bristol the following year, when Wilberforce offered another motion for abolition. In April 1791 local newspapers dutifully reported the debate but little else. The breaking news concerned France, where King Louis had been forced back to the Tuileries palace for fear he would join a counterrevolution with this brothers and kin who were flocking at the border. Amid the panic and rumour generated in Paris, the liberal Marquis de Lafayette was losing his grip on the increasingly volatile situation.[59] The importance of the international situation was registered in the British parliament as well, where a division over a possible alliance with Prussia drew the attention of 75 per cent of the members. The corresponding vote on abolition drew only 45 per cent.[60]

In Bristol much attention had centred on sport in the run-up to the 1791 abolition debate. The day before the motion, Bristolians had an opportunity to watch a prize fight between Hales and Snailman at Marshfield Downs, where the combatants slugged it out for one hour and forty minutes before the latter capitulated. For the genteel set, there was a benefit concert for the Magdalen Hospital at the Oratorio, St James, although it was unseemly disrupted by a mob throwing stones at the windows.[61] The next day the crowd would have more to celebrate: the defeat of the abolition bill. Bristol celebrated with a cannonade, fireworks, a bonfire and a half-holiday. The elite, at least, had spoken. Writing to the pro-abolition *Bath Chronicle*, 'Mentor' was outraged to witness slave traders congratulating each other outside the Exchange. He hoped their 'indecent joy' would be suitably admonished before the 'tribunal of God'.[62] For some slave captains, and by extension slave merchants, other tribunals beckoned.

2

The accusation

On 2 April 1792, William Wilberforce, the parliamentary voice of abolition, exposed Captain Kimber in the House of Commons, singling him out for the vicious, atrocious and fatal whipping of an enslaved African girl. What he actually said is not altogether clear. This may surprise some readers, but the fact is there was no official record of the Commons debates in the eighteenth century. Reporters had only been admitted to the Commons' chamber in St Stephen's Chapel in 1771, and a designated reporters' gallery did not appear until 1835. Before that, writers jostled with one another in the overhead galleries to hear speech after speech, and in the absence of shorthand committed much to memory.[1] In earlier decades, when the publication of debates was illegal, clever scribes like Dr Samuel Johnson fabricated much of the debate. In the *Gentleman's Magazine*, he wove a tapestry of speeches delivered to the 'Senate of Lilliput' that was predominantly Johnsonian; what the good doctor imagined or remembered people saying. Reporters strove for more authenticity in the 1790s; they had to cater to a curious public who expected a reasonably accurate account of what went on in the House in the middle pages of the tri-weeklies. Yet speeches had to be edited to accommodate the allotted space for parliamentary debate in four-page productions, and they were printed off quickly for an attentive market. In the 2 April debate on abolition, William Woodfall of the *Diary* admitted he produced his version with 'more than common haste', offering only a 'sketch' of its character.[2] He didn't need to apologise. Transforming a debate of twelve hours into four columns of newsprint entailed savage edit-ing.[3] Disagreement of what should be emphasised and what was said was inevitable, especially if the House was noisy and crowded. In fact, since the House could only sit 427 of the 558 British MPs, people stood in the gangways during an especially important discussion and muffled the voices of the major speakers.

Captain Kimber's name surfaced on two occasions in Wilberforce's long speech to the Commons on the evening of 2 April. These were centre stage in most accounts. In stressing the brutal and anarchic conditions in which the slave trade was conducted, Wilberforce trotted out some incidents that had unfolded during the Commons inquiry, including a disputed transaction over the price of slaves that escalated into a series of reprisals in which a captain was taken hostage for attacking an African trader's lodging at night and killing his wife and three children. Wilberforce used this story to show how dishonourable the traffic in slaves could be. He argued that if there was any credit in coastal trading, it often emanated from the African deal-ers, the so-called 'savages', rather than the slave captains. Wilberforce then offered a fresh example of the anarchy of the coast, an episode that had not been part of the two inquiries into the slave trade by the Privy Council and the House of Commons. This concerned a confederacy of Bris-tol and Liverpool ships that had bombarded New Calabar in August 1791 in an attempt to drive down the price of slaves. In the three-hour cannonade from the 66 guns of six vessels, some 20–50 people had been killed before the traders capitulated. Wilberforce described this attack as 'a mockery of all feeling, and an insult on the opinions of Parliament and the sense of the people'.[4] He claimed that captains had already been 'furnished with fresh berths, as if they raised their estimation by this instance of their activ-ity'.[5] The episode reaffirmed the notion that the trade was

4. Karl Anton Hickel, *The House of Commons, 1793–4*

inherently violent, conducted, as John Newton had written earlier, in a semi-state of war.[6] There was no honour to slave trading; it frequently degenerated into violent scenarios in which hostage taking and reprisals were commonplace and taken for granted. When called upon to name the captains involved in this outrage, Wilberforce at first hesitated to do so, or perhaps he affected to do so to heighten the drama of the disclosure. But he eventually cited Captain Kimber of the *Recovery* as one of the three Bristol-based commanders involved in the bombardment. No newspaper recovered all the names amid the clamour of the House, at least no newspaper recovered them all accurately, and Kimber's name was sometimes lost in the uproar. William Woodfall managed to catch his name, but the reporter from *Lloyd's Evening Post* declared that 'the general indignation and murmur that was expressed prevented the hearing of any more than the ships Thomas, Betsy, Wasp and Recovery, and the names of Captain Thomas and Captain Reid.' Likewise, the *Evening Mail* reported that Wilberforce 'named several of the Captains, but we only heard the name of one distinctly, which was that of Captain Phillips, who commanded the Thomas of Bristol.'[7] Had Kimber's been associated with this outrage alone, he might have been buried in historical obscurity.

But Kimber's name cropped up again, in an equally controversial context. Having expatiated on the violence of coastal trading, Wilberforce turned his attention to the Middle Passage, the voyage from Africa to the slave ports and landings of the Americas. The mortality of slaves during this transatlantic journey had been slowly declining over the course of the eighteenth century. Historians calculate that it stood at 15 per cent before 1750 and 11 or 12 per cent in the two decades before 1790.[8] This was hardly a cause for congratulation, and indeed the public was probably unaware of the decline. Abolitionists tended to emphasise the accumulating toll of fatalities from slave ship to plantation 'seasoning'. This was devastatingly high – some put the cumulative toll at fifty per cent – for one had to take into account the decrepit state of slaves upon embarkation in the Caribbean and the toil of plantation work, not just deaths during the Middle Passage.[9] The British public's imagination was in any case seared by the dramatic scandal of the *Zong*, a slave ship that overshot its destination in Jamaica and had to address the possibility of death by starvation or dehydration as she tacked back to the island.[10] The captain, a former surgeon named Luke Collingwood, decided to throw 132 sick slaves overboard to shore up supplies of water. The owners of the ship, the Liverpool syndicate of William Gregson and company, then had the audacity to claim the insurance on the dead slaves. When the insurers discovered that the water supply had been relieved by rainfall, they countered with a law suit, and in 1783, the grisly details of the case spilled into the public domain; slowly, because insurance cases rarely attracted a large audience.

The Zong atrocity might never have come to light had it not been for the endeavours of the black abolitionist, Olaudah Equiano, who alerted Granville Sharp, the future chair of the London Abolition Committee, to the importance of the case. Quobna Ottobah Cugoano, a freed slave working as a servant to the miniature artist, Richard Cosway, and his wife Maria, thought the incident conclusively confirmed the slavers' insensitivity to human suffering. They considered the captive Africans 'as their own property,' he remarked, 'that they may do with as they please, in life or death; or that the taking away of the life of a black man is no more account than taking away the life of a beast'. Along with Equiano and other 'persons of colour', he commended Sir William Dolben for refusing to 'suffer the rights of humanity to be confounded with ordinary commodities, and passed from hand to hand, as an article of trade'.[11]

Dolben was an architect of a 1788 act regulating the slave trade, which was annually renewed until 1795 and after a hiatus of two years, finally made permanent in 1799.[12] The act restricted the number of slaves by a ship's tonnage; three slaves to every 5 tons for vessels under 201 tons, and one slave per ton thereafter. It also insisted that qualified surgeons be present on slave ships and offered bounties to captains and surgeons if they delivered slaves to the Caribbean islands at 'respectable' rates of mortality, that is, under two or three per cent. The act was partly a policing operation, for ships had to register their tonnage and report the number of deaths incurred at the coast and during the Middle Passage. It tightened up the regulations governing the insurance of slaves and demanded that ships were commanded by men with previous experience in the trade; a reaction, no doubt, to the Zong atrocity, brought on by a surgeon with no experience of running a ship. Abolitionists were divided about the merits of the Dolben Act. Olaudah Equiano supported it, believing it a stepping-stone to the abolition of the slave trade.[13] Wilberforce and Clarkson were more sceptical. Clarkson felt enforcement would be a problem in a world of legal pluralism and profit-minded cruelty. Anticipating the problems that confronted the prosecution of Kimber, he felt that ordinary sailors lacked the time and financial resources to prosecute brutalities in the slave trade.[14] Wilberforce felt Dolben's regulatory machinery was a double-edged sword. It offered temporary relief in a despicable trade, but it also let slavers off the hook. They could hide behind 'regulation', and contend, along with colonial amendments to slave codes in the West Indies, that abolition was unnecessary.

Wilberforce's 1792 speech asserted the imperative of immediate abolition and strove to show why 'regulation' was not working. To the anarchy of coastal trading Wilberforce added the murderous cruelties of the Middle Passage. Drawing on the testimony of surgeon Isaac Wilson before the Commons committee, Wilberforce produced figures that suggested that the mortality on the Middle Passage was actually as high as 28 per cent.[15] He also reiterated Wilson's observation that slaves were so overcome with grief on leaving their homelands that they sometimes considered suicide, with the result that some captains erected safety nets around their ships. No 'benevolent' treatment below deck would erase that feeling. He then produced a story about the cruelties of the Middle Passage, which he said, surpassed his imagination, one that he felt compelled to relate without paying deference to the 'squeamishness' of the House. 'If it be too bad for me to recite, or for you to hear, it was not thought too bad for one of those unhappy creatures to suffer, of whom I have the honour to be the Advocate.'[16] He then told the story of a fifteen-year-old girl who was hoisted to the mizzen stay of a slave ship and whipped until she collapsed in convulsions and died. She was a dejected young girl who tried to hide her nakedness and refused to stand up straight, burying her head in her hands. The House cried for the name of the perpetrator. 'Name, name the monster', resounded from all parts of the House'. And so Wilberforce did. He was Captain Kimber of the *Recovery*.

Reporters differed on the cause of the girl's plight. To some she was simply trying to hide her modesty, which Kimber thwarted by exposing her to the whole crew with devilish delight, suspending her by one leg after another as well as by her wrists. In this account, which was favoured by the London Abolition Committee because they ordered copies to be distributed to the public, the young woman was 'overcome by shame and sensibility'.[17] In another report, which found its way into Cobbett's *Parliamentary History* and Symonds' *Senator*, the youngster had a 'disorder ... incident to women of that age', or 'incident to her sex'; a phrase which historians have usually interpreted to mean she was menstruating, perhaps for the first time given the age of menarche in the eighteenth century.[18] This narrative was reproduced in the *Bath Journal*. It was also found in the *Evening Mail*, although circumspectly, because the newspaper would only report the facts as far 'as decency would permit'.[19] In a third version of the story, the girl had 'contracted' a disorder that 'rendered her a peculiar object of commiseration', a discreet reference to a malady that was subsequently disclosed as gonorrhoea.[20] This version appeared in a pamphlet recalling the whole debate in some detail. It was probably introduced in the light of further revelations about the Kimber case that surfaced at Bow Street a week later. Wilberforce might have been told of this infection, but I very much doubt that he had wanted to speculate on the sexual commerce of the ship and the rape of this particular fifteen-year-old girl. It was enough that she had been tortured and humiliated in all her nakedness. This silence or ellipsis was commonplace in slave-trade stories before parliament, which tiptoed around the issue of sexual assault.[21] In Thomas Clarkson's printed version of the depositions he had solicited from seamen, there is not one reference to rape or sexual assault.[22] Frank admissions of sexual predation did surface in personal accounts of the trade, although they sometimes replicated the false gaiety of a brothel-monger. Captain James Barbot of the *Albion* frigate, for example, claimed sexual restraint on board ship was difficult because the 'young sprightly maidens, full of jollity and good humor, afforded an abundance of recreation'. Recreation for sailors perhaps, hardly for their captives. Surgeons like Alexander Falconbridge were more candid. He noted that 'the common sailors are allowed to have intercourse with such of the black women whose consent they can procure' while the officers were 'permitted to indulge their passions among them at pleasure, and are sometimes guilty of such brutal excesses as disgrace human nature'.[23] John Newton believed the sexual 'licence' was 'almost unlimited' as long as the captain agreed. 'When the Women and Girls are taken on board a ship, naked, trembling, terrified, perhaps almost exhausted with cold, fatigue and hunger, they are often exposed to the wanton rudeness of white Savages'. Thomas Cooper also thought the sexual encounters were rampant, although in terms that today would raise eyebrows. He talked of the 'unrestrained commerce of the sailors with the female slaves during the voyage, circumstances which are like the small dust in the balance of iniquity'.[24]

Wilberforce was reluctant to delve into the rape of the girl; perhaps his sources, Thomas Dowling and Stephen Devereux, kept this from him. A devout Christian, he was more comfortable clothing her in the rhetoric of sensibility, and it is within this trope that she was most often reported. 'The innocent simplicity and modesty of this poor creature, reflecting upon the inhuman indecency with which she had been exposed, affected her so much, that she fell into convulsions, and in three days she died!'[25] In this version it is the shame of the exposure rather than the beating that destroyed the African girl. It reads a bit like a bad sentimental novel, although when the torture is added – the hoisting, the ropes, the enforced postures, the lashing of the naked body, the 'cruel inventions' of the captain who turned her this way and that – the disclosure could certainly be read in a titillating way. It was by Isaac Cruikshank in his memorable print, but it was not the narrative Wilberforce intended. Wilberforce's rhetoric was not wanton, even if the public-school boys in the House, familiar with Mistress Birch'em or Mr Thwack'um, got off on it. As one Etonian mused two months later, 'The birch, they aver, is the true tree of knowledge./ Rever'd by each *school*, and remember'd at *college*.'[26] This was not Wilberforce's perspective. He had helped pioneer the Proclamation Society, a new campaign to reform the nation's manners and clamp down on gambling dens and disorderly houses. He was a straight evangelical, or evangelically straight, not an MP who frequented the bagnios of Drury Lane or indulged in flagellation fantasies. His version of the story was a form of sentimental realism, an appeal to his audience across time and space to imagine and shudder at the brutality and perversity of the punishment.[27]

Between the sentimental and the pornographic the story took off. Coupled with the bombardment of New Calabar the story raced through Britain and across the Irish Sea. It could be found in Edinburgh, Newcastle, Leeds, Whitehaven, Manchester, Derby, Birmingham, Bath, Bristol and Lewes among other towns, and also across the Irish Sea in Dublin and Cork. It also surfaced in America, where the *Salem Gazette* claimed the 'tale required no comment', for its 'universal abhorrence needed but to be related'.[28] That judgment was premature, because the story was not simply about the inventive cruelties of a sadistic captain; it also addressed the fact that his crime, like others, had thus far eluded legal censure.

This was the basic question that emerged from these atrocities. What was one to do with the anarchy of the Guinea trade? Cannonading New Calabar made waves in public, but it was not easily judiciable.[29] Abolitionists made the case that slaves were often taken in unjust wars, in effect kidnapped, and that transatlantic slavery was essentially piratical. A 1750 act regulating the African trade did address the possibility of taking Africans by 'fraud, force, or violence or by any other indirect practice' but did so in terms of civil suits, for which the offender would be fined £100 for every infraction.[30] Essentially the act was concerned with slave captains cheating one another, not with the lives of Africans. There were no international courts of justice, and no treaties with African kingdoms about peacetime reprisals. Britain had no jurisdiction over African codes of law and could not easily impose penalties upon the 'violators of human liberty' on the African coast. In 1724 lawyers pondered the case of a Guinea captain who beat two of his sailors to death because they had broken a jar of palm oil while trading for slaves. The incident occurred ten leagues upriver from the estuary of the Calabar. Was this judiciable, because neither beatings nor deaths occurred on the 'high seas'? Eventually the government decided it was, although the relevant acts from the Tudor era privileged murder on the high seas.[31]

Indicting Kimber for the murder of a slave was thus theoretically judiciable, in that the death occurred on a British ship in the high seas, *provided* the legal personality of the slave and the common-law liability of killing one could be established. It had in a number of cases before 1792: two involved black cabin boys, which will be addressed later in the book; and a third occurred on board an actual slave ship. In a case before the Court of Admiralty in 1759, Captain William Lugen [or Lugan] of the Bristol snow *Hope* was indicted for ordering a live four-month-old baby be thrown overboard. The surgeon on board testified that the baby's mother had died of dysentery and that her offspring was ailing fast. Together with commendations from the Bristol corporation as to Lugen's character, this was enough to acquit him. The jury regarded the act as a mercy killing, necessary to prevent the spread of dysentery on the ship.

5. Calendar of Prisoners, March 1759, William Lugen,
'for the Murder of a female Negro Child'.

According to the very brief account in the *Proceedings*
Captain Lugen did not even bother to offer a defence.[32] The
judgment in fact reflected the very ambiguous nature of
slaves, human but also chattel, or cargo.

It is not clear Granville Sharp knew of this case when
he tried to indict Captain Collingwood and his crew for
murdering the slaves who were tossed into the ocean from
the *Zong*.[33] In this instance, Sharp came to know of the case
when it entered the courts as an insurance dispute, and he
had to face Lord Chief Mansfield's notorious reluctance
to move beyond the narrow construction of the issue. He
didn't get any sympathy from the Lords of the Admiralty,
who declined to address his arguments for making it a
common law suit for murder. Captains believed they were
immune from such accusations as long as it could be shown
that the killing of slaves was necessary to the health and
safety of the ship. In practice this left slave captains with
wide discretionary powers.

Kimber probably thought he could get away with a
murderous whipping under the Dolben Act as long as the
protocols of surveillance were observed: that is to say, as
long as the death was registered in some innocuous way
in the Caribbean. Many were. The surgeons' returns published in the Commons inquiry gave little away about a real
circumstances of a slave's death: most specified 'dysentery',
the 'flux', 'bilious fever'; Joseph Buckham, the surgeon of

the *James*, even wrote 'lethargy', 'sulkiness' and 'suddenly' against some of the deaths in his voyage of 1788–9.[34] Entries demanded by the Dolben Act left plenty of scope for malicious death, assuming, of course, that captains and surgeons saw eye to eye.

Besides, Captain Kimber didn't think he was involved in a human rights violation, if indeed he knew what that was. The incident scarcely scratched his 'Christian' conscience, for after this exposé he resumed life in the slave trade with gusto. Whipping slaves who would not eat or dance to improve their saleability was what slave captains and their officers did, as well as ramming funnels down their throats in order to force-feed them.[35] To Wilberforce, Kimber's arrogance underscored the fact that regulation would not work as long as the minds and manners of the captains were corroded by slavery, its brutality and racism. This issue was not new. Thomas Clarkson had addressed it directly in a pamphlet three years earlier, one that the London Abolition Committee had circulated widely. Clarkson believed that the regulation of a trade as nefarious as slave trafficking was ultimately self-defeating and fundamentally perpetrated the evil it was designed to contain. 'Regulation implies *continuance* upon stated terms,' he argued, 'and *so long as the trade continues*, so long will there be temptations, ... so long will the needy and avaricious embrace them, to obtain the persons of men.'[36]

In accusing Kimber of murdering a slave, Wilberforce clearly hoped to check the customary abuses of the Trade and seize a moral high ground that potentially carried a legal punch. If murdering a slave were indictable and could be made to stick, then a great many slave captains would be on the hook. In broader political terms, the problem for abolitionists was how they could persuade the legislature to abandon a trade that was morally objectionable yet still economically significant and viable in what was an increasingly tense international situation. How, as Edmund Burke put it, they could reconcile the humanity of abolition with its impact upon imperial policy?[37] Although abolitionists had made great headway among the public at large in terms of social justice and humanitarianism, winning over the legislature was proving a more difficult problem.

Wilberforce, who was born in Hull and inherited a mercantile fortune in the Baltic trade, represented the largest county in Britain: Yorkshire, with 20,000 voters. When he presented his motion to investigate the slave trade in April 1792, he had 519 petitions supporting him. This was an unprecedented mobilisation, involving about 400,000 signatories. Many flowed from the leading industrial towns and cities, the slave ports of Liverpool and Bristol excluded.[38] Although civic bodies promoted a third of all petitions, relatively few were narrowly elitist, perhaps a sixth. Roughly half hailed from the 'inhabitants' of cities and small market towns. They included small Scottish townships and places like Great Marlow in Buckinghamshire, which had 3,238 inhabitants in 652 families in 1801; and Crediton in Devon, a market town with a declining serge industry, that had just over 4,900 residents. They also featured Bishop's Stortford, a small malting town on the road from London to Colchester, with a population of just over 2,300. To Wilberforce, this 'provoco ad populum',[39] this mobilising of the people, gave his crusade great moral force. The people had spoken, although Wilberforce would have preferred to hear the 'educated and religious classes' who convened at orderly county meetings, not the urban artisan and worker.[40] Indeed, early on Wilberforce advised the London Abolition Committee to rein in the provincial ones for fear that 'forced or unnecessary Associations' would alienate the legislature.[41]

Predictably the Trade condemned the broad support of the petitioning campaign as rabble-rousing. It gave vent to the 'raving enthusiasm' and abolitionist ranting that misled ignorant people. The *Bath Journal* asserted that many signed out of deference to their landlords and civic leaders, 'for we in the Country know nothing of what is doing in India

and Africa, and those parts, but what we are told'.[42] Others
emphasised the scouring of the slums for signatures. At least
two asserted the petitioners solicited 'people of the lowest
class, sought for in Brothels, Jails, and Tippling Houses'.[43]

Of course, petitioning on a large scale did not arise from
nowhere. This particular campaign, which in geographical
scope surpassed those of the radical associations of the 1770s
and 1780s when they agitated for peace with America or
parliamentary reform, relied on a network of abolition committees, co-ordinated by the Old Jewry group in London.
These committees were largely composed of urban, middling nonconformists or Methodists, some of whom had
been actively promoting abolition for several years. This
was especially true of the Quakers, who had strong links to
their brethren in Philadelphia and to prominent abolitionists there like Anthony Benezet. From these hubs, the social
penetration of abolitionism ran deep, deeper than in the
first abolition campaign of 1788. 'There was never perhaps
a season when so much virtuous feeling pervaded all ranks',
reminisced Thomas Clarkson. 'Great pains were taken by
interested persons in many places to prevent public meetings.
But no efforts could avail.'[44] In some parts of Britain as many
as a quarter or third of adult males signed up; in Manchester, where the signatories exceeded 20,000, the proportion
climbed to nearly 50 per cent.[45] And although women were
generally excluded from signing petitions, there were places
like Belford in Northumberland where they were allowed 'to
shew their abhorrence of this abominable trade'.[46]

The heavy participation of Manchester and outlying
towns like Blackburn and Oldham registered the fact that
the abolition campaign had strong moral foundations. It
pulsated with the politics of affect. The rapidly growing
Lancashire towns were dependent upon British slave-grown
cotton for their products; supporting the trade was in their
economic interest. Yet this does not seem to have deterred
workers from supporting abolitionism under the banner of

'humanity, religion and justice', a familiar triad in the language of the petitions. A Shropshire association declared that abolition was indispensably required by 'Religion, Morality' and 'every principle of sound policy'.[47] Slavery was morally reprehensible, whatever casuists could conjure up from the Old Testament about its biblical legitimacy. It was a blight on national honour that money should be made from the chattel labour of 'fellow-creatures', people wrenched from their homelands and families and condemned until death to unremitting toil in a foreign land.

Thomas Clarkson, in a series of letters penned in Paris, talked of how Africans were transformed into a 'mere instrument of labour' in the Caribbean whose work rhythms were governed by the bell, the whip and the physical toil of harvesting tropical crops. Denied the pleasures of conjugal domesticity, unable to watch their progeny grow in a climate of freedom, these workers were discarded in old age, 'dead weight' to their owners.[48] These themes were reiterated in the testimony before the Commons, especially by former doctors, overseers and bookkeepers disenchanted with the cavalier way in which slaves were worked to death on plantations, mere beasts of burden to their owners. They found popular circulation in abridgments of the evidence and in popular tracts like the *Short Sketch* by the Tewkesbury abolitionist, William Bell Crafton.

Thomas Cooper's *Letters on the Slave Trade*, first published in serial form in *Wheeler's Manchester Chronicle*, laid the groundwork for the ferment against the slave trade. Cooper was a radical cotton merchant from Bolton who rose to prominence opposing Pitt's fustian tax of 1784. His anti-slavery tract of sixteen pages opened with a verse from his near namesake, William Cowper:

I would not have a Slave to till my ground,
To carry me, to fan me while I sleep,
And tremble when I wake, for all the wealth
That sinews bought and sold have ever earn'd.

The verse on the title page underscores the decadent luxury and arbitrary power of slavery: the tilling, the pampering, the trembling when the master wakes, the fear of his anger, the loss of freedom. It depicts a human being reduced to a chattel, to 'sinews bought and sold'. In popular extracts of these letters, which in October 1791 were sold for a penny or sixpence for one hundred, great emphasis was laid upon the brutal regimen of plantation labour, the caprice of Caribbean punishments, and the hypocrisy of so-called codes of law which afforded whites unprecedented and virtually unregulated power over the life and death of a slave. Thomas Cooper cast slavery and slave traffic as a gross affront to human liberty and independence, just as he described the 'manufacturing system' three years later. Along with the routine punishments inflicted for slack work and unpunctuality – one witness at the inquiry reported that a slave was hoisted to a crane and whipped for simply taking too long to run an errand – these images registered with Cooper's immediate audience, who themselves struggled against the new work discipline of the industrial revolution.[49]

It is worth emphasising these issues because they are sometimes marginalised in a historiographical debate on abolition and emancipation that pitches humanitarian motives against macro-economic. In the literature Reginald Copeland is set against Eric Williams, and so on. Indeed, the debate has sometimes taken an almost idealist turn[50] – how capitalist was humanitarianism? how humanitarian was capitalism? This meta-analysis, important in exploring the relationship between abolition and free labour, unfortunately obscures the micro-dynamics of the agitation. If we want to understand what motivated ordinary people to campaign for the abolition of the slave trade, then we have to attend to the petty productions that saturated the public sphere, to arguments and signifiers that might have registered with Manchester operatives and artisans, not simply with conscientious Quakers and those above them. In this context Cooper's contribution was important.

Cooper's comments had clear radical resonances, linking slavery with arbitrary power and the denial of human rights to freedom. At the same time, abolitionism flourished in a milieu of popular evangelicalism and spurred men and women to agitate for an end of the trade, sometimes for an end of slavery per se, a goal that leading campaigners found commendable though strategically troubling. Clarkson told William Dickson, who was in charge of recruiting support in Scotland, to continue 'pressing the distinction between emancipation and abolition' for fear that the campaign would incur strong opposition from people outside the plantation complex.[51] At crucial points in the campaigns of 1791 and 1792, the Old Jewry Committee openly assured the public it was not agitating for emancipation.[52] The abolition of the slave trade not slavery was the goal, even though the agitation for the one leeched into the other. The Old Jewry tried to keep ardent abolitionists in line, especially during the sugar boycotts, a particular province of women, when the image of blood-drenched sugar fuelled emancipation sentiment.

In the five years of campaigning from 1787 to 1792, the abolition movement had made great strides. It distributed cheap tracts and digests of the parliamentary inquiries, and cleverly mobilised the mass media of the day. The seal of the abolition committee, the kneeling slave in chains with the motto 'Am I not a Man and a Brother', was given a new life by Josiah Wedgwood, decorating snuff boxes, bracelets, hair-pins and middle-class pottery. 'At length the taste for wearing them became general;' recalled Thomas Clarkson, 'and thus fashion, which usually confines itself to worthless things, was seen for once in the honourable office of promoting the cause of justice, humanity, and freedom.'[53]

Abolition cameos were not the only means by which the campaign to end the slave trade was promoted. The cross section of the *Brookes*, a large Liverpool ship crammed with slaves, row after row, was distributed gratis by the thousand. Originally conceived as a way of illustrating the inhumanity of the Middle Passage by abolitionists in Plymouth, the idea was taken up by Thomas Clarkson, who had a Captain Parry search for the appropriate model on Merseyside and the publisher James Phillips construct an imprint. It 'seemed to make an instantaneous impression of horror upon all who saw it,' Clarkson recalled, and 'it was therefore very instrumental ... in serving the cause of the injured Africans.'[54]

So, too, was William Cowper's poem, *The Negro's Complaint*, in which a slave laments the loss of 'home and all its pleasures', smoulders in bondage, and reminds English men and women that 'Fleecy locks and black complexion/ Cannot forfeit Nature's claim;/Skins may differ, but affection/Dwells in black and white the same.'[55] This 'fugitive piece', as Clarkson termed it, might have remained in manuscript had not some enterprising abolitionists in London printed it on the 'finest hot-pressed paper' and disseminated it widely. The poem combines sentimentality with the sublime, with images of 'wild tornadoes' wrecking a landscape where sugar is brutally extracted from tortured slaves, a reference no doubt to the six hurricanes that swept Jamaica in the first seven years of the 1780s. These were often interpreted in evangelical discourse as a providential punishment for slavery. The poem was even set to music, both as a drawing-room glee and a popular ballad that could bridge the gap between oral and literate culture.[56] It was a production that served the wide and diverse constituency of abolitionism. Indeed, Cowper's poem inspired a number of women to pen sentimental rhymes about the devastating way in which the slave trade destroyed families and female integrity. 'When'er to Afric's shore I turn my eyes' reflected the Bristol-based Hannah More,

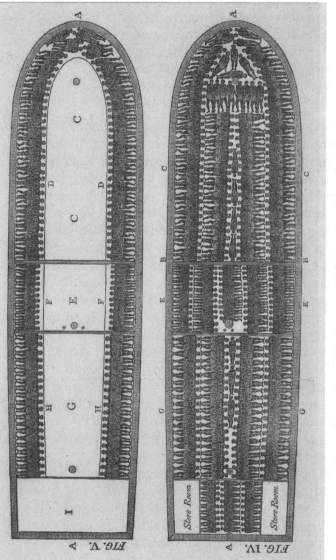

6. Cross section of the Liverpool slave-ship, the *Brookes*, 1788

Horrors of deepest, deadliest guilt arise;
I see, by more than Fancy's mirror shewn,
The burning village, and the blazing town:
See the dire victim torn from social life,
The shrieking babe, the agonizing wife!
She, wretch forlorn! Is dragg'd by hostile hands,
To distant tyrants sold, in distant lands!
Transmitted miseries, and successive chains,
The sole sad heritage her child obtains.[57]

When Wilberforce addressed the Commons on the evening of 2 April, he knew he was speaking to more than a gathering of MPs. 'The people of England had expressed their sense against the trade,' he declared; their petitions should be heeded.[58] Wilberforce saw himself speaking to and for the nation, especially to that body of evangelical sentiment that fuelled the abolition movement. The Middle Passage story was tailor-made to evoke horror and sympathy for the girl, an innocent creature subjected to the gaze and abuse of a sadistic captain for whom the rules of civil society simply didn't apply. The emphasis upon the girl's modesty and vulnerability, her struggle to hide her nakedness or menstrual condition, would have appealed to the women who constituted a significant section of the abolition movement. They could identify with her distress, her shame, which in the British imagination was as much about her inner emotional state as the beatings she received. Those beatings would have been beyond the pale, too, because the flogging of women before the cart's tail was rapidly declining in Britain.[59]

Wilberforce knew he had the moral force of the public behind him when he opened the debate, and it seems he wanted to shame his very different audience, men of property, into conceding to the will of the people and to Christian benevolence. It is interesting to speculate on why he chose the atrocity he did to bring home the brutality of the Trade. There were others he could have chosen from the evidence brought before the Commons committee, evidence that the London abolitionists had published as an abstract. These detailed some horrific instances of abuse. Isaac Parker, now the ship-keeper of the *Melampus* frigate, but a former seaman in the slave trade, recalled an incident on the *Black Joke*, where the captain tortured to death a nine-month-old African infant because she refused to eat the rice given her. The captain is said to have exclaimed: 'Damn you, I'll make you eat, or I'll kill you.' The captain scalded the child's swollen feet in hot water, to a point that the skin fell off; he then beat her with a cat o' nine tails and purportedly forced her to wear a 12 lb weight around her neck. When the child died, he ordered the mother to throw the infant overboard. She was beaten when she refused, but Captain Marshall 'forced her to take it up, and go to the ship's side, where holding her head on one side to avoid the sight, she dropped her child overboard, after which she cried for many hours.'[60]

The savage cruelty of this story is beyond belief, but Wilberforce declined to use it even though it circulated in a Scottish pamphlet by the Unitarian botanist, Theophilus Houlbrooke, and had been briefly mentioned by William Smith in the abolition debate a year before.[61] Perhaps he felt it was too ghastly for a British audience, even to mobilise grief for the mother. It was so horrific it could not be set in a sentimental mode, that is, within terms with which British mothers could identify. Perhaps Wilberforce felt it was the kind of horrific tale that would immobilise rather than provoke action. In a later statement critical of excessive sentimentalism, he would argue that 'true humanity' did not involve 'starting or shrinking at such tales' but 'in a disposition of heart to relieve misery', and this required a judicious mix of reason and emotion to promote meaningful reform.[62]

Yet another reason for avoiding the Parker story was that this story was enmeshed in disputes between the Trade and abolitionists about the credibility of the evidence brought before the select committee of the Commons. Curiously historians have not made much of this engagement, perhaps because the Trade seems so odious to a twenty-first-century audience as to warrant immediate dismissal.[63] David Brion Davis describes the inquiries as a 'ritual of expiation', a hand-wringing exercise 'that temporarily exorcised the slave trade's worst evils'.[64] This assessment only addresses the abolitionists; it ignores the staunch defence of the trade and slavery advanced by their opponents; and the alleged respectability of their witnesses. Slave traders made much of the fact they mobilised seven admirals and six governors on the condition of slavery in the Caribbean and disputed abolitionist accounts of the trade with the testimony of captains of considerable experience.[65] They also argued that the hazards of the Middle Passage were little different than those experienced in troop transports; overcrowding made both vulnerable to diseases like dysentery and smallpox.[66] Both sides spent money promoting their evidence, with the Trade lobby distributing 5,000 copies of their own *Abstract* in the month before the debate. Copies of the Abolition abstract were distributed to all the coffee houses in Bath. Publicity mattered, to both sides, and newspapers joined in.[67] The slave trade wasn't simply exorcised at the court of conscience as Davis suggests.

According to Clarkson, the Trade reviled the Abolitionist *Abstract* as much as radical Tom Paine's *Rights of* Man.[68] It tried to discredit it at every turn. John Ranby, possibly the son of a Chelsea Hospital surgeon of the same name,[69] disputed the veracity of Parker's story and wondered whether his memory was faulty after twenty-odd years. The notion that a nine-month-child would have to wear a wooden harness of that weight was incredible, he thought: 'it would be the conduct of an absolute lunatic'.[70] The same reaction came from John Fenton Cawthorne, MP for Lincoln, who thought the story too extreme to be believable; in this respect, he opined, it was characteristic of other so-called 'atrocities'

swirling through the public sphere. It was 'fake news'. Sir
George Thomas, MP for Arundel, chimed in. Why did
Parker keep this story from the public until now? No doubt
this errant seaman – he deserted on his second voyage to
Africa and for a time worked as a slaver's assistant – was the
beneficiary of the largesse that the Old Jewry had distributed in securing evidence.[71] He was as crooked as some of
the witnesses before the Old Bailey.

Wilberforce did not want to get into these choppy
waters. It would be too distracting. Besides, he needed to
counter the arguments of people like Robert Norris, a Liverpool slave captain of five voyages between 1769 and 1777,
who had offered a roseate picture of the Middle Passage.
Norris argued that every effort had been made to promote
the 'Health, Cleanliness and Chearfulness' of the slaves,
whose survival and fitness increased profits. 'Interest, is
so much blended with Humanity in this business,' Norris
averred, that 'every Attention is generally paid to the Lives
and Health of the Slaves that Circumstances will permit.'[72]
This was a familiar refrain among some of the more experienced masters who gave evidence on behalf of the slave
trade lobby, including James Fraser of Bristol, who had been
20 years in the trade. He was not uncritical of some trading practices: he disliked the pawn system of sureties, for
example, because it could easily lead to misunderstandings
and slights to the status of African traders.[73] He admitted
that the most intractable of slaves needed to be corrected;
a predicament, he claimed, which was also acknowledged
by abolitionist witnesses like the surgeon Alexander Falconbridge. But basically, Captain Fraser thought that it was
not in the interest of slavers brutally to mistreat their slaves
because of the commissions and 'head money' involved; the
bonuses offered to captains and surgeons who delivered
slaves capable of enduring the rigours of plantation labour.
This line of argument was in the spirit of the Dolben Act,
which offered state douceurs for minimal mortality on slave

ships, even if it took an optimistic view of the self-regulating practices of most captains.[74]

To counteract this evidence Wilberforce needed the element of surprise. Most of the atrocities reported to the Select Committee were pre-Dolben; that is to say, they took place before 1788. To drive home the argument that regulation was not working and immediate abolition was necessary, Wilberforce needed fresh examples; examples that belied the urbanity of captains like Fraser, whose command of slave ships won the begrudging respect of even Falconbridge, Clarkson's sidekick in Liverpool.[75] He needed an atrocity that could not be written off as singularly exceptional, but one that signified the brutal habits of the trade *in extremis*. It seems Wilberforce secured it at the eleventh hour, the day before the debate, through the auspices of Clarkson and the printer and abolitionist activist, James Phillips. It was in his office in George Yard, Lombard Street, that the witnesses Dowling and Devereux told their stories.[76] They had been summoned to give evidence about the bombardment of New Calabar. The Middle Passage story was an incidental bonus.

It was not enough to sway the vote. William Pitt, who had initially tried to dissuade Wilberforce from launching his motion, came out in support of his friend. He argued that the colonial legislatures could adjust to the change, that the demographic deficit of the plantations could be made up quickly if current trends continued; that is to say, if slave women had more surviving children, as some of the Jamaican evidence seemed to suggest. He also believed the continued importation of slaves was potentially explosive in the light of the unrest in St Domingue, where the mobilisation of slaves in the bitter dispute between whites and free blacks had led to some appalling scenes of butchery. But ultimately his peroration was for justice and humanity. Britain should abolish the trade to atone 'for our long and cruel injustice towards Africa'.[77] The House was not convinced.

As Matthew Montagu, the nephew of the celebrated Blue Stocking, Mary Wortley Montagu observed, the vote would be determined by the middle ground, by those 'who admitted the injustice of the trade, but who feared the danger and impolicy of an abolition'.[78] When Henry Dundas moved an amendment for gradual abolition, the majority warmed to it, and the amendment passed by 230 votes to 85. Lord Mornington attempted to thwart this amendment by suggesting a terminal date of 1 January 1793, but this was defeated by 49 votes. Eventually the House settled on terminating the slave trade on 1 January 1796.[79]

Gradual abolition met with a mixed reaction. The London and Newcastle Abolition societies rejected the compromise. The *Sussex Weekly Advertiser* believed that parliament had thwarted the will of the people and suspended justice for over three years 'at the fiat of Borough corruption and Personal Interest in the Council of the Nation'. Meanwhile, it raged, '60,000 wretches will be consigned to slavery and 6000 will be murdered by "Kimber-kindness"'.[80] Others, however, thought the Dundas amendment was a fair compromise. 'The temperate determination of the House of Commons … bids fair to gratify all parties', intoned the *Derby Mercury*. 'The friends of humanity' would eventually see an end to the trade; 'the friends to our commercial happiness' economic security. The paper hoped that 'every subsequent step will be rationally, and we hope calmly, discussed'.[81] People thought Wilberforce should be elated. He had lost the debate but had secured the principle that the slave trade should be abolished; amid mounting insurgencies in the Caribbean that were far from propitious. Yet Wilberforce was not satisfied. 'I cannot help regretting we have been able to do no more,' he wrote to John Clarkson, Thomas's brother, 'yet on the whole we have reason to be thankful for what we have obtained.'[82] He feared the wily Dundas had out-manoeuvred him. The Lords would likely oppose abolition, and so gradual abolition could well mean another eight to twelve years of slavery, as Speaker Henry Addington had assumed during the debate. Wilberforce regretted not calling Dundas's bluff.

In any case, gradual abolition was really another form of 'regulation'. In order to make the West Indies demographically viable, Dundas's scheme involved financial incentives to the Trade to secure a better ratio of female slaves from Africa. And it would only work with the cooperation of colonial legislatures, who would be urged to give baby bonuses to slave mothers, and perhaps offer freedom to slave mothers who reared five children to the age of seven, to an age when their bonded labour would commence.[83] To a man who thought slavery was morally wrong, these proposals were extremely distasteful. It meant that Wilberforce and the abolitionists would have to tolerate the forced migration of tens of thousands of Africans every year of the transition.

Precisely why did members of the House opt for Dundas's solution? There were probably 55 to 60 MPs who had a clear vested interest in the slave trade and slavery, as colonial agents, planters, merchants, and men who held mortgages or bonds on Caribbean estates. As we now know from the recent University College London project on slave compensation in the 1830s, the tributaries of slave money ran broadly through elite society; they were not confined to a narrow rump of absentee planters and merchants, but also to people who had a financial stake in plantation assets. Sugar merchant George Hibbert specified seven classes of creditors to the Commons committee, including shippers and annuitants by will or marriage who had some stake in the plantation complex. He added that his own merchant house had debts of 40 or 50 years standing, which it propped up by giving planters advances to purchase slaves.[84] This meant he had plantation shares in his portfolio.

Fifty-three MPs in 1792 can be identified as having some financial interest in slavery from the UCL list, and there are others who should be included as active members of the Trade phalanx. These include Banastre Tarleton, MP for

Liverpool, whose family owned plantations; and John Baker
Holroyd, Lord Sheffield, MP for Bristol. They were two of the
most vocal supporters of the slave trade. They were joined
by Sir George Thomas, MP Arundel; John Dent, MP for
Lancaster; John Fenton Cawthorne, MP for Lincoln and the
Recorder of Lancaster, who seems to have had some involvement in the Trade. They also numbered James Lowther, MP
for Westmorland, who was married to an illegitimate daughter of Sir William Codrington, a slave owner. This brings the
total to just below 60, roughly the same number identified by
McCahill in his study of Stephen Fuller and the slave-trade
advocates of this era.[85] This group could be counted on to
side with Henry Dundas in 1792 if his amendment meant
postponing abolition for some years to come.

Yet the slave trade could win broader support because
slavery was imbricated in Britain's capitalist economy. It
fuelled the raw materials of the industrial revolution. A
third of Britain's raw cotton in 1787 came from its West
Indian colonies; the rest was supplied by Turkey, Brazil and
other islands in the Caribbean, some of which depended on
British slaves for their labour.[86] The Trade, and by extension the plantation economy, provided a lot of jobs in the
processing and export industries. The West Indian share
of British exports was never less than 10 per cent after the
American war; its share of imports ran at roughly a quarter.
A significant part of the Bristol and Liverpool economies
were bound up with the slave trade and slave-based industries, and London's financial services were heavily engaged
in managing shipping insurance, mortgages and plantation
exports as well as offering credit through bills of exchange
for the purchase of slaves.[87] Through sugar revenues, in
particular, slavery contributed mightily to Britain's taxes,
an important consideration in the light of the French Revolution and the very real possibility that the island would
soon be at war again with its traditional enemy; as indeed it
was within a year. Did the dominant group in the House, the

landed gentry, want to take up the slack of a collapsing sugar economy? Did it want to foot more of the tax bill necessary for war? Not really.

Equally important, there was a very good chance the British Caribbean economy would falter with immediate abolition. The motion for radical abolition came at a difficult time. The principal sugar island in the Caribbean, French St Domingue, was in flames. Over a thousand estates had been burned to the ground in a complex insurrection that pitted whites against free blacks over political and civil rights and prompted estate owners on both sides to mobilise slaves in support. In this contested space, St Domingue's half a million slaves would ultimately gain the upper hand, forcing emancipation on the agenda of the French Revolution. More will be said about this monumental revolt later in the book, but suffice to say here that the explosive situation in St Domingue, little more than a day's sail from Jamaica, raised genuine doubts that immediate abolition could be effected smoothly, predicated as it was on a robust and adaptable slave economy. In the months before the debate in the Commons, Jamaica had mobilised the militia to contain a possible contagion of unrest from across the water, and government officials were pondering which British islands were vulnerable to French revolutionary and emancipationist ferment.[88] Newspapers openly suggested that abolitionist agitation had already fuelled a revolt in Dominica in 1791, and feared the rolling thunder from St Domingue would do the same, precipitating a collapse of the sugar economy and disruption on the scale of the South Sea Bubble. It would affect every member of the community, claimed Woodfall's *Diary*, 'the high and the low, the rich and the poor'.[89] Wilberforce tried to head off these arguments by insisting it was slavery that was to blame for the Caribbean insurrections, not radical or abolitionist agitation.

At the time of the debate there was no consensus in Britain about the causes of the St Domingue revolt or its potential consequences. A lot of conservative opinion blamed abolitionists and their counterparts in France for fuelling unrest. Historians now believe there was some substance to the charge, not in terms of direct involvement but in inadvertently generating rumours of emancipation that catalysed unrest among the slaves.[90] Wilberforce's speech in April 1792 tacitly recognised that the outbreak of the French Revolution and civil war in St Domingue unsettled the push for abolition, although he parried the argument by insisting that a ban on slave trading was an honourable move that would take the heat out of the crisis. What Wilberforce's speech did not recognise was that the revolutionary circumstances of the early 1790s encouraged self-emancipation among slaves, of which the Dominica revolt of 1791 was arguably the first example on British imperial soil. Although there is some disagreement among historians about the aspirations of the rebel slaves on the Windward side of that island, whether or not they were inspired by revolutionary or abolitionist ideas, there seems little doubt that maroon-slave collaboration and the influx of mulatto refugees from Martinique fuelled outrage against white planters and generated talk of rights. Certainly the governor of the island, John Orde, was troubled by the possibility of Dominica becoming embroiled in the mounting unrest in the French Caribbean.[91]

Quite apart from the rapidly changing political context, abolitionist arguments for a smooth transition to a self-sustaining plantation economy were wildly optimistic. Its advocates underestimated the complexies of the demographic transition if the slave trade was eliminated. Although there were some Caribbean estates that were demographically self-sustaining – Thomas Clarkson had mentioned twenty in the *Impolicy of the African Slave Trade* – the vast majority were not, and would not be for at least a decade under the most optimal conditions. The Jamaican assembly calculated that it needed six new slaves per plantation every year to sustain the current levels of labour power.[92] Witnesses before the Commons inquiry suggested that planter indebtedness undermined long-term plans to adjust the demographical balance, which in Jamaica ran at a ratio of 127 males to every 100 females.[93] Indeed, the Caribbean preference for male slave migrants actually increased as the eighteenth century advanced and the pro-natalist policies of the early years of settlement were abandoned. Planters and their creditors wanted immediate profits from fresh African labour, not the trouble and extra expense of bringing children into the workforce. They persisted in this policy in the face of substantial losses among new African immigrants, a quarter to a third of who would die within three years. Before the abolition campaign was underway, Anthony Benezet had stressed that slaves were disposable labour; if they worked eight to nine years on a plantation, their labour was 'reckoned a sufficient compensation for the cost'.[94] As Henry Coor, a millwright in Jamaica for fifteen years, candidly remarked, overseers 'work slaves out and trust for African supplies than work them moderately and keep them up by breeding'.[95] Quite apart from the economic imperatives of bringing in a good profit, it would take years to wean managers and overseers from the custom of using 'expendable' labour on the plantations.

Cutting off the labour supply would thus compromise existing ventures and also those devoted to cultivating cotton and coffee in the newly acquired islands of the Lesser Antilles. 100,000 acres of land in Dominica had been sold on the expectation that it would be cultivated, and without fresh supplies of African labour, this project would fail. Some contemporaries calculated that the total amount of British Caribbean capital in jeopardy might be as high as £70 million [£10.5 billion today].[96] This would be disruptive enough, but abolitionists also underplayed the knock-on effects of slave-driven economies, pretending that the domestic importance of the slave trade could be reduced to a matter of exports to Africa and shipping. They overlooked the repercussions in the Caribbean sector and the lines of credit that sustained it. And they were blithely optimistic about the possibilities of crafting alternative economies to slaving in Africa. This was evident in the Sierra Leone projects of the late 1780s and 1790s, which were promoted as a sanctuary for displaced Africans, a missionary effort to bring Christianity and 'civilisation' to the continent, and a bridgehead for new British commodity trade in Africa; in effect, a free labour counterpoint to the slave trade. Granville Sharp's initial venture, the attempt to establish a self-governing, utopian 'Province of Freedom' collapsed when many of the original settlers were wracked by disease or disappeared without trace. The sequel, the Sierra Leone Company of 1791, could not reconcile the democratic aspirations of black loyalist settlers from Nova Scotia with the hierarchical government imposed by abolitionists in London. John Clarkson's dismissal in 1793 for sympathising with black loyalists over land policies illustrated this all too well. With a divided command and the persistence of ties between white administrators and slave traders, the company struggled to retain a foothold in Africa.[97]

Besides, the British slave trade had just received a boost from the decision of the Spanish crown to open up its slave markets to the English and to encourage its own traders to purchase more slaves from the British islands. This was followed by an *arrêt* from the governor of St Domingue opening up the southern coast of the island to the free importation of slaves for a period of five years.[98] The slave port of Nantes opposed the move and had the governor arrested, but the rapidly changing political context made metropolitan regulation difficult. In effect, demands for more slaves were made on the British, and Jamaica, in particular, was fast becoming an international entrepôt for the Trade. Hard on these changes in policy came the collapse of the largest sugar economy in the world, in St Domingue.

This collapse offered untold opportunities for British plantation economies provided the contagion of insurrection could be contained. Britain and France accounted for 80 per cent of the North Atlantic sugar market in 1790, and the loss of France's major producer redounded massively to Britain's advantage.[99] One estimate claimed St Domingue produced 130,000 hogsheads of sugar compared to 212,800 from all of the British Caribbean islands, not to mention one million lbs of coffee, one million lbs of indigo and 12 million lbs of cotton.[100] In sum, there were rational economic reasons for postponing the abolition of the slave trade in 1792. The calculations were unprincipled and unjust, but MPs salved their consciences by voting for gradual abolition while protecting their pocketbooks.

David Brion Davis sees the vote for gradual abolition as a pivotal event in constructing the hegemony of humanitarianism in an era of rapid social and political change.[101] It made the unreformed Commons look like a beacon of benevolence. Perhaps, but many MPs understood the vote to mean postponing abolition for a long time; in the light of the known opposition of the Lords and the King, probably longer than specified in the Commons' final resolution. The 1792 vote was altogether more cynical than Davis's interpretation allows. To adapt a famous phrase from Marx, MPs drowned the fervour of abolitionism 'in the icy water of egotistical calculation'.[102]

As we shall see, the movement for abolition faltered and slowed considerably after 1792. Yet there was the possibility of salvaging something from the pyrrhic victory of April, beyond pressing for immediate abolition. And that was dealing with slave captains like John Kimber. This might be a way of reining in the slave trade and increasing the pressure upon Parliament. At the very least a prosecution might reinforce the criminal possibilities of the Dolben Act.

3

The man and his crew

John Kimber is sometimes described as a Bristol captain, but strictly speaking he was the captain of a Bristol ship, the *Recovery*, owned by the merchant James Rogers and three others.[1] He hailed from Bideford, a north Devonshire port which had seen better times. In the 1680s Bideford was a leading port in the cod fishery of Newfoundland and the tobacco trade of the Chesapeake. By the time Kimber was born, in 1751,[2] it had lost ground to Poole and Glasgow. When Kimber took to the sea at the age of fifteen, Bideford was considered a 'decayed town'.[3] Trade to foreign parts had declined at the turn of the century, from almost 6,300 tons in 1701 to 2,220 in 1751, falling below 2,000 tons after 1755.[4] The port's main commerce was now coastal, transporting coal from South Wales to local industries, and shipping wheat to regional centres like Bristol.

It was predictable that a boy with maritime ambitions might gravitate to Bristol, unless he was interested in the Royal Navy in which Devonshire men played a conspicuous role.[5] Kimber first appears in the Bristol muster rolls as a seaman on the *Brickdale*, a brig that made a five-month voyage to Virginia and back in 1772. He is listed there as previously sailing on the *Polly*, although which *Polly* is unclear.[6] He made another trip to Virginia on the *Caesar* in 1774, and then, in what was likely his first slaving trip, as the first mate of the *Sally*, a schooner bound for Africa and Antigua in May 1775 under the command of James Hodnett. He was 23 years of age. What happened to the *Sally* is a mystery. It lingered on the Slave Coast for a long time. The muster roll reveals it only reached Antigua in April 1777, nearly two years after its departure from Bristol, before moving on to Montserrat. Four seamen lost patience with the captain in African waters and switched boats; so eventually did Kimber, who on 24 September 1776 entered the *Constantine*, a larger vessel under the captaincy of Archibald Robe. That ship successfully delivered 600 slaves from the Gold Coast to Grenada after beating off two American privateers during the Middle Passage.[7] By the time the *Constantine* sailed again she was armed with a letter of marque, an Admiralty licence to maraud enemy shipping as well as buy and sell slaves. Kimber was not part of that crew, but it was the sort of opportunistic strategy that attracted him.[8]

Our man first attracts public attention as the mate of the Bristol privateer, a ship like the *Constantine*, one licensed to ply the waves in search of enemy shipping and profit from the prize.[9] She was the *Hornet*, a Bordeaux boat originally designed as a Guineaman, a slave ship, but now designed for war. The *Hornet* was a 300-ton vessel with a square stern and three masts. It mounted 32 carriage guns on its main and quarterdeck, capable of firing off 24 lb or 12 lb cannon balls. One enthusiast sketched a picture of vessel in the style of Nicholas Pocock, a leading eighteenth-century British painter of naval battles and admirals. The portrait presents a sleek vessel, armed to the teeth, gun portals open, powered by billowing sails.[10]

Kimber joined its large crew as the first lieutenant in the spring of 1780 and when the captain of the ship died four months later in St John's Newfoundland, he assumed command at the age of 28. Privateering ventures were a bit like snakes and ladders; a lot was left to chance because while crews of letters of marque were paid monthly for their labour, the real rewards came from the prize.[11] You could score or you could come up empty-handed. The volatility of the enterprise was reflected in the muster return: within the first year, it tracked six deaths, twenty desertions, fifteen impressments and high turnovers at ports like Tryall, Jamaica, and St Kitts.[12] The crew may have initially numbered 80, but over 120 names crop up in the first year.

Fortunately for Kimber he secured a prize very early on. Within months he captured the *New Defence*, an American vessel out of Maryland bound for St Eustatius with 320 hogsheads of tobacco. This newly launched ship, on its first run, was sent to be condemned at the Admiralty court in St Kitts and later sold in Bristol. Then Kimber ventured further south to Surinam, where Admiral George Brydges Rodney was engaging the Dutch, who had only recently joined the war coalition against the British. As Dutch forces crumbled in what is now modern day Guyana, Kimber and three other Bristol privateers entered the Demerara and Essequibo rivers and seized Dutch shipping. Initially the privateers informed the Dutch colonists that they came to confiscate shipping on the orders of Rodney, which was untrue, for the admiral had sent Captain Francis Pender of HMS *Berbuda* to cruise the river and seize the property of the United Provinces.[13] The privateers beat Pender to it, a cheeky move that might have incurred Rodney's wrath had he not been consumed with the illegal trade that British merchants were conducting through St Eustatius; people he execrated as 'Smugglers, Adventurers, Betrayers of their Country and Rebels to their King.'[14]

The privateers also pushed their luck by going ashore and pillaging two plantations. A report from the Dutch authorities alleged 'they took everything they liked' and freed all criminals, some 'under Sentence of Death which did put us in the greatest anxiety for our own Negroes, who would be glad of such an Opportunity to rise against the Inhabitants.'[15] This incursion could have had international repercussions. The Dutch officials at Demerara argued that the seizure of their effects was unauthorised and illegal. Fortunately for Kimber, the owners of the *Hornet*, the merchants William

Jones and William Randall, ensured that his credentials were above board. His letter of marque was signed and sealed a month before the raid, as was the case with the *Bellona* and *Mercury*, two of the other Bristol privateers.[16] No one could challenge the heist, for the terms of surrender that guaranteed resident colonists their property was not signed until March 1781. Some thirteen ships were taken in the two rivers, one bound for St Eustatius but most destined for Holland, particularly to Amsterdam and Middelburg. Nine were laden with valuable cargoes of coffee, sugar and cotton, the principal exports of the colony.[17] What share the *Hornet* accrued from this raid is not clear. Kimber's vessel was the largest ship, twice the size of the *Mercury* and the *Bellona*, but it had run aground at the mouth of the Demerara River and did not come up until Dutch surrendered there.[18] Nonetheless a memorandum affixed to Admiral Rodney's letter of 3 May 1781, shows that Kimber was accredited with capturing vessels on the river along with the other two Bristol boats. There is no indication that the Dutch were able successfully to contest these claims.[19] When Captain Edward Thompson of HMS *Hyena* was sent in to settle the formal terms of capitulation, the only privateering venture he disallowed was that of James Walcott, the commander of the *Regulator* privateer at Berbice. Kimber and company had plundered the Dutch ships and plantations in the nick of time. By early 1782 the settlements in Guyana had fallen to the French, with the result that official British seizures there, which according to Thompson amounted to a phenomenal £140,000, in addition to some lucrative properties of Amsterdam merchants, were stillborn.[20] These seizures excluded the prizes of Kimber and company.

1781 was a good year for Captain Kimber. 1782 was probably even better, as there were no negotiations surrounding prizes that might have diminished Kimber's share. Early on he picked up the *Puríssima Concepción*, a 350-ton Spanish ship bound for Buenos Aires with a rich cargo of linens,

7. Nicholas Pocock, *The Hornet privateer*, c. 1782

silks, woollens, wine, bar iron and olive oil worth £70,000. This prize was taken to Bristol in March.[21] Later in the year Kimber captured *Les Trois Frères*, a French boat out of St Domingue with a cargo of sugar, cotton and indigo, tortoiseshell and mahogany.[22] These were the principal hauls, although there were others, including an American brig, the *Betsey*, which carried 2,000 gallons of rum and 11,000 gallons of molasses from Guadeloupe to Boston. Quite apart from the cargoes, the ships themselves were worth something. *Les Trois Frères*, for example, was advertised as a 'remarkable fast sailor' by the Bristol brokers, Meyler and Maxse, with a copper bottom and ports for ten guns. It was suitable for privateering, or for sailing in the Newfoundland or African trade.[23]

By the time the *Hornet* itself was put on sale in March 1783, Kimber must have been a wealthy man. It's impossible to know just how much he had made up through his sea

adventures. A good chunk of the prize money after expenses
and fees went to the owners or investors in the enterprise; in
this particular case, as much as 75 per cent.[24] Under the terms
of agreement signed in April 1780, the captain was entitled
to three-eighths of the crew's share, which amounted to
9.4 per cent of the total venture.[25] In these circumstances,
and given the 'capital' prizes Kimber brought in, it is not
inconceivable that he gained £10,000 in prize money [about
£1.5 m in today's currency]; even allowing for the fees and
possible legal disputes involved in the condemnation of
the seizures. This was enough to set him up as a gentleman
of property. He had commanded a major privateer and
made spectacular hauls in longer-than-average ventures.[26]
Apparently his motto was 'Who'd have thought it?' one that
signalled his good luck and aspiration to upward mobility.[27]
For several years after 1782 Kimber disappears from the ship
muster rolls. The St James's Chronicle reported he 'kept his
carriage' in Bristol, 'having obtained a considerable fortune
by privateering in the last war'. At 5 feet 9 inches, tall for
the eighteenth century, with dark eyes, black hair and a dark
complexion, he must have cut an imposing figure.[28] He certainly gained a reputation as a big spender. Perhaps he hoped
to emulate patrician merchants like the MP Henry Cruger,
whose pretensions to fashionable gentility were lampooned
by Thomas Chatterton.[29] Kimber became a sought-after
creditor, for in 1783 he underwrote a lease on stables owned
by the Bideford Bridge Trust.[30]

The next time we hear of John Kimber he is commanding the Levant, a ship bound for Newfoundland in the
summer of 1786.[31] He may well have had a personal stake
in this venture, although the principal proprietor was the
up-and-coming merchant Walter Jacks, who financed three
successful slave voyages to the Bight of Biafra in the mid-
1780s and bought plantations in Antigua and Dominica,
shipping sugar back to Bristol. Jacks also invested in transatlantic shipping to New York and Rhode Island, and dealt

in flour and wheat from his warehouse on Bristol Bridge.[32] A churchwarden of St Maryport, he ingratiated himself with the Bristol bigwigs by joining the local Marine Society. Among its vice-presidents and stewards in 1788 were prominent slave owners, members of the Society of Merchant Venturers, and the incumbent Bristol MP and sugar refiner, George Daubeny.[33]

Kimber entered a partnership with Jacks in the cod-fishing business, selling the fish in Leghorn [Livorno] and Sicily. It didn't last. One of the firm's vessels, the *Flora*, captained by William Matthews, became embroiled in a dispute over fishing rights at Perlican, a Newfoundland outport. Kimber lost the suit, which dragged on into the 1790s.[34] In February 1789 his company was dissolved, with Jacks settling the outstanding accounts. In April, he agreed to settle Kimber's bills drawn at Newfoundland, along with James Bonbonous, a broker in Corn Street, and Henry Cook, a merchant and sailmaker in Prince Street, Bristol. Kimber and company was no more.[35]

So Kimber decided to take command of a slave ship, the *Recovery*, one that was partially owned by Jacks. He was able to do this under the Dolben Act because he had been a chief mate on a slaving voyage.[36] By eighteenth-century standards he was old to take his first command of his first slave-ship, 39 when the median age was 30 and when nearly half [48 per cent] of all captains had begun in their twenties. To put it more starkly, 85 per cent of all first-voyage captains in this era were younger than Kimber.[37] By this time, Bristol's involvement in the trade had declined considerably. Many of the elite families who profited from slavery in the heyday of Bristol's influence, from roughly 1710 to 1745, had moved out or diversified their portfolios. The rump of the trade was carried on by a few notable merchants and a smattering of self-made men who had previously worked as mates or captains in the trade; men like James McTaggart, a former naval lieutenant and brute of a captain who drew the contempt of

Falconbridge for intimidating seamen from giving evidence
to the abolitionists about the recruitment and condition of
slaves and slave-ship crews.[38]

Bristol's share of the slave trade was now a slim version
of what it had been. In the last two decades of the century
Liverpool absorbed about 73 per cent of the trade, tower-
ing above its rivals.[39] Still, there were profits to be made.
Slave prices were buoyant. Prices had more than doubled
since Bristol's entry into the trade, reaching a peak in the
years 1785–1789 at around £55 for a healthy male and quite
possibly £57–59 by 1792.[40] The demand for slaves was high,
because planters became increasingly anxious about the
drought of slave imports if abolition caught on and started
buying for the future. In fact, the aftermath of the American
War of Independence saw increased activity in the Bristol
slave trade, with an annual investment of £285,000, higher
than in the 'golden age' when investments reached £150,000
per annum. Since sugar prices were high as well, the possibilities of raking in an 8–10 per cent profit on investment in
sugar, tobacco and slaves were good. The total profit from
the Bristol slave trade and associated commissions was
around £60,000 pa.[41]

Kimber clearly hoped for a slice of this pie. Slave-ship
captains were paid a nominal £5 per month for a voyage,
but there were perks. They were allotted several 'privileged
slaves' to dispose of as they wished and were normally
granted a healthy commission on the slaves collected, delivered and sold in the Americas; often 4 per cent on coastal
commissions and a further 2 per cent on sales. In 1784, Captain Bostock of the *Bloom*, a Liverpool slave ship, received
just over £778 for 307 slaves; Captain Roberts of the *Thomas*,
£1,000 for delivering 530. Captain James Fraser, reckoned
to be the most responsible captain of Bristol slave ships,
received £962 for commanding the *Emilia* on a voyage to
Bonny and Grenada in the late 1780s, plus a share of over
£880 with other officers.[42] Captains did better in the 1790s as

slave prices rose and demand remained high. In 1791 Captain Charles Molyneux of the *Christopher* raked in a commission of over £1,100 on 270, plus four privileged slaves at average prices. Three years later Captain Young of the *Enterprize* received over £1,200 in commission for 360 slaves plus his slave perquisites.[43] Captain Kimber, with a 'cargo' of over 300 slaves, could expect an equivalent reward. With a few successful voyages under his belt, and perhaps the opportunity to invest in his own voyage, something that 10 per cent of all captains managed to do, Kimber might climb into the mercantile class, as he had clearly hoped to do in the Newfoundland venture.

There were risks. Trading for slaves had become an increasingly complex business; 'one constant train of uncertainty', claimed one insider.[44] At the beginning of the eighteenth century, the Royal Africa Company complained of private traders who seized 'all the Negroes whom they could surprise along the Coast, robbing Canoes on the water, forcing Women, Boys and Girls along with them from the Shoar, shooting at Boats, and Killing such Negroes as refused to answer their call.'[45] Those marauding forays declined a little over time. With the expansion of the trade in the eighteenth century and the decline of the forts on the Gold Coast, there was a shift from trading through European middlemen to negotiating with local rulers and their designated clients in places like Benin and Biafra.[46] This shift in locale required some knowledge of local custom and protocol in which deals were conducted in a festive atmosphere of ritualised mutual respect.[47] Alexander Falconbridge recalled that when a ship arrived at Bonny the slave captain went ashore to make his presence known to the king and the principal men. A day or two later the king came on board the slave vessel 'with a band of music to break trade.'[48] The chieftain was given some presents called 'dashes' and once permission to trade was granted, the dealing commenced. Small clusters of African captives were exchanged for goods and large canoes, armed with small cannon, ventured up country for bigger batches of potential slaves.

Critical to these negotiations was the building of trust and credit. By the middle of the eighteenth century, in places along the African coast like Old Calabar, it was commonplace for slave captains to take human 'pawns', often kin of their clients, for the credit they advanced until the transactions were completed.[49] This was because local merchants or their middlemen could take months searching for slaves upriver or collecting them from the inland fairs and markets, and British merchants wanted some collateral for their credit. If the deal went sour, captains had to decide what to do with the pawns, whether to punish the middlemen by taking their kin as slaves on the Middle Passage, or transferring them to another European boat on the coast in return for some of her slaves. In the logbook of the *Black Prince*, trading at Annamaboe [now Anomabu] in late 1764, Captain William Miller recounted that he had released two traders on the delivery of two more slaves and hoped that a Liverpool captain would redeem the remaining two pawns so he might set sail.[50]

The delicate balance between trust and enmity could easily slide into violence and anarchy. Thomas Pye, a naval captain on the African coast in 1750, said the abuse of the pawn system by slave commanders generated reprisals from African dealers 'who always make one White Man [as they call them] suffer for another'.[51] The seizure of men for security became so common that traders adopted an old Portuguese term for the custom: 'panyar' or 'panyarring'. To compound matters, dealers remembered those commanders who broke the conventions of trade. Pye cited the example of an errant American captain who had to change his name and disguise his boat in order to return to trading at Cape Mount.

The instability of the trade was still evident in 1788, as the story of Captain Joseph Williams of the *Ruby* illustrates.[52] Williams had been involved in some tricky negotiations regarding the pawns of some dealers in Bimbia, a slave port in the Cameroons. This resulted in some reprisals against British captains because some pawns had been sent into slavery. Williams was excluded from these attacks because he had agreed to release his pawns. Even so, he had the reputation of making hard bargains, and when he confined a principal trader called Bimbe Jack because he was not getting the deal he wanted, he was repaid in kind. At the bar of the river Captain Williams was captured by Bimbe Jack's followers, taken ashore, and stripped naked, that is, down to his drawers. He was then tied to a tree and forced to wear the neck collar he had previously forced on the trader. Williams was detained three days at Bimbia, and eventually released on condition his credit be cancelled. The captain didn't have much choice in the matter, but he swore 'if he had a ship of sufficient force, he would have laid siege to the island and have taken away all he could'.[53]

The Williams story revealed how explosive bargaining with middlemen could still be, although elite African associations such as the Ekpe society sought to bring order to fractious bargaining.[54] An alternative method of trading was to deal directly with merchants on shore, but this could involve captains in countless transactions. Captain Potter, a Liverpool commander once purchased 499 slaves over the course of 131 days in some 316 transactions. He averaged only four slaves a day.[55] Whatever method was chosen, trading for slaves took time, more time as the century advanced, and a lot could go wrong.

The African merchants whom Kimber would encounter became increasingly picky about the European goods offered in exchange. They wanted particular textiles and would not be fobbed off with inferior guns from Birmingham. Hard experience, the loss of fingers and thumbs, underscored the sale of defective weapons.[56] Africans had their own information about the price of slaves in the West Indies and bargained hard. In the period 1763–1788, prices for slaves in Africa rose faster than those in the West Indies, with the result that the margin of profit for European sellers fell from around 100 to 57 per cent.[57] For their part the captains and their surgeons were not always happy about the slaves on offer. 'Many of them appear half-starved when brought down for sale', claimed one contemporary.[58] The supply of slaves was reaching capacity in the Bight of Benin when Kimber began to trade. Slaves sickened on the long journey to the coast; adult captives sometimes looked a poor bargain and so more children became part of the quota, even though planters were not always keen to take them. And the clock kept ticking.

Time was the slavers' worst enemy on the African coast. This was widely recognised. Writing in 1751, the owners of the *Chesterfield* told Captain William Earle they depended 'on your Prudent management with Natives and Ships in the River in your Trade for our best interest; should you[r] purchase be very tedious and slaves scarce we think it advisable that you leave the river when you have 350 slaves rather than risk your own lives by such long detention.'[59] As this letter suggests, the mortality of crews as much as slaves was at stake. This also emerged clearly in a letter that Thomas Leyland wrote to Charles Molyneux when he set sail in the *Christopher* in 1791, the same year Kimber ventured to Africa in the *Recovery*.[60]

> The success of our adventure appears to depend entirely on your having a short passage out and by that means securing an opportunity of quitting the Congo before the Rains set in and your Crew and Negroes become sickly; to avoid such a misfortune to the Voyage must be your particular attention.

Long anchorages on the African coast increased the likelihood of malaria and other diseases among crews, especially when seamen had to shift for themselves on deck and sweat and shiver under small canvass coverings in order to accommodate slaves in the holds. As part of an industrial carrier complex, seamen were put at risk for the profits of the 'cargo'. Seamen who were not 'seasoned', or tippled a lot to boost their morale, could go down like ninepins.

Thirteen of the fourteen first voyagers on the *Brothers* on its journey to Africa in 1785–7, died.[61] Harry Gandy, the lawyer and former seaman from Bristol who gave evidence on behalf of the abolitionists, said his early ventures to Africa convinced him that crews became 'exceedingly sickly owing to their intemperance and want of fresh provisions, and sending them up the River in Boats'. Sir William Yonge attributed the death of seamen to the 'unhealthiness of the climate, the lingering in rivers amid rain, the bad accommodation aboard ship' and 'the frequent want of provisions'.[62]

Rain, mosquitoes, harsh conditions and poor food undermined immune systems. Whatever the specific cause, there is no doubt that slaving voyages were dangerous to seamen, debilitating, if not killing them, and sometimes rendering them blind from ophthalmic disorders contracted on the coast; very probably onchocerciasis or river blindness, contracted from tropical black fly or ticks.[63] John Davis, who served as a cabin boy on board the *Iris* in 1748, told a committee of the Bristol Merchant Venturers that fellow seaman Josiah Holland was 'afflicted with a soreness in his eye' off the coast of Bonny, which 'soon deprived him of his eyesight'. Similarly, John Abercrombie, the surgeon on the *Hope*, was said to be 'afflicted with a distemper which then reigned amongst the slaves' he attended. He lost his sight also.[64] Straightforward mortality figures consequently underestimate the health hazards of the slave trade for seamen, as doctors in the Bristol and Liverpool infirmaries were well aware.[65] Even so, those figures are daunting. In the 84 voyages from Bristol to Africa for which we have figures in the years 1788–1791, the average mortality for crews was a shocking 21.2 per cent.[66] In 1784 it had been marginally higher, 23.7%. No wonder the slave trade was regarded as the graveyard of seamen.

In these years, the mortality of Bristol crews was often proportionately higher or as high as that of the slaves. In the 57 voyages for which we have comparable figures between 1788 and 1791, crew mortality was higher in 54 per cent of all cases. Of course this is not to discount the appalling mortality in the holds. On 20 of 53 known voyages [38 per cent] the mortality rate exceeded 20 per cent, a fifth of all Africans on board. In some of the worst cases, such as the *Sarah* [1789] and the *Thomas* [1791] where the mortality rate was 44 and 39 per cent respectively, long stays on the coast were certainly a contributing factor, weakening slaves before the Middle Passage. The worst-case scenario was that of the *King George* [1790], where the mortality rate was a phenomenal 78 per cent. This was because 280 slaves drowned when the vessel sank off the rocks near Barbados. Only 80 slaves were saved along with 34 of the 36 crewmen.[67]

Against this it should be noted that 55 per cent of all well-documented voyages from Bristol in the years 1788–91 had slave mortality rates of under 10 per cent and 26 per cent had mortality rates of under three. The wide variation is obscured in many accounts of slave-trade mortality, because historians tend to construct average mortality ratios over the long term, sometimes refining their figures by region; creating, in effect, comparable serial data.[68] Yet the wide variation is important if we wish to consider the lure of profits that kept sea captains in this obnoxious trade, and the optimism with which new captains like Kimber entered into it.

One other factor must be considered in assessing the risk of slave voyages; that is the status and experience of the crews. After visiting Bristol in the summer of 1787 and conversing with seamen who were bold enough to talk, Thomas Clarkson came to the conclusion that many were coerced into the service, often by crimps who offered them the choice of paying off their debts on a slaving voyage or facing an indefinite term in prison.[69] Gunner James Morley testified before the Commons that a Bristol publican named

Sullivan deliberately ensnared his sailor customers in debt and confronted them with the choice of 'Guinea service or gaol'.[70] This was a critical mode of recruitment, yet there were a few captains who were able to build up a loyal following by virtue of being 'fair-minded' commanders. Alexander Falconbridge thought James Fraser was one, at least the only one he happened to work with; indeed, a deputy clerk in Bristol, sympathetic to abolition, tartly remarked that Fraser was the only captain from the port 'who did not deserve to be hanged'.[71]

The muster rolls of Bristol tend to confirm Fraser's popularity. In 1786 and again in 1787 Fraser began his ventures to Africa with seamen he knew. In each case over half of his crew had sailed with him before, although some of them departed the ship in the West Indies before the voyage was over, an indication perhaps that the pressures of handling slaves required some sort of cathartic release in the pubs and brothels of the tropics, or that seamen found better-paid berths for their homeward-bound voyages. Or that Fraser's self-proclaimed paternalism, which he paraded before the Commons committee investigating the trade, disguised the fact that he dumped decrepit seamen in Caribbean ports when it suited him, paying them off on the cheap in local currency. Part of Fraser's success likely stemmed from the fact that he recruited some of his key men from his native Scotland. In 1790, when he captained the *Hector*, his steward hailed from Aberdeen and his chief mate from Carron, near Stenhousemuir, close to the estuary of the River Forth.

Yet very few other commanders in Bristol were able to emulate him. Edward Robe retained six of his crew for a second voyage on the *Alfred* in 1786.[72] Thomas Phillips also gained a modest following. In his early voyages to Africa he was able to win back seamen, but his record was uneven. During his voyage to Cape Coast Castle and Bonny as commander of the *Thomas* in 1789, six of his crew mutinied and had to be put on board the *Pomona*. Subsequently few of his crew stayed the course, less than half by the time the vessel left Jamaica.[73]

The fact is that aversion to the slave trade ran high among seamen. Bilateral trips from Bristol to the West Indies could attract a regular crew; voyages to Africa could not. The mortality differential was huge; in the 1780s, an average of 21.5 per cent of seamen died on slaving ships compared to 1.5 per cent on West Indiamen.[74] On the *Wasp*, a former privateer that made two runs to the Slave Coast in the years 1790–2 under the captaincy of William Hutcheson, only the cook and the carpenter returned for the second voyage. On the first trip four men died of fevers at Calabar, two others at sea, and ten of the crew deserted at Jamaica. Hutcheson had to bring in four 'runners' to help man the ship on the homeward run. Experiences like that made seamen averse to chancing their luck in the 'black business'. Clarkson noted how reluctant seamen were to enter the *Brothers* after a disastrous voyage to the Bight of Benin where the captain 'dreadfully' abused the crew, with the result that many seamen died while the vessel lingered on the coast for eight months.[75] Twenty-five of the 34 men who hailed from Bristol died on that venture; and 95 per cent of the original crew.

To be sure, there were a few attractions to working on a slave ship. Seamen were offered two months advance in pay, and it was marginally better than on other mercantile vessels; although such margins disappeared when seamen were paid off in Caribbean currency at the end of the Middle Passage.[76] At the same time the risks were huge. Thomas Clarkson believed that if one compared voyages of equivalent length then more seamen died in three slavers every year than in the rest of Bristol's transatlantic fleet. This was likely an exaggeration but a compelling one. 'Beware and take care/Of the Bight of Benin;' ran one popular jingle, 'For one that comes out,/There are forty go in.'

The result was that slave merchants scrambled to find crews where they could. There were some exceptions. On the well-documented muster roll of the *Cornwall*, 1766–8, half of the crew seem to have been a-slaving on their previous trip.[77] This was unusual. Quite a number of muster rolls for the 1780s and 1790s suggest hasty recruitments. They register a large number of 'unknowns', which I interpret to mean last-minute entries whose place of origin or last port of call was simply not recorded for lack of time or inclination. On the *Brothers*, in her disastrous voyage of 1785–7, the percentage of unknowns among the outgoing crew was as high as 43 per cent.[78] One suspects these were reckless seamen in debt, perhaps even in prison, coerced into joining a slave ship at the caprice of a crimp; or restless seamen like Isaac Parker, who had been injured on a coastal vessel and 'had taken a fancy to go upon the coast of Guinea'.[79] He entered under Captain Pollard, but upon Pollard's death he fell under the command of the mate, John Marshall, the man who tortured and killed the black infant, forcing the mother to throw the child overboard.[80] Crews had to stomach outbreaks of sadistic, psychotic behaviour such as this, and more routinely deal with the disagreeable task of keeping captive Africans free from the bloody flux and other diseases that could sweep through the lower deck. The hold 'was so covered with the blood and mucus' of sick slaves, noted surgeon Alex Falconbridge upon an outbreak of dysentery, 'that it resembled a slaughter-house. It is not in the power of the human imagination to picture ... a situation more dreadful or disgusting.'[81] A slave ship was mired in puke, blood and shit. It was a Sisyphean task to keep it tolerably clean. It was not a job for the faint-hearted and it seared the conscience of many. A typical slave crew featured a sizeable number of disgruntled, disoriented men bound for an unpredictable, dangerous and brutally distasteful voyage. In Bristol, in particular, the unsavoury nature of the trade and the high rate of casualties in the early 1790s made recruitment difficult and stretched the available pool of maritime labour.[82]

So who joined Kimber when he set sail in the *Recovery* on 10 April 1791? There were no 'unknowns' among his 27-man crew, but there were a relatively large number of very young men on board, even for a transatlantic vessel.[83] Nearly half of the crew [46 per cent] was under twenty years of age, which was unusual for a slave ship. The two other Bristol vessels that traded in New Calabar at the same time, the *Wasp* and the *Thomas*, had proportionately fewer in that age cohort, 21 and 12.5 per cent respectively. They had more seamen concentrated in the twenty-year-old cohort, 58.5 and 65 per cent, as did the *Brothers* [71 per cent] and the *Prince* [62 per cent] both of which sailed in the same year. A strong cohort of twenty-year-olds, in fact, was typical of transatlantic vessels and men of war.[84]

Two-thirds of Kimber's crew was under 25 years of age, although this did not necessarily mean they were inexperienced, which was important because the *Recovery* was undermanned compared to Liverpool vessels.[85] Justinian Symes, the third mate from Poole, aged 24, had spent thirteen years at sea. Robert Mills, a Scottish seaman, had sailed for twelve of his twenty-two years. Ten members of the crew [including Kimber] had spent ten years or more at sea; that is, over a third of the company. The *Recovery* was crewed by a solid minority of experienced men; the average number of years at sea was seven, with over 70 per cent having five or more. As far as I can tell, this experience was rarely on a slaver. Kimber had at least two slaving voyages under his belt, but of the others we know very little. Of the two principal witnesses against Kimber at his trial, only Stephen Devereux had been on a slave ship before.[86]

Kimber's crew was distinguished by the fact that it hailed entirely from the British Isles, with three from Ireland and the rest from Britain. This was a little unusual because most Bristol crews of this era had a smattering of foreigners, even on the outward run, although they were hardly as 'multi-ethnic' as is sometimes alleged. Mike Breward has shown that only 7 per cent of all seamen aboard Bristol slavers in the years 1790–5 were 'foreigners', that is, people born outside Britain and Ireland. Stephen Behrendt came up with comparable figures.[87] Indeed the latter has suggested that only 3 per cent of Bristol and Liverpool crews were men of colour. The *Thomas* had a Prussian on board when it left Bristol in February 1791, and three blackjacks from Africa: Ambrose Franaire, James Jones and Jean Baptiste, the latter hailing from Annamaboe. They were seaman who had been recruited on a previous run and decided to remain in the trade, for there is a record of their return to Bristol a year later. The *Albion* had an all-British crew when it left Kingroad in April 1790, although the death of eight men on the African coast and a slave insurrection at Cape Mount in January 1791 forced it to take on others. These included a third mate from New York, two Scotsmen from Glasgow, and two Portuguese seamen from Lisbon.[88] The diversification of crews was often the product of such contingencies. Black seamen who took advantage of these opportunities did so at some risk, for there was a chance they might be re-enslaved.[89]

Half of Kimber's crew hailed from the South West, which is a little over the average Mike Breward has assigned to Bristol slave ships in this period, although slightly less than those in Stephen Behrendt's sample.[90] In the circumstances it is doubtful whether Kimber's reputation as a privateer made any difference to the composition of his crew. Certainly there were no crewmen from the *Hornet* on Kimber's *Recovery* a decade later.[91] It is more likely that seamen entered this slaving venture out of poverty rather than the lure of a Kimber captaincy. Among the crew was a boy aged thirteen from Shepton Mallet who had no maritime experience at all. He hailed from a depressed woollen town where alternative forms of employment, in the Mendip pits in particular, were dangerous and precarious.[92] Other members included illiterate sailors who initially took to the sea in their pre- or early teens, possibly children from broken homes or orphans sent off to relieve the family budget. Other sources, such as the Ordinary of Newgate's account, suggest that children from marginal families were often sent to sea, and Bristol had a huge orphan population at the beginning of the century. Almost a quarter of all households with children were single-parent operations. There is no reason to suspect that number diminished substantially as the century progressed.[93] In the one parish just east of Bristol for which we have a detailed record, 20 per cent of poor-law recipients were either unwed mothers or from broken homes.[94]

Another index of marginality is literacy, and here the figures are striking. Forty-three per cent of Kimber's crew could not sign their names, a higher percentage than on the *Hornet* [32 per cent], the *Thomas* [32 per cent] and the *Prince* [38 per cent], but roughly similar to the *Wasp* in her 1790 voyage [41 per cent], the *Crescent* in 1791 [45 per cent], and the *Pearl* and *Sally* in 1785 [47 per cent and 41 per cent].[95] These figures reveal that sailors were marginally more literate than soldiers, more literate than labourers and servants, but never on a par with artisans, even in the populous textile trades.[96] Relatively high rates of illiteracy spoke to the proletarianisation of seafaring, as did the fact that seamen boarded their first vessel at any time between the ages of 10 and 24. They were not conspicuously clustered in their early teens, which one would expect if they took up articles of apprenticeship.[97] In the sixteenth and mid-seventeenth century seafaring was still regarded as a craft. A mariner served a regular apprenticeship; he was trained by a master. By the eighteenth century so-called 'mariners' were often a select breed, putative mates or masters of a ship. Only 77 appear in the 1734 poll book, when sailors in port numbered in the hundreds if not thousands.[98] Most seamen were wage earners who learnt their skills on the fly. George St Lo thought the main qualification for a seaman was that he should learn the 'mechanic part' of the job, which was to 'Reef and Furl, and take his Trick at Helm, and to be a Man at all Calls'.[99]

Although seamen could earn better wages than agricultural labourers in the late seventeenth century, that gap closed and the prospect of good earnings at sea diminished. Sailors were increasingly drawn from poor families who could not place their children in apprenticeships or from those who broke craft indentures for the vicarious excitement and freedom of the waves. The precariousness of seafaring was registered in the Bristol probate inventories, in the meagre holdings of men lost at sea: John Daniel, 'mariner', left 7 months' wages on the slave ship *Society* and his 'wearing apparel' totalling £9-9-6d, or about £9.47; Thomas Walling's wealth amounted to only two months' back pay on the slaver *Freke Galley*; Peter Welch had five months' pay on the *Calabar Merchant*, a slave ship sailing to Africa and Rappahannock river, Virginia. These three seamen left nothing or virtually nothing beyond their outstanding wages and what was on their backs or in their sea chests.[100] And sea chests were not always permitted on slavers because they took up room assigned for the slaves.[101] Imagine what that would do to your 'wardrobe' when the sweat of the day on the Guinea coast was followed by the chill of night.

In April 1791, the *Recovery* left Bristol and reached Cape Coast Castle in early June, sailing on to trade in New Calabar [Elem Kalabari] in the Niger Delta. In previous decades Bristol ships had traded further south at Old Calabar on the Cross River, partly because of the options of buying ivory and palm oil as well as slaves. Some vessels were still dealing there in 1791, despite the fact that the demand for slaves was beginning to exceed the capacity of local Efik merchants and despite the fact that the heavy rains rendered it an area of high mortality. Kimber was instructed to go to New Calabar and Bonny, where the prospect of buying slaves was better, where the credit mechanisms were more efficient and often eliminated the need for pawns, and where the loading rates were faster.[102] These two stations ranked first in the trade, delivering on average 14,500 slaves per year.[103] Yet for some reason in 1791 Kimber found trading hard going. Even the experienced Captain Phillips of the *Thomas* had trouble getting the slaves he wanted, for he smouldered over an unfulfilled contract for 27 slaves and the refusal of locals to provide him with water.[104] As one subsequent report put it, 'There was little traffick carried on for slaves for some time, as too high a price was demanded of them.'[105]

In 1767 Bristol and Liverpool merchants had resolved this sort of conflict very ruthlessly. They manipulated the rivalry between Old and New town, Old Calabar, entrapped several Efik traders on board the *Duke of York*, and colluded with New Town traders in the massacre and enslavement of their rivals. As we have seen, this massacre still resonated in public memory fifteen years or so later.[106] Wilberforce alluded to the incident in the Commons' debate in April 1792, and Houlbrooke printed it up in his *Short Address*. A Captain Hall mentioned the massacre, too, this time before a Commons committee. It led him to conclude that the trade 'was founded in Blood and perfectly illegal'.[107]

What the slave captains did in early August 1791 was just as ruthless if not as sanguinary. The six captains in the Calabar river, three from Liverpool and three from Bristol, including Kimber, held a meeting in which they decided to soften up the Kalabari by bombarding the town. Once a French vessel had ceased trading in New Calabar, the six vessels came abreast of the town and opened fire. A good volley of cannonballs, it was believed, would resolve outstanding contracts and force down the price of slaves. This practice was not unprecedented. Alexander Falconbridge overheard Captain Vicars of Bristol remark that when his traders were slack, he fired a gun over their town 'to freshen their way'. Captain Jeremiah Smith did so as well during a dispute with traders at Old Calabar in 1766.[108]

Whether the vessels fired on or over the town in 1791 became a matter of dispute. Wilberforce railed about the bombardment. It was nothing more than 'bloody and inhuman butchery' to drive down prices and gratify the greed of captains and their avaricious employers.[109] Banastre Tarleton, the MP for Liverpool, retorted that Wilberforce sensationalised the incident. On the authority of another vessel that entered the river, the *Enterprize* of Liverpool commanded by Roger Leathom [Latham], he claimed that the slavers fired over the town to secure legitimate contracts. In his account the slavers inflicted no casualties, and trading resumed quickly after the cannonades, with no reprisals. Even so, the affair was said to have troubled merchants at home, to the extent that some considered prosecuting the captains for murder and piracy off New Calabar at the High Court of Admiralty. If there had been irregularities, Tarleton contended, the Liverpool investors would dismiss the three captains from the port once they returned home; namely, Doyle [*Betsey*], Huson [*Martha*] and Lee [*Amacree*].[110]

None of this happened. No suit regarding the New Calabar bombardment came before the Admiralty Court. The prospect of a mercantile prosecution was a rumour, nothing more. Sir Sampson Wright might have considered committing Kimber for the bombardment in his pre-trial examinations at Bow Street, but he focused on the floggings instead.[111] So the captains evaded criminal censure for firing on New Calabar, and those from Liverpool were not dismissed from their commands, as Tarleton anticipated. All three resumed sailing in slavers, two for the same owners, although Roger Lee took a year off before sailing in the *Bolton*.[112] As for the bombardment, it seems that the intention was to inflict some damage, for the perjury trials of 1793 reported that a few cannonballs of the *Recovery* were heated so they would explode upon impact and set fire to buildings.[113] The Kalabari had to be taught a lesson; don't mess with British captains from the leading slave ports. Six vessels with a total of 66 guns fired off cannonades for two to three hours. They then parleyed with an intermediary who scurried to negotiate with them in a canoe, fired again to hurry along the agreement, and eventually secured one. There were casualties. Kimber's surgeon, Thomas Dowling, was sent ashore to assess the situation. He noted one dead victim and two who were dangerously wounded. The final death toll was calculated at between 25 and 50, although the figure was fiercely contested by the slave traders.[114]

Kimber concluded trading at New Calabar within three and a half weeks of the bombardment. He was on the coast for 91 days, fewer than average even when trading was reasonably brisk.[115] There were conflicting reports as to how many slaves he took on board. One suggested 325 with a high percentage of children, some 57 per cent; another 304 with only 19 per cent under four feet four.[116] The discrepancy can be explained by the fact that Kimber was trying to pack as many slaves as he could into the hold of the 189-ton *Recovery*. Under the terms of the Dolben Act, the maximum number of slaves he could accommodate without penalty was 315.[117] He had ten more than that, and so he classified many as 'children' in order to come under the bar, for five children were regarded as the equivalent of four adults in the Dolben formula. In Grenada, the captives were reclassified, revealing that there were actually over 250 adult slaves on board, but enough children under four feet four to satisfy the 1788 act. Kimber's 'cargo' eventually came in at around 313, two under the bar, probably with a little help or advice from the local customs commissioner. Even so, he didn't get any bonus for low mortality. Had his ship registered a 2 per cent mortality of slaves, Kimber would have received £100 from His Majesty's Treasury. His mortality ratio was 7 per cent.

Compared to the other vessels involved in the New Calabar bombardment, Kimber's *Recovery* did not lose a noticeably high proportion of slaves. All of the ships save the *Thomas* lost 6–7 per cent of their slaves in the Middle

Passage, a figure that was slightly higher than average for this region. The transatlantic trips were shorter, moreover. They ranged from 57 to 75 days, when a typical Middle Passage was 76 days in the late eighteenth century.[118] As the least experienced captain, trading in difficult circumstances, Kimber did reasonably well. He had left Bristol weeks, even a month after the other Bristol boats, and arrived at New Calabar on 2 June 1791, six weeks after the *Thomas* and probably three after the *Wasp*. He missed out on the early trading. Two of the Liverpool vessels came to the coast a month later than Kimber, but they planned to trade at Old Calabar on the Biafran coast as well as the Bight of Benin.

I suspect Kimber's sights were really fixed on the *Wasp*, which was the only other ship destined to sell slaves in Grenada. An ambitious man, Kimber was probably keen to reach the island first and sell, sell, sell. He had the shortest Middle Passage of the group, some 57 days, yet in acquiring 'good quality' slaves he had to reckon with Captain Phillips of the *Thomas*, a man who had been in the Trade for twenty years, had previously commanded five ships to Africa and was a known entity on the coast.[119] He had been bargaining for 450 slaves, over a hundred of who were transferred to another vessel. I can only speculate here, but I suspect that Phillips bought the best slaves. This likely rankled with Kimber. Phillips was a Bideford man like himself. Younger by six years, he had rapidly risen through the ranks on Bristol's slave ships and was clearly outshining Kimber on this trip. It seems likely that Kimber hurried his purchases and did not get the slaves he wanted. At the very least he agonised that they wouldn't sell for the price he hoped. Four died before the vessel had sailed, and dysentery was beginning to break out on the tightly packed ship.[120]

This was an extra inducement for Captain Kimber to leave the coast before the others: eight days before the *Thomas*, and weeks, even months before the rest. My impression, and it is only an inference derived from sailing schedules, is that

Kimber was determined to recoup what he could from this first voyage and plan a quick turn around. He was well ahead of the *Wasp* in selling his slaves in Grenada; in fact, he was back in Bristol before Captain Hutcheson had even reached his port of call. Kimber anchored in Kingroad, at the estuary of the Avon, on 22 December 1791, and was ready to sail out again in less than three months.[121]

Certainly Kimber's behaviour on the Middle Passage registers acute frustration. He quarrelled with Thomas Dowling, a surgeon from Cashel in Ireland, who had accused the carpenter, John Hamly, of stealing six shirts. Kimber dismissed the charge and struck Dowling for his 'impertinent' accusation. When the 25-year-old surgeon retaliated by collaring the captain at his cabin door, Kimber had him confined in irons for 24 hours and sent to mess with the topmen on salted food.[122] Kimber also threatened to stop half of Dowling's wages and deprive him of one of his privileged slaves. This deepened the rift between them and undermined the health of the ship because the surgeon's mate, Miles Meredith, had died of a fever in mid-July at New Calabar. The only medical care available now came from a disgruntled surgeon; described as five feet six inches tall, with brown hair, grey eyes and a fair complexion.[123]

Beyond his altercation with Dowling, Kimber drove the crew hard, very likely because his ship was undermanned. Given his target of over 300 slaves, Kimber should have had a crew of at least thirty at the outset. As it was, he began his voyage with 25 seamen and lost two while trading: Meredith and the third mate, Justinian Symes.[124] Symes was replaced by Devereux from the *Wasp*, which relieved some of the pressure. Nonetheless, with a full 'cargo' of slaves and a smaller-than-average crew, Kimber doubtless felt he had to run a tight ship. Consequently, he withdrew the crew's grog ration during the Middle Passage and chivvied the men to do their duty.[125] John Wilkins, a nineteen-year-old from Tenby who had already served seven years at sea, declared

Kimber was 'a very bad captain to deal with' for he cuffed or whipped the crew for the slightest offence. As he colourfully put it, Captain Kimber 'flogged every morning for breakfast', a turn of phrase that echoed punishments in the plantations, where magistrates supervised whippings over their repasts.[126] In the face of this hard discipline, six seamen considered leaving the boat at Grenada, but Kimber pre-empted a mass desertion by having a magistrate in Grenada threaten them with a spell in jail.[127] In the end only one member of the crew left the ship: Ted Williams, an ordinary seaman from Bristol, aged 19 years. He felt he had a right to desert on account of the 'ill-usage'.[128]

Kimber was uncompromisingly harsh to his crew, although he was not as pathologically brutal in his punishments as others. In the Commons inquiry on the slave trade we encounter a captain who forced his Portuguese cook to eat cockroaches because he served up mean fare. The cook was then whipped and brine was poured into his welts.[129] In 1787 the incorrigible Captain Williams of the *Ruby* tied his cooper, Thomas Wyatt, to the shrouds and gave him twelve lashes because he complained of lack of sleep. Two months later he beat him again with a double inch rope and punched him in the face. James Arnold, the surgeon, said he 'found contusions on his back, breast and downwards to his thighs'. His head and face were 'much swelled'.[130] Kimber did not victimise members of his crew with such noteworthy brutality. He reserved this for his slaves.

All the indications are that Kimber began to worry about his likely profits from the voyage. His time on the African coast had not been spectacularly long, just three months, yet the death of four slaves and the dysentery troubled him.[131] The prospect of losing more and not getting a good return on his 'cargo' seemed to haunt him as he sailed to Grenada. He became enraged when slaves refused to eat or dance on deck, an aerobic imperative designed to raise their spirits and keep their muscles honed. Those refusals threatened to lower their price, for weak slaves had to be sold at scrambles at lower-than-average rates and refuse slaves at a pittance. And slaves who died from dejection or refusing to eat could not be claimed on insurance policies.[132]

An old slave called O'Kiebra or O'Keibra was flogged because she would not eat her allowance of beans and yams; so severely that her flesh mortified. She survived two-thirds of the Middle Passage, 'gradually declining in health and spirits' as the journey progressed.[133] The same happened to a well-proportioned female whom the crew called Venus, presumably because she was sexually desirable and vulnerable to the sailors' lust. How many of the crew assaulted her is unclear, but Thomas Dowling, whose job it was to inspect the slaves and who had 'danced' with them, reputedly had. He was a sexual predator, a man whom the surgeon of the *Thomas* accused of professional 'improprieties'.[134] Members of the crew alleged that Venus infected Dowling, and that Dowling passed on his venereal complaint to another attractive girl brought on board by the African trader, Jackamacree.[135] Whether Venus poxed Dowling or vice versa, she did not want to be part of the sexual commerce of the ship. She went on hunger strike and she was flogged for it. She also fouled herself; perhaps to reduce her attractiveness or simply because she was sick. What is certain is that the abuse killed her. After four or five days of flogging she fainted way at the sight of Kimber standing with his thong whip in the gangway. She expired soon after.[136]

These brutalities formed part of the initial charge against Kimber, who was indicted for three murders, those of O'Keibra and two unnamed females, one nicknamed Venus. We know this from the recognisance signed by Sampson Wright, the Bow Street magistrate, requesting that Thomas Dowling and Stephen Devereux give evidence against the captain.[137] In the end, the trial centred on the unnamed girl. She was thought to be 14 or 15 years of age, although one account believed she was a few years older.[138] Wilberforce argued that she caught Kimber's attention because she refused to dance on account of her 'modesty', but the sordid truth was that she had contracted a severe case of gonorrhoea and had, because of her captivity, her rape, and her illness, fallen into a lethargic melancholia. Where and by whom she was raped is unknown. Dowling claimed that she had the clap when she came on board which produced 'no sore or ulcer but a simple discharge'.[139]

Dowling probably steered clear of the diseased girl; yet given his silence about other sexual assaults on board the ship, his testimony about her sexual history is unreliable.[140] What we do know is that she was too depressed to eat the food given her and unwilling to dance on the deck. The treatment she received from Dowling did not help. It produced a 'salivation', it inflamed her head and tongue, which lolled outside her mouth, and induced drowsiness.[141] According to Devereux, who believed the girl also had the flux, Kimber lost patience with her a week or so after the *Recovery* left New Calabar for Grenada. Perhaps he feared her actions might prompt a general hunger strike. Dowling claimed 'she did not eat as hearty as the rest of the prisoners' with the result that Kimber 'flogged her frequently with a thong whip'.[142] This was later corroborated by crewman Ted Williams, who testified that No-name was flogged every day for a week; 'sometimes with a bit of rope, and sometimes with a whip'.[143]

On 22 September Kimber adopted a more dramatic strategy. The girl bent her knee inwards and walked crookedly. She could not dance with the other female slaves.[144] So the captain tried to stretch out her limbs before the ship reached Grenada; that way she would fetch a better price. He had her hoisted from the mizzen stay and bounced or jerked, to straighten her out. First one arm, then another, then one leg, then another, and finally by both hands so that her toes barely touched the deck. According to Thomas Dowling she was suspended for roughly half an hour in total, and in each position she was flogged with a thong whip of roughly six feet in length.[145] She would not straighten out; even when Joseph Pearson, the ordinary seaman who was ordered to assist, pulled hard on her limbs and massaged her joints with palm oil. After each suspension No-Name collapsed on the floor, her head below her knees. Dowling said 'she was welted in several parts of her body' with 'marks of Whip on Arms & Legs' and her hands swollen.[146] Kimber thought her a 'sulky bitch' for not dancing, and when he had finished lashing, prodding, slapping and stretching her, to no avail, he told Pearson not to bother helping her to the hold.[147] She crawled to the hatch, took a few steps, and slithered down the ladder. She collapsed in convulsions, desolate and deranged. Dowling tried to revive her with 'vital spirits' without success. No other female slave would comfort her on account of her condition and within three or four days, she died.

Kimber thought nothing of it. He had lost a disposable slave who would have fetched a poor price. As John Newton recognised, the Trade could quickly 'efface the moral sense' and 'rob the heart of every gentle and humane disposition.' Kimber's attitude, in fact, anticipates the 'banality of evil' that Hannah Arendt attributed to Adolf Eichmann at his 1961 trial for his role in the Holocaust.[148] That is to say, he displayed a mundane indifference to the suffering of his slaves; disciplining them, and disciplining them harshly, was simply part of his job. Others declined to contest the captain's actions, as well. Surgeon Dowling did not report the incident at Grenada, although he was supposed to under the Dolben Act. The crew remained silent. The whipping occurred on the awning or upper deck, which was separated from the main deck by a seven-foot barricade, a precaution against sudden slave insurrections. Consequently, most of the crew would not have witnessed the flogging; but they must have heard it, and No-Name's groans.[149]

4

The trial

Captain Kimber was arrested within days of Wilberforce's denunciation of him in the Commons. The arrest surprised members of the Trade, who believed Wilberforce or the Abolition Committee was behind it.[1] In fact the prosecution was public not private, noteworthy because the Board of Admiralty, who were responsible for murder on the high seas, had resisted calls for a criminal prosecution in the Zong affair some nine years earlier. Prosecutions for murdering slaves were not unknown in Admiralty courts, but they were extremely rare. As I have already mentioned, the only instance I have discovered at the Old Bailey itself occurred in 1759, when William Lugen, the captain of another Bristol ship, the *Hope*, was indicted for throwing a four-month-old baby overboard.[2] He was acquitted because in the jury's view the child had the bloody flux [dysentery] and had lost her mother. She was dying anyway, so the jurymen thought; in the language of insurance, from 'natural causes'.

Precisely who pushed for a state prosecution is not at all clear. I have found no hint in the Pitt papers or the Admiralty records, whether those of the Board or the Admiralty Solicitor, or in the letters to the Admiralty from the Privy Council and the Secretary of State. What I do know is that by virtue of a warrant issued by the High Court of Admiralty, Bow Street runners Thomas Carpmeal and John Miller were dispatched to Bristol to arrest Captain Kimber on Friday, 6 April 1792. They called at his house at 27 Redcross Street, but Kimber seems to have made himself scarce. The runners could not find him all day Saturday, and so they left a message on Sunday morning that they wished to talk to him about shipping some goods and would meet him at the Exchange between 12 and 1 pm. Kimber was likely in hiding, and may only have agreed to turn himself in at the behest of some Bristol merchants. When he arrived at the Exchange, the runners took him into custody. By the time the runners left the Bush Tavern in Corn Street for London, word had circulated that Kimber had been arrested and the streets were crowded.[3]

Kimber was taken to London to be examined by the Bow Street magistrate, Sir Sampson Wright.[4] He was scheduled to command the *Recovery* again; he had been entered on the muster rolls as the master in late February, and the owners scrambled to find a replacement. One newspaper suggested that had the *Recovery* not been delayed from sailing by an accident on the River Avon, Kimber would have been on the high seas, not in London's principal criminal prison.[5] As it was, Kimber found himself in Newgate on the night of 9 April, along with 400 other inmates, fifteen of who were under a sentence of death.[6] Wright examined Kimber regarding the bombardment of New Calabar and the floggings of three 'negro women' on the Middle Passage. According to the *Bath Herald*, Kimber admitted that he had beaten the women, but only to 'make them eat, which was frequently a necessary conduct'.[7] On this second set of charges Sampson Wright was satisfied that the pre-trial examination merited a committal, the testimony against Kimber coming from the surgeon Thomas Dowling and the third mate, Stephen Devereux, formerly of the *Wasp*, who had joined the *Recovery* on 26 August 1791. Kimber had counsel at this pre-trial examination in Bow Street, and his lawyer, Mr Morgan, was confident that he would be acquitted. He insinuated that Wilberforce and company had misconstrued the facts and declared he would gather 'some of the first people in Bristol' to prove it.[8] John Baker Holroyd, one of Bristol's

MPs, believed the arrest had been altogether too hasty and the charge 'severe and impolitic'. In his view, Wilberforce's accusations and the rapid arrest prejudiced the case against Kimber from the start because of the adverse publicity.[9]

Publicity there certainly was. Kimber sought to contain the outcry by announcing that he would publish his own account of what happened on the *Recovery*. On 5 April 1792, he published a notice imploring the public not to assume he was guilty 'of the atrocious crimes then laid to his charge'. He assured his readers he would 'submit the facts to public discussion' within a few days. Once arrested, his lawyers advised against it.[10] A published defence might backfire. Wilberforce's emotive comments about Kimber in the Commons, he was a 'barbarous wretch' whose indifference to suffering typified the slave trade, reverberated around Britain. Within two months it had reached the shores of America, surfacing in newspapers from Portland, Maine, to Maryland.[11] As far as the Yorkshire philanthropist was concerned, people like Kimber were despicable individuals inured to cruelty, robbery and even murder. His crime ran high in the annals of depravity. Newspapers across the British Isles covered the accusation very closely.[12] The *Newcastle Courant* produced a supplement of the debate while the *Derby Mercury* and the *Hibernian Chronicle* [Cork] seem to have had their own reporters in the gallery; they did not simply echo reports from the metropolis.

Three London newspapers detailed the Bow Street examinations, although the *Chronicle* declined to do so for fear of prejudicing the jury.[13] Sir Sampson Wright was similarly concerned that the advance publicity given the trial would compromise a fair one.[14] Indeed, some supporters of the slave trade, fearing that Kimber's behaviour might compromise the argument that the regulations under the Dolben Act were sufficient to contain murderous acts of violence, published a piece of fake news.[15] He suggested that Bristol's West India merchants had actually arrested Kimber at the

Exchange, a seemingly responsible act designed to rein in a reckless slave captain. If those merchants played any part, it was to encourage Kimber to observe the law.

John Baker Holroyd feared Kimber would fester in irons until December, but in fact Kimber's trial came up considerably earlier, on 7 June 1792 at the High Court of Admiralty. There was huge interest in the trial and the courtroom at the Old Bailey was 'crouded at an early hour'. One newspaper reported that the court filled up within minutes of opening its doors at noon.[16] Among the spectators were merchants and admirals who had given positive testimony about the slave trade to the Commons committee. Particularly noticeable was the royal vice-admiral, William, Duke of Clarence, the third son of George III. By virtue of his rank he was allowed to sit on the right hand of the chairman of the sessions, Sir James Marriott.[17] This concession to rank was a concession to the slave-trade lobby, for Clarence was a strong opponent of abolition. In his maiden speech to the Lords a month earlier, Clarence declared himself 'an attentive observer of the state of the negroes', having been on naval duty in the Caribbean during the 1780s with Horatio Nelson. In his opinion the blacks there were in a state of 'humble happiness' and if the slave trade was lopped off, other nations would cash in and destroy a valuable commercial asset of Britain. He demanded a 'full and substantial proof' of the 'enormities' complained of by the abolitionists in the Commons and urged his fellow peers to stand up to popular pressure. He had even been prepared to give evidence to the Privy Council on behalf of the slave trade, based on his limited experience in the West Indies.[18]

Clarence took a keen interest in the trial. He had read some of the depositions in Kimber's favour, and he was disposed to giving advice to his counsel. At the trial itself he was not an impartial or silent observer. Although one writer thought he helpfully clarified some maritime terminology for the court, others felt he was an unseemly meddler, smirking and laughing when the prosecuting witnesses sweated under tough questioning. One edition of the trial thought it reprehensible that the duke should show such a partiality for Kimber and for the slave trade, which could only signify his love of 'uncontroulable tyranny'.[19] Another, printed by the radical H. D. Symonds, deplored his indifference to the whippings. It noted that when a witness faltered under cross-examination, 'his Grace was almost convulsed with a species of merriment, which in any other person would be deemed unfeeling and ridiculous. He bit his lips, smiled, shook his head in exultation', and 'winked at some of his slave friends in the gallery'.[20]

Brycchan Carey has found the trial a disappointing foray into the sentimental rhetoric of the slave trade debate, largely because court records 'remain legally blind to tone, nuance and innuendo'.[21] If Kimber's trial had simply left the bare bones of a legal record, Carey's remarks about what he terms 'forensic rhetoric' might have held some weight, but in fact the trial record spilt out to the public in the form of newspaper reportage and rival accounts, of which four survive.[22] These are full of nuance, intertextual engagement and dialogue, as we shall see. The Kimber trial, in effect, was an event, a spectacle in which abolitionists confronted the slave trade over the evidence of slaving atrocities; in this case the brutal and fatal flogging of a young girl. The stakes were high, as Clarence's appearance on the bench indicated.

Clarence's presence signified that the slave-trade interest would stand by Kimber, who many believed was the unwitting victim of Wilberforce's wild and extravagant accusations. Horatio Nelson joined the duke at the trial. He had married into a planter family from Nevis and described himself as a member of 'the good old school' that was 'taught to appreciate the value of our West India possessions'.[23] Kimber's supporters included Robert Harrison, a London banker and likely investor in a slaving venture in 1802;[24] and Lord Sheffield, the Bristol MP who had written a pamphlet against abolition and denounced Wilberforce's so-called exposé of the captain. 'A melancholy instance of malice and credulity', so he asserted.[25] Also present was William Jones, now a retired Bristol merchant. He was the former owner of the *Two Brothers* slave ship and part-owner of the *Hornet*, the privateer that brought he and Kimber a lot of money.[26] Among the admirals present was Samuel Barrington, who had commanded the Leeward Islands squadron during the American war, and whose maternal grandfather, Sir William Daines, had been a tobacco merchant, Merchant Venturer, Bristol mayor and MP. Also in attendance was George Daubeny, the former MP for the City, a sugar refiner, banker and glass manufacturer. He had been a member of Bristol's original abolition committee, but it seems he switched sides the following year for he attended an anti-abolitionist meeting convened by the Merchant Venturers.[27]

Completing the Bristol group was John Noble, a Newfoundland merchant, insurer and current mayor of the City.[28] A day after Kimber's arrest he had deliberated over the signing of depositions in support of the captain. He did this as the mayor and major magistrate, but one suspects it was not a vexatious task given his occasional investment in slavery. Although Noble was principally involved in the cod trade, he had from time to time dabbled in multilateral voyages to the middle colonies of America. He owned or had a major stake in seven privateers during the American war. On one of these ventures his ships captured a French prize, which was subsequently converted into a slave ship. In 1785 the *Hector*, as the vessel was called, embarked on a journey to the Gold Coast and picked up over 500 slaves for Dominica and Jamaica.[29] Noble was so interested in Kimber's trial that he took the extraordinary step of travelling down to London to claim a seat on the High Court bench, on the grounds that Bristol's ancient charters entitled him to sit as an Admiralty judge. He appeared before the astonished judges in his full regalia, only to withdraw once his right was admitted.[30] This pompous spectacle was clearly designed to flag mercantile Bristol's support for the captain and intimidate the prosecuting witnesses.

The slave-trade lobby did not simply back their man; it mustered evidence exculpating Kimber from the charges against him. Ten petty officers and seamen aboard the *Recovery* swore Kimber was a humane captain who had never flogged the girl. She had been suspended from the mizzen stay on the orders of the surgeon, Thomas Dowling, to improve her circulation and tone up and stretch her muscles. Her death was not caused by Kimber's cruelty, they deposed, but from a combination of disease and medical incompetence. Dowling had put her in such a state of salivation as to endanger her life; and by feeding her tropical fruits had brought on dysentery.[31] These statements constituted a robust rebuttal of the prosecution's case. To press home the point, the defence team had the witnesses travel to London within days of Kimber's committal in order to be examined by Wright. They were housed near the Old Bailey, at the Bell Savage Inn on Ludgate Hill. The seamen stayed there for several days and then moved to cheaper quarters in Chelmsford, but not before they had made themselves public, on the street and on the river. Sir James Marriott was made aware of their presence two weeks before the trial began. They were called 'Captain Kimber's witnesses'.[32]

The question arises as to whether 'Captain Kimber's witnesses' were cajoled or bribed to give evidence on his behalf. Just how much pressure was put upon them to testify? Bristol's slavers were a powerful group, linked to the levers of local power and well placed on institutions like the Merchant Venturers that managed charitable aid for seamen and their families. One can imagine that the two mates who testified, John George of Bristol, and James Corrick of Dartmouth, both aged 30, might not have wanted to rock the boat and testify against a captain who was liked by many merchants. They had their families, jobs and the prospect of being promoted to commander to consider. In fact, John George appears to have gone on to command a small slaver to Annamaboe in 1793.[33] If they had only heard the suspension and flogging of the girl – a seven-foot barricade separated most of the crew from the quarterdeck – they might have given the captain the benefit of the doubt. In the fourteen years they had both been at sea, they must have seen quite a few cuffs and beatings, so what was one more?

I don't write this callously or cynically. Even Thomas Dowling, the surgeon who accused Kimber of murder, declared that beatings and occasional deaths were so 'customary on board slave ships' that seamen sometimes shrugged them off.[34] In the cut-and-thrust of cross-examination in this trial and those that followed, it is clear there was a high tolerance or resigned acceptance of violence on board ship. On a slave ship, in particular, the casual beating of slaves and sailors was habitual. At various points in these trials a sailor swore there no floggings, meaning no formal floggings. Elias Mansfield, the armourer on the *Recovery* claimed in the perjury trials that Kimber did not flog No-Name, but he did 'touch' her with the whip. 'You don't call that flogging with a horse-whip?' counsel asked. 'It was correction', he replied, not 'punishment', inferring that a slave who refused to eat or dance could expect a few strokes, as might a sailor for slovenly work. 'If you strike a man once on board a ship, is that a flogging?' interjected Thomas Erskine. 'No', replied Mansfield, 'when a man is hauled up, and flogged with a cat [o' nine tails], that is a flogging.'[35] No-name was not 'flogged' when suspended, Mansfield continued, at least not in his presence, although she was 'touched up'; in more ways than one, one suspects, because she was rubbed down with palm oil. Tolerance or familiarity of violence could work in Kimber's favour.

Even so, there was a wide discrepancy between those who thought No-name was 'corrected' and those who believed she was beaten with 'uncommon severity'. A few

seamen on the *Recovery* thought Kimber's behaviour despicable enough to merit legal action. Two of them, Robert
Mills and Evan Richards [sometimes Pritchard], considered
committing Kimber's cruel actions to paper while they
were on board ship during the Middle Passage. We have
this on the testimony of Ted Williams, who deserted the
ship in Grenada, but gave evidence at the perjury trials.[36]
And when the ship anchored in Bristol around Christmas
1791, other members of the crew huddled at the Chepstow
Boathouse on Welsh Back to consider what they might do.
According to Ann Grace, the landlady of the pub, Mills
was still keen to take Kimber to court: 'he has done worse
than beating us, for he has murdered a Black Woman', he is
said to have declared.[37] Most agreed: one lodger at the pub
observed that the general sense of the company was 'if ever
there was a woman murdered in the world, Captain Kimber
killed that girl.[38] The only seaman reluctant to push the
issue was Harry Watkins, the cook, but others wondered
how they should go about it. 'What use is it going to law?'
one remarked, 'we have no money.[39] One of them proposed
that they should send the information to 'the gentleman in
Parliament', namely Wilberforce.

In the end no one in the company did this. Although
the story circulated through Bristol in the first half of 1792,
it was Dowling and Devereux who eventually informed
Clarkson and Wilberforce of the death of the slave girl. Bob
Mills, in fact, turned coat. He had entered for the *Triton*
after the slave voyage, but he was sent for by Kimber's supporters at the White Hart in Union Street and offered £5
or five guineas to change his story. Anne Grace chided him
for changing his tune, but he replied that 'before he swore
for Captain Kimber or anybody else, he would have cloaths
on his back and his Landlady should be paid Three Pounds'.
The pressures of hand-to-mouth living eroded his resolve.
He was embarrassed by his volte-face. He tried to pretend
that the money he received was back pay, and he alleged he

was 'nonplussed' when he came to sign the affidavit exoner-
ating Kimber, scarcely knowing what he was doing. 'I did not
know hardly what it was', so he claimed.[40]

Mills was not the only seaman courted by the Kimber
faction. It won over two key witnesses, the armourer Elias
Mansfield and ordinary seaman Evan Richards, who had
both witnessed No-name's suspensions. It strove to win
over Stephen Devereux, who alleged that Kimber's brother
or brother-in-law approached him in Bristol, a fact that the
defence team tried to suppress. When Devereux blurted this
out under cross-examination at Kimber's trial, the defence
counsel quickly switched topics.[41] Kimber's supporters
also tried to corner the deserter, Edward Williams, on his
return from a voyage to Sweden. He had been responsible
for fetching the tackle to hoist up the girl, and according
to one account he had been ordered to bounce her up and
down to try to stretch out her limbs. He complained that a
Captain Goodridge came to his lodgings in Wapping and
attempted 'to draw words out of my mouth'.[42] He resolutely
refused to co-operate, but he was too isolated from the legal
prosecution to pose much of a threat to Kimber. The defence
only contacted him the day of the trial, when he arrived in
the Thames from a voyage in the Baltic.[43] The prosecuting
counsel probably did not know where he was after Grenada.
Marshalling evidence from mariners was a perennial problem. They were too mobile for the process of the law: often
at sea when they were required to testify. This was the case
with Joseph Pearson, who had helped hoist up No-name and
rubbed her down with palm oil. He had taken another ship
to Africa, sailing on the *Royal Charlotte* in February 1792
and not returning until the end of the year.[44]

Still, the strategy of the Kimber camp was clear: buy
off as many key witnesses as possible, intimidate his most
vocal critics, and make a great parade of those who would
offer an alternative narrative to Wilberforce's account in
the Commons. In the event Kimber's back-up boys proved

unnecessary. The slave traders wanted to make this trial a test of abolitionist evidence. In this respect it is important to note that when *Felix Farley's Bristol Journal* reported Wilberforce's accusations about the behaviour of slave captains, the brutality of the trade, and the hardships of plantation slavery, it immediately countered by printing extracts from the Privy Council inquiry where noteworthy admirals reflected on the benign character of West Indian slavery. It even cited commentators who maintained the slave trade stanched the bloodbaths of African sacrifice. In this far-fetched scenario, the slave trade 'civilised' Africans who otherwise would have been beheaded to satisfy the egos of kings and princes. To abolish it, perversely maintained James Boswell, would be to 'shut the gates of mercy on mankind'.[45] As it was, slavers were pleased that Kimber's defence team zoned in on the issue of evidence, because they had felt that the most recent testimonies of the Commons inquiry had left them at little vulnerable on that score.[46] Delving into the fatal beating of the girl was likely to be toxic in the summer of 1792 when so many people were up in arms about the slave trade.

In his charge to the jury, the chairman of the Admiralty session, Sir James Marriott, stacked the deck in favour of Kimber. He began by urging the jury to divest themselves 'from everything which popular and general opinion, inflamed at any time by particular circumstances, may suggest'. This was a reasonable request for some sort of impartiality in the wake of the publicity surrounding Kimber's arrest and committal, although the 'inflammation' could easily have been construed as a veiled critique of Wilberforce's emotive accusations in the Commons and the frothy rhetoric of some abolitionists. Sir James then went on to allow Kimber a wide range of discretionary violence by suggesting that captains were sovereigns of their ship to whom everyone should defer. 'A ship is a little government', he told London's jurymen, 'compressed into a narrow compass, in which there can be no hope of security for any man who is embarked in it, without a rapid and strong occasional exertion of an absolute power, placed in one man ... The original passions of human nature operate there in their full violence, and all on board of a ship is too often nothing but one scene of misery and terror, disorder, disobedience, confederacy, resentment and revenge.'[47] The imagery played to a propertied jury panicked by developments in France, where Louis XVI was fighting for his life, and where popular unrest was taking a violent turn. It played, too, to the carnage at St Domingue. And in the light of what emerged in the trial about the Kimber's relationship with the two material witnesses, Thomas Dowling and Stephen Devereux, the charge gave the captain a concessionary uplift. On a plane such as this, criticisms of the captain's actions could easily be construed as malicious, and both witnesses had run into trouble with captains on board ship.

It was on the actions and character of the two witnesses that the defence rested its case. After an urbane introduction from the prosecuting counsel, Sir William Scott, in which he admitted that Dowling's evidence was inconsistent if not contradictory, the leading defence counsel, Arthur Leary Pigott, went for the jugular. Pigott was a Foxite Whig, a member of the Friends of the People, which eventually got him in trouble with the Prince of Wales, for who he was solicitor general. But unlike Fox, Pigott was an advocate for the slave trade, a Barbadian who began his legal career in Grenada. He had opposed Sir William Dolben's bill to regulate the slave trade on the grounds that the slave-to-tonnage formula would make the trade 'impracticable'. And he had acted as counsel for the Liverpool merchants petitioning against the bill.[48] He was not about to pass up an opportunity to discredit Wilberforce and expose his extravagant denunciations of slave captains, despite the fact that in the Zong case some nine years earlier he had acted for the insurers not the traders. In that suit he had ironically urged that Captain Collingwood and his crew be indicted for murder and had expatiated on the humanity of slaves.[49] Pigott could clearly press the abolitionist case when called upon to do so. He was one of those lawyers excoriated by Granville Sharp for arguing cases 'diametrically opposite to their own declared opinions of law.'[50]

In Thomas Dowling Pigott had a relatively easy target. Whatever the truth of Dowling's allegations about the treatment of No-name, Dowling had grudges against Kimber that might colour his judgment. They had fallen out; Dowling had suffered a humiliating punishment; and he had lost his perk of a second privileged slave.[51] Moreover, Dowling had not denounced Kimber in a clear, consistent manner. He had not objected to the suspension of No-Name or the whipping. In Grenada, where he was obliged to render an account of the deaths on the African coast and the Middle Passage, he had only reported the seamen lost on board, not the slaves. At the trial he peevishly admitted he did not 'kiss the book', that is, formally swear to the facts on the bible.[52] Dowling had not wanted to alienate Kimber any further on the homeward journey. He told Pigott he was worried about his safety. 'When I gave in my journal at Grenada,' Dowling testified, 'I wished to omit every mention of the Negro Girl, from the apprehensions I was under for my safety, not knowing what the prisoner [Kimber] might have done.'[53]

Yet back in Bristol, Dowling took no immediate steps to prosecute Kimber. When he produced a copy of his journal to release his bond at the Customs office, he mentioned the death of only one slave, who died of dysentery.[54] In fact, it seems he was partially placated by the ship's owner, Walter Jacks. In early January 1792 Jacks compensated Dowling for the wages Kimber had denied him, but he refused him the second privileged slave.[55] It was not until late March 1792, when he was asked by a Mr Charles Lloyd, a Birmingham banker, to provide evidence about the bombardment of New Calabar to the Abolition Committee in London, that he mentioned the murder of the girl at all; and then as an afterthought.[56] This behaviour hardly strengthened his testimony. It reinforced the suspicion that he had something to hide; that perhaps his treatment of the girl had been partially responsible for her death. The defence argued that Dowling's smouldering resentment towards John Kimber really prompted his accusation that the captain had murdered the girl, and it did not have any difficulty finding reputable people to back this up. Walter Jacks, the owner of the *Recovery*, Billingsby Riddle, the surgeon on the *Thomas*, and Thomas Laugher [or Laughter], a factor from Birmingham, all noted his vengeful spirit.[57] Jacks testified that when Dowling came to settle his wages, the surgeon had said Kimber was 'a rascal and a cheat' and swore he would 'ruin him if it was in his power.'[58]

Stephen Devereux was a different kind of witness. He had no ostensible grudge against Kimber; in fact, he was obliged to him for taking him on board the *Recovery*. As he said at the trial, 'Captain Kimber had behaved to me as a friend.' He had 'used me well.'[59] Devereux had been the chief mate of the *Wasp*, but he had fallen foul of the captain, William Hutcheson [sometimes Hutchinson], a 24-year old, six years his junior, with less experience at sea. While Hutcheson was ashore at New Calabar, Devereux had allowed two boys on board to settle their differences with a round of fisticuffs. When Hutcheson returned from the coast and confronted the mate about the punch-up, Devereux denied it happened, a lie that led him to be charged and convicted of mutinous behaviour by a board of officers in the river and ejected from the ship.[60] Hutcheson likely feared that any remissness by his chief mate would reverberate through the ship. In the light of the poor returns on his previous voyages and a slave insurrection under his predecessor, he was probably anxious to run a tight operation.[61] Kimber took Devereux on because three weeks earlier he had lost his third mate, Justinian Symes, to tropical fever.

Devereux may have been a troublemaker – he was later accused of 'corrupting people's minds'[62] – but he was hardly about to commit an act of piracy and take control of the ship. The relatively trivial nature of his offence, however, was concealed from the jury by the skilful cross-examination of John Sylvester, the Common Sergeant, who read an extract of the original charge against Devereux, that he was a 'pernicious, dangerous and troublesome fellow', without going into specifics.[63] Devereux denied he had been formally charged with anything; he clearly thought light of the matter. I was a 'little remiss in giving him [Hutcheson] the lie', he admitted, and 'begged his pardon for it'.[64] As far as Devereux was concerned, Captain Hutcheson should have handled the incident more tactfully, not gone over the top. This nonchalance undermined Stephen Devereux's credibility; and so, too, did the fact that while he had 'delicately' mentioned No-name's death to the magistrate at Grenada, he did not accuse Kimber of murdering the girl in the pre-trial examinations at Bow Street.[65] Why was he doing so now? Was it simply that he had been summoned by the Abolition Committee, for some versions of the trial suggested he was a diffident witness for the prosecution.[66] By damning the reputation of the witnesses, the defence team absolved itself of fully confronting the actual evidence of the suspension, the flogging, and the bruises and welts that were inflicted on No-name. There was, in fact, a significant concordance of testimony from Dowling and Devereux about the floggings, one which the prosecution could have pursued more aggressively; either by finding corroborative evidence from other witnesses, or by insisting the defence bring forward its own witnesses for cross-examination, since some of them were spectators to No-name's punishment.

Yet the crown was lethargic and complacent in prosecuting this case. Perhaps the crown counsel had little enthusiasm for pleading it. Politically the barristers were divided about abolition. The Attorney General, Sir Archibald Macdonald, had tried to postpone a motion on Dolben's bill when it was first introduced in the Commons in 1788. The Solicitor General, Sir John Scott, opposed abolition in 1791; his brother, Sir William, the Admiralty's advocate general at the trial, was the only one in favour.[67] Perhaps the problem was that the case was not well prepared. James Dyson, the Admiralty Solicitor, had been ordered on 26 April to prepare the prosecutions for the next Admiralty session on 7 June 1792, but with two murder trials and one case of piracy to handle, he might not have had enough time to build a case against Kimber and muster more evidence.[68] Five to six weeks is not a lot of time if you are trying to track down sailors in the eighteenth century, and Dyson had to reckon with the fact that the defence team had corralled ten of the crew. The welter of testimony that emerged from Devereux's perjury trial in February 1793 suggests this might well have been the case, although if the defence team managed to find Ted Williams, why hadn't the prosecution? And what about James Cruise, the sixteen-year-old boy from Newcastle who had witnessed the punishment on the awning deck? Where was he? By having to rely solely on Dowling and Devereux, who could be cast as dodgy, disreputable witnesses, the crown prosecution was taking a chance. It allowed the defence counsel to indulge in character assassination.

Indeed, having watched these lawyers discredit Devereux and Dowling, Sir James Marriott peremptorily stopped the proceedings. In a trial of just under five hours, he had heard enough. He didn't need to hear more evidence from the defence, which had thus far simply presented merchants and commanders who vouched for Kimber's character. Marriott urged the jury to find the captain not guilty, which they promptly did, without retiring. In the main they were local tradesmen and merchants, all resident in the City. One was a warehouseman, two were highly skilled instrument makers and another with the remarkable name of Onesimus Ustonson sold high-end fishing tackle for anglers from his shop in Bell Yard, Temple Bar. Ten of the twelve were livery-men, although only Joseph Rose junior was a member of the elite twelve companies.[69] One juryman was later said to have West Indian interests, a matter that should have merited a challenge from the prosecution. Basically, the jury appear to have been solid burghers, not the sort of people who would rock the boat.

At the end of the trial, Judge William Ashhurst enter-tained a motion to prosecute Dowling and Devereux for perjury. This reinforced the idea that Wilberforce had cobbled together untrustworthy witnesses in his crusade against Kimber. Overall, the slave lobby was elated by the result, and celebrated at the Bell Savage tavern.[70] Other defenders of the trade present at the trial, such as James Boswell, 'gloried in it'.[71]

Srividhya Swaminathan has described the trial as 'far-cical', a 'sham', which I take to mean that it was a travesty of justice.[72] In general terms I would agree, but it is worth reminding ourselves that the law does not always deliver justice, and when it does, the terms of legal culpability often narrow or occlude the moral compass. In the language of the law, Kimber's contribution to the murder of No-name was a little inconclusive. As I said at the beginning of the book, we cannot be completely bowled over by Cruick-shank's image of a sadistic captain slavering over a slave, however incessantly it insinuates itself into the story. There was no possibility that Kimber could be charged with man-slaughter because that offence was not judiciable at the Admiralty Court until 1799.[73] It was thus up to the prosecu-tion to prove *mens rea*, to show that Kimber had maliciously intended to kill the girl. The burden of proof rested with the prosecution, and yet No-name was not in good shape when she embarked on the *Recovery*. Dowling testified that she had a severe case of gonorrhoea and was 'in a disezed [dis-eased] state all the time on b[oar]d'.[74] The crew said she was 'violently afflicted with the venereal disease' and her arms

and legs 'were daily becoming more contracted'.[75] There
was also some doubt whether the surgeon had dispensed
the appropriate medicines, or possibly had the appropriate
medicines, because there were complaints about the poor
medicine dispatched by Bristol apothecaries to another
slave ship of James Rogers, the part-owner of the *Recovery*
along with Walter Jacks.[76] Dowling denied giving No-name
mercury, although symptoms of salivation suggested he
might have. He did confess to dispensing saltpetre and gum
arabic, but in what quantities is unclear.[77] In the crude phar-
macology of the day, these would only have brought down
No-name's temperature. Saltpetre could 'coole the violent
boyling of the blood', claimed John Woodall in the early
seventeenth century.[78] Combined with a tartar emetic it was
used to reduce fevers, while gum arabic was a cooling agent
and intestinal stabiliser. From the testimony of the seamen
it appears this treatment was ineffective, for No-name had
all the symptoms of a raging fever from dysentery. Dowling
may have added to her discomfort by giving her fresh fruit,
which Captain Phillips of the *Thomas* believed brought on
the bloody flux.[79] The girl was in rough shape and she didn't
improve under Kimber's lashes. Stephen Devereux believed
No-name might have survived the Middle Passage had she
not been whipped.[80] Perhaps. What we can say for sure is
that the slave trade killed her: the long harsh journey to the
coast, the rape, the venereal disease, the dysentery, the poor
medical attention, the lashings, the painful humiliations.
Kimber contributed greatly to her death.

Calling the trial a 'farce' also minimises its political
import. The trial was always bigger than Kimber. As the
Stamford Mercury remarked, the 'trial had in it much of
party'. It proved 'a kind of victory obtained by the advocates
of the slave trade over the *abolitionists*'.[81] To the abolitionists, the Kimber affair was a synecdoche of the slave trade; it
epitomised its callous brutality, a habit of authority in which
atrocities were unrestrained by law and too frequently

beyond its reach. This is what Wilberforce stressed when he said the slave trade sanctioned 'robbery and murder' and bred up characters like Kimber whose 'habits and conduct could not be eradicated'.[82] Tinkering with the Dolben Act would not stop this brutality. As one Scottish reformer argued, the affair reaffirmed 'the moral necessity of an entire and speedy abolition'.[83]

Yet to the slave traders, the Kimber case underscored Wilberforce's wild, extravagant allegations about the traffic in slaves. It was emblematic of the falsehood abolitionists were spreading. A print representing this perspective appeared about the month after Wilberforce's speech in the Commons.[84] Etched by Richard Newton, a young engraver of publisher William Holland, it portrayed the well-known parliamentary figure as a zealous reformer whose pieties and moralistic judgments would do untold damage to Britain's Caribbean economy. Wilberforce is portrayed as a blindfolded fool with the ears of an Ass and a cap covered with the bells of 'Humanity', 'Justice', 'Piety', 'Credulity', 'Calumny' and 'Enthusiasm'. His fiery denunciations of the slave trade simply fuel unrest in the Caribbean, something that the philanthropist cannot see in his quest for a black humanity. Wilberforce himself clutches petitions from Newgate prisoners, Cornish miners and Manchester schoolboys; in the slave-trade lexicon, people of no account.[85] Alongside the philanthropist, a female figure of Justice, also blindfolded, suggests two of his polemical targets – a sailor and a planter – are not guilty of the crimes he attributes to them. The sailor, dressed as an officer rather than a jack tar, no doubt refers to Kimber, with Newton anticipating his acquittal.

The print may have been a satire of pro-slavery argument rather than a defence, for Holland was a publisher whose radical prints put him in trouble with the authorities and finally propelled him into Newgate prison. But this one was ambiguously framed, timely and polemical. Wilberforce had asserted in the Commons that Kimber's

THE BLIND ENTHUSIAST.

8. Richard Newton, *The Blind Enthusiast*, May 1792

fatal flogging of the young African girl was 'beyond dispute a fact', and yet at the Old Bailey that fact had proved to be shaky, if not false.[86] Captain Kimber had been acquitted of murder in the High Court of Admiralty by that 'palladium of British liberty', the jury, and pro-slavery pamphlets drove that fact home. This statement had some purchase in 1792, not simply because the jury's authority was soon to be augmented in libel trials, but because many at the time contrasted the British rule of law with the anarchy of Jacobinism across the Channel. This was graphically represented in Thomas Rowlandson's print, *The Contrast*, which appeared at the end of the year.[87] It depicted Britannia holding Magna Carta and the scales of justice, with a ship departing or defending Britain's shores. The French image featured Fury with a Medusa's head; she trampled on a body whose decapitated head was stuck on her trident. A gentleman hung from a lamppost in the background.

If Wilberforce's charge against Kimber was rejected by a British jury, some of his collateral claims were suspect, too. His assertion that Captain Kimber had been so harsh to his men that only six or seven of the original crew returned to Bristol, was plainly wrong.[88] It would have rung true on Kimber's next voyage, where he began with a crew of 32 and returned, through death, desertion and discharge, with only eight of the original members. But not on this one. Of the 24 members of Kimber's crew on the *Recovery*, two died in Africa, one deserted in Grenada, and the others returned.[89] This was a good rate of survival for a slave ship. Clearly Wilberforce had his facts wrong and this fortified the suspicion that his allegations about Kimber and the bombardment of New Calabar were hastily drawn up. One MP suggested Wilberforce should have reflected a little before he 'suffered his humanity' to 'run away with his judgment'.[90] The philanthropist only knew about these incidents the day before the debate in the Commons on 2 April 1792, April Fool's Day no less, he had no time to check his sources as thoroughly as he would have wished. Perhaps that fact was registered in Newton's fool. Dowling had testified that he 'communicated this Business to Mr. Wilberforce the day before his Speech in the House of Commons. I never told anybody of it or ever intended to appear as an Evidence.'[91] Both Dowling and Devereux intended to talk to Wilberforce of the bombardment; the murder came out inadvertently.[92] Wilberforce insisted he had corroborated his evidence on the murder and examined Dowling and Devereux separately, but he was clearly flying by his breeches. He misnamed the mate in the Commons, calling him Jefferies.[93] It is also possible he confused the captains and their affiliations in the New Calabar cannonade when he exposed the incident in the House. They are scrambled in the newspapers and the parliamentary record, but, as I have already suggested, that was probably because the reporters had difficulty lining up the captains and their ships amid the uproar of the Commons.

Transcripts of the trial poured off the presses within a week. The pace was set by Edward Hodgson, the shorthand writer to the Old Bailey, who had just produced his own manual of the skill, entitled *Swift Writing*. His account, the official *Whole Proceedings on the Admiralty Session*, was announced just two days after the trial, and seems to have come out on 12 June.[94] Other accounts of the trial quickly followed, at least four, possibly five, by my count, one written by a student of Middle Temple.[95] None of them offered a verbatim report of the trial itself; a five-hour trial was impossible to compress into 35–40 octavo pages, especially on presses that could only produce large print. Rather the pamphlets were designed to appeal to the public's curiosity about the case and to deliver compact versions of the trial, with some dramatic dialogue, for the price of one shilling. The pro-slavery newspaper, *Felix Farley's Bristol Journal*, also offered an abbreviated version of one of these productions that ran for over five columns of print.[96]

Printers vied for an audience keen to learn about Kimber. Their advertisements pressed their claims for authenticity and they even edited their titles in an effort to poach readers from their rivals.[97] Two of the tracts were explicitly partisan. Kimber's defenders produced a version in which the captain was tried 'for the supposed murder of an African girl'. It emphasised his 'honourable' acquittal before that 'sacred deposit of the subject's liberty, A BRITISH JURY'.[98] William Lane, the printer, vowed he would not abridge the trial 'to answer one party', but let the public judge for itself whether it was to depend on an 'unfounded DECLAMA-TION ... under the specious pretence of HUMANITY'; in other words, whether the public would buy Wilberforce's version of events hook, line and sinker. The pamphlet luxuriated in the predicament of the two witnesses as they tried to wriggle out of their inconsistent testimony concerning

Kimber's culpability. It zoned in on Pigott's barbed remark that Thomas Dowling had 'mutinied' against Kimber because he had tried to strike him. It emphasised that his disclosure of this 'EXTRAORDINARY MURDER', a phrase drenched in sarcasm, was 'casual' and half-hearted. In Sylvester's cross-examination of Stephen Devereux, the editor singled out the third mate's admission that he had been 'sent for' by the Committee for the Abolition of the Slave Trade. This implied that Devereux was an abolitionist toady, a man who had never tried to ascertain the views of the rest of the crew.[99] Both witnesses were depicted as disgruntled outsiders, fodder for the abolitionists.

By contrast, Charles Stalker of Stationers' Court, Ludgate Street, the printer who produced an edition of Olaudah Equiano's *Narrative*, sought to play down the legal decision. His trial of Kimber 'for the wilful murder of a Negro girl' or 'for the murder of two female negro slaves' began by noting that the 'unnatural and abominable custom' of the slave trade had already been denounced by a majority of the Commons, albeit in the qualified terms of gradual abolition. It hoped the obstructive stance of the Lords, and the unseemly zeal of Clarence at Kimber's trial, might precipitate another demand for immediate abolition, for which the people of England had already mobilised in an impressive fashion. As for the trial itself, the pamphlet viewed it as 'a necessary and a useful measure' despite the verdict, a 'salutary lesson' to slave captains who attempted to commit such 'horrid outrages' as Kimber was charged with. Crews could no longer treat the 'barbarous treatment of slaves' with 'indifference'.[100] After Kimber, no commander of a slave ship or crew could cavalierly torture slaves; they would be held to account. One newspaper claimed Kimber pleaded to the general issue of murdering slaves, not to the specific indictment, although I have found no evidence of this in the trial transcripts.[101] Either way, the charge of murder acknowledged that slaves were people, not simply 'cargo', as in the Zong scandal, where dying slaves had the same status as horses.[102]

Predictably, this pro-abolitionist version of the trial did not belabour the embarrassment of the witnesses. It pointed out that Thomas Dowling was thoroughly disgusted with the slave trade and swore this first voyage would be his last. In Stephen Devereux's testimony, it focused upon Kimber's brutality, how the captain slapped No-name on the face when she collapsed on the ground after the first round of suspensions and simply declared 'the bitch is sulky'. Kimber then 'ordered her to be raised by both hands ... and in this posture flogged her severely'.[103] The tract reiterated Devereux's conviction that No-name would have survived the Middle Passage had it not been for Kimber's punishments. It picked up Devereux's comment that members of the crew 'were all taken up at Bristol and sent away'; in effect corralled, so that they would not incriminate the captain.[104] This served as a segue to questions in the postscript, questions prompted by the final remark of the Solicitor General at Kimber's trial. Why had Kimber's counsel failed to bring forward a single witness to contradict the substantive charges of his accusers? As the *Derby Mercury* remarked, the trial would have been more convincing 'if but one of the numerous crew of of the ship who attended in the gallery of the Sessions house, men who could not be ignorant of the business, had come forward to disprove a plain tale'.[105] Did Kimber have something to hide?

This question troubled Kimber's supporters. No-one expected unanimity on the verdict, but the suggestion that Kimber had cheated justice rankled. Two weeks after the trial, the Kimber camp drew up a leaflet that listed those members of the *Recovery* who had rallied to their captain and had formally repudiated the charges laid against him.[106] This paper, four pages in length, was distributed gratis from William Lane's printing house in Leadenhall Street, London and extracted in pro-slavery newspapers like *Felix Farley's Bristol*

Journal. It was subsequently appended to the second edition of the pro-Kimber trial tract, now renamed *Genuine State of Facts*, which was also printed by Lane. This was done to counter public doubts of Kimber's innocence, doubts raised by the absence of defence witnesses concerning No-name's death.[107] To Kimber's supporters the answer was clear: the jury was satisfied before those witnesses became necessary. *The Times* even suggested it had been satisfied 'for above an hour'.[108] The defence witnesses were always there, waiting in the wings. 'Let truth prevail,' the paper concluded, 'and let an innocent man stand justified in the eye of the public.'[109]

What impression this move made is unclear. Wilberforce, of course, had never been persuaded of Kimber's innocence. He had been told by Sir John Stonehouse, a friend and confidant of Hannah More in Bristol, that Kimber was 'a very bad man, a great spendthrift; one who would swear to any falsehood, and who is linked with a set of rascals like himself'. Wilberforce wrote to Lord Muncaster that Kimber was in no way acquitted '*in foro conscientiae* [morally rather than legally] of the cruelties with which he is charged'.[110] He blamed the verdict on the 'remissness' of the prosecution. He also believed the verdict was influenced by the 'indecent behaviour' of Clarence, the royal duke. Consequently Wilberforce was not disposed to offer any kind of apology for his remarks in the Commons. Kimber attempted to extract one, along with £5,000 in compensation and a government place to make him 'comfortable'. When that offer was rejected the captain lurked around Wilberforce's residence and tried to confront him personally. On one occasion he was described as 'very savage looking ... muttering and shaking his head' as he left the scene.[111]

Rumours ran that Kimber contemplated legal action against Wilberforce, and failing that, wanted to challenge him to a duel. In fact the only man to demand satisfaction of Wilberforce was Robert Rolleston, part-owner of the *Brookes*, the ship made notorious for its image of slaves sardined in the hold.[112] Even so, the philanthropist's friends feared for his life at the hands of Kimber, to a point that Lord Rokeby found it necessary to accompany Wilberforce to Yorkshire. Eventually Lord Sheffield intervened and advised Kimber to restrain his behaviour. By December 1792 the captain was out of the country, bound again for New Calabar, and he did not return until early 1794. He commanded the *Levant*, another slave ship owned by Walter Jacks. This was a welcome interlude for Wilberforce, because as late as the spring of 1794 he was still troubled by the 'awkward business of Kimber'; one, he reflected, 'in which my life is perhaps at stake.'[113] He did not shake off the apprehension of violence by Kimber for another two years.

Other members of Wilberforce's circle shared his sentiments about Kimber's culpability. On the evening of the trial Henry Thornton wrote to John Clarkson to say that 'Capt. Kimber is this day acquitted – the cruelties charged upon him seem to me however to have been indisputably committed, but the charge of murder was not thought to have been established.'[114] This was most certainly the view of committed abolitionists, of which there were many in the country, as the huge wave of petitions to the Commons had confirmed. People who signed those petitions would have agreed with the *St James's Chronicle* that Kimber should have at least produced the 'boys' who hoisted up and stretched the girl, his accomplices to her punishment. As far as this paper was concerned, there was not 'one tittle of evidence to contradict the account of the cruelty inflicted by him on the helpless wretch. The long parade of oaths made by the rest of the crew, who from their situation are entirely precluded from being eye witnesses to the fact, can be of no importance one way or another.'[115]

Yet some newspapers echoed the slave lobby in condemning Wilberforce's extravagant accusations. The *Evening Mail* went so far as to accuse Wilberforce of being 'an agent of oppression' for forcing an innocent man to undergo imprisonment and a trial for his life; his charges had been loose and fuelled with 'sanguinary malice'.[116] This view was shared by some newspapers in the United States, where there was considerable interest in the initial exposé of Kimber. Two newspapers went so far as to suggest that the 'pious frauds' of Wilberforce had fuelled slave unrest in Virginia and Carolina.[117] Philadelphia's *Federal Gazette* was strongly critical of Wilberforce as well. It hoped the trial would 'dispel from the public mind those visions of inhumanity which have been most probably presented by malice and misrepresentation'.[118]

It is doubtful it did. One knock-up version of the trial, printed in Edinburgh and purporting to be the *Whole Proceedings*, laboured Wilberforce's ruthless pursuit of Kimber. It was actually a hack production modelled on the *Genuine State of Facts*. Running at half the price of the others, it allegedly went through ten editions in the course of six months.[119] This strains credibility. The production seems more of a confidence trick designed to dissipate the strong Scottish support for abolition so evident in the petitioning campaign; either that, or a backhanded attempt to use the trial to discredit Wilberforce, whose attack upon Kimber is sandwiched between the trial and the Bristol depositions.[120] I rather doubt it made a big impression. Constant vindications of the verdict did little to disrupt the view that the slave trade was a despicable institution. One writer wondered how the slaves who witnessed Kimber's brutal flogging of the girl would have reacted if they knew the captain were acquitted. 'When we hear of Captains of slave ships pleading in excuse for their cruelties that they are obliged to flog the negroes on their passage to the West Indies in order to make them eat,' declared another, 'it must give us an extraordinary idea of the happiness which the Slave Traders so often assert that they enjoy'.[121] In response to one attempt to reassert Kimber's innocence, a 'juryman' remarked that 'all persons on board a slave-ship are tainted with the villainy of the traffick. Let us not hear any more talk about *honourable acquittals*.'[122]

Interest in the Kimber affair had ebbed a little by the time the perjury trials came around. In early 1793, the newspapers were absorbed with the execution of Louis XVI, the French Terror, and the impending war with France. Even so, a fair number of London and provincial newspapers covered the trials at King's Bench. The *Derby Mercury* did so quite extensively, anxious that the trials might be misreported, as did the *Cumberland Pacquet* and the *Sheffield Register*.[123] Thomas Dowling's case came first, on 19 February 1793. There were over forty assignments of perjury, but the presiding judge, Kenyon LCJ, directed the special jury to two: namely, Dowling's claim that Captain Kimber's suspension and flogging of the girl killed her; and his denial that he sought revenge. On the first assignment Kenyon decided not to proceed, because the shorthand writer acknowledged that he did not take down all that was said, and without a complete transcript it was impossible to determine whether Dowling perjured himself or not. But he did proceed with the second because the issue of revenge was not related to the general merits of the cause, and could be determined on the cross-examinations alone.[124] Here Thomas Erskine, the prosecuting counsel, had little difficulty showing Dowling had sworn revenge on Captain Kimber to Walter Jacks and others, and on that testimony he was found guilty. While Dowling was out on bail awaiting his sentence, his lawyer, Mr James Mingay, KC, the Recorder of Aldborough, a small pocket borough in Yorkshire,[125] tried to arrest the judgment on legal technicalities. He argued that the original commission to try Kimber was irregularly constituted, and consequently his client was not tried before a competent jurisdiction. Mingay also claimed the perjury did not affect the material parts of the cause against Kimber, which centred on his treatment of the girl.[126] Both arguments were denied by the court and Dowling was left to face the wrath of Justice Ashhurst, who expatiated on the enormity of a perjury that was designed to deprive an 'entirely innocent' man of his life. He sentenced the horrified surgeon to one month in Newgate and seven years' transportation. Eleven of the twelve jurymen who heard the case petitioned for Dowling's pardon, and ultimately his sentence was mitigated to seven years' banishment. He was not sent Down Under to Botany Bay. Eventually an abolitionist from Birmingham helped Dowling set up a new life in America.[127] Summing up the sentence, the *Morning Post* believed Dowling 'the unhappy victim to the Slave partisans'.[128]

Some thought the abolitionists had been cavalier in their treatment of Dowling, abandoning him to the Traders; among them the radical Robert Watson and Lord George Gordon, notorious for leading the London Protestant Association and inciting the anti-Catholic riots of June 1780. From his cell in Newgate prison, Gordon went out of his way to publicise the character references that had been mustered for the Irish surgeon, although an open letter to Captain Kimber from the bishop and mayor of Cashel stressed they had commended Dowling's character as a sixteen-year-old, when he was resident in the town, not on what he did subsequently.[129]

Stephen Devereux's trial came up on 20 February 1793. It focused on his claim that Kimber's flogging was responsible for the death of No-name. Kenyon proved a little pedantic about the assignment, because Devereux had never been accused of perjury in the 'course of judicial proceeding', only in the aftermath of Kimber's trial.[130] But he allowed the trial to proceed; and the objections he raised in Dowling's case did not obtain in this one because John Dalby, Edward Hodgson's assistant, assured the judge he had accurately taken down Devereux's cross-examination.[131] Thomas Erskine again led the crown prosecution. He claimed that Devereux had self-evidently perjured himself, because he had denied Kimber had killed the girl before Sir Sampson

Wright in Bow Street, and then argued the contrary at the
trial. But Kenyon would not entertain this proposition. He
wanted more evidence to be brought to bear on the issue
of Kimber's treatment of the girl, evidence that had been
alluded to in the cross-examination.

This meant that some of Kimber's witnesses were heard
for the first time. Their testimony in court could be checked
against their depositions before John Noble, the Bristol
mayor, which had been written down before Kimber's trial.
The first prosecuting witness to appear, Elias Mansfield the
armourer, did not fare well under cross-examination by
Devereux's counsel, Mr James Mingay. In his original deposition, Mansfield had denied Kimber suspended No-name
by the arms and legs; now he admitted it. When asked about
the flogging, which he had also denied, he equivocated.
'She might have a touch with a whip at different times', he
conceded, and with 'a common horse-whip' to boot.[132] Yes,
No-name was slapped about a bit; but so, too, were all slaves
who didn't co-operate by eating and dancing. No-name was
suspended with the 'greatest tenderness', insisted Mansfield, so that her naked body could be rubbed down with
palm oil and her legs straightened. Kimber treated her with
'great humanity'.

All this was said before an evangelical judge of the
strictest morals, who abhorred adultery, sexual licence and
the libertinism of his age.[133] One can imagine his reaction.
Kenyon was, in fact, an ally of Wilberforce and believed
the slave trade to be 'cruel and nefarious'. Enter Bob Mills,
who now developed a complete amnesia about his conversations at the Chepstow Boathouse, and forgot that he had
heated cannonballs so they would explode upon impact in
New Calabar. At least Mills admitted that No-name had
been suspended, although if she was bounced, he protested, she could have easily eased herself down 'with what
trifle of strength she had'.[134] And on it went, amnesia and
equivocation: 'I cannot tell'; 'I cannot rightly say'; 'She was

not licked much'.[135] After Mills, the same refrain came from Bill Phillips and Joe Pearson. Lord Kenyon was beginning to lose patience. 'Did the Captain strike her at all with a thong whip – no stroke, no tap with any whip, or any thing?'[136] Kimber's witnesses established that Dowling had consented to the suspension of the girl, but on the actual whipping, evasion reigned.

Until Ted Williams appeared for the defence. He had left the boat at Grenada, and he had refused to co-operate with Kimber's party on the day of his trial. He was forthright and pretty graphic. No-name 'was fastened by one hand first to the mizzen-stay, taken down again and tied by both hands; then she was taken down, and the Captain walked on the deck and flogged her with a whip.' He continued: 'I have seen him flog her when she has been lying down upon the deck, and she has not been able to stand.' When flogged 'she moan'd inwardly, and cried out'.[137] Thomas Erskine tried to discount Williams' evidence by painting him as a petty thief and deserter, but in the course of his cross-examination more evidence of the punishments oozed out. Kimber moved back and forth when he whipped her; she was suspended three inches from the deck; she was jerked up and down.

Stephen Devereux was a silent witness to all this because he was 'abaft the wheel', that is, between the helm and the stern of the ship.[138] He was allegedly supervising the dancing of the female slaves, but all were fixated on the flogging. His account squared with that of Ted Williams and put pressure on those members of the crew who had sworn otherwise before the Bristol mayor, John Noble. By the time the Chepstow Boathouse witnesses took the stand, namely Israel and Anne Grace and the lodgers in their pub, it was clear that some of 'Captain Kimber's witnesses' were lying through their teeth: specifically, the reprobate Bob Mills, a 22-year-old Scot, who was living a marginal existence; and Bill Phillips, an eighteen-year-old Bristolian, who had likely been pressured by the Bristol slavers into backing Kimber. William Garrow, who was member of the prosecution team, a hired gun rather than the Enlightenment liberal of 'Garrow's Law',[139] tried to undermine Anne Grace's testimony by wondering how she could remember a conversation in December 1791 so clearly. He insinuated she was an ally of Stephen Devereux.[140] But after other witnesses had undermined Mills' and Phillips' testimony, Kenyon stopped the trial. Newspapers reported he was 'much affected' by Devereux's witnesses. The evidence for the prosecution had been so undermined by their testimony, he declared, that Devereux's acquittal was 'absolutely necessary'.[141] The jury agreed. His lordship added that in retrospect Dowling was not as culpable as he might seem, a judgment that certainly paved the way for his pardon. Kenyon then ended on an evangelical note: 'the Searcher of all Hearts only knows on which side the truth lay'.[142]

The Devereux verdict blew the Kimber case wide open. It became increasingly difficult to argue that Kimber was not in some way culpable for the death of the girl. This was recognised by Niel Douglas, an abolitionist from Scotland. 'It is hence easy to see in what light we are to view the Captain,' he remarked, 'notwithstanding his acquittal, and tho' he may escape the punishment ... from the hand of man, yet the equitable Judge of all will not suffer him ... to escape his righteous judgment.'[143]

Not everyone accepted this logic. When Wilberforce moved for another discussion of the slave trade a few days after the Devereux trial, two pro-trade MPs, Fenton Cawthorne and John Dent, argued against it. They claimed that Wilberforce had misled the House over Kimber, and that his denunciation of the captain had critically swayed the vote for gradual abolition last session. Now that Kimber had been honourably acquitted and one of his prosecuting witnesses successfully indicted for perjury, Wilberforce should apologise and desist from these anti-slave-trade motions.

Wilberforce stood his ground. He had helped finance the defence of Dowling and Devereux and he was convinced of Kimber's guilt.[144] He was angry about the verdict in Kimber's favour but he had not felt humiliated by it. Kimber 'had undoubtedly been acquitted *in point of law*,' Wilberforce declared, 'but by no means in such a manner as to convince him of his innocence'. Otherwise he would have made amends. Fellow abolitionist William Smith concurred. Kimber had been acquitted on collateral evidence; the courts had never investigated the real merits of the indictment; and besides, the trial of Devereux had not gone 'honourably' for the captain.[145] The *Northampton Mercury* echoed these sentiments, bluntly. The Kimber and Dowling trials sidestepped the floggings; only Devereux's brought them to light.[146]

The abolitionists won the argument; they did not win the debate. In a thin House, an amendment to postpone the abolition motion for six months passed by 61 to 53 votes, a majority of eight. Despite the new evidence reaffirming Kimber's brutality and his likely culpability in the murder of No-name, the abolition campaign seemed to be losing momentum. Why was this?

5

Abolition and revolution

Storm clouds were already on the horizon when the first wave of abolition reached its peak. These were related to the revolutionary situation in France and its major sugar colony, St Domingue, both of which became violent and volatile places as the breakdown of the most prominent *ancien régime* in Europe proceeded after 1789. Historians are divided on what impact these events had on the course of abolition, but it will be argued here that while the initial challenges to the status quo seemed to boost abolitionist fortunes, the longer term prospect undermined them.

The Declaration of the Rights of Man established in principle the notion of secular human rights and made the very existence of slavery problematic. It reinforced the notion that slavery could not be simply justified as an economic necessity but was ipso facto an abuse of human, or in eighteenth-century parlance, natural rights.[1] Before 1789, abolitionist writers generally framed this argument in terms of Christian benevolence: it was morally wrong to deprive God's subjects of the opportunity to live a righteous life. Within these terms, slavery was a Christian sin; it made Christ's wounds bleed; yet rather perversely it also brought it within the moral pale. In the spectrum of Christian sin, slavery was intolerable, inviting irrevocable damnation, yet it had to be nobly borne until such time that the law was changed or God's deliverance intervened. Some Methodist missionaries in the Caribbean could even argue that the 'loss of liberty was more than compensated by the inward freedom from the law of sin and death.'² And for the slaver it was always possible to ask God's forgiveness and redeem oneself. Slavery thus paradoxically offered spiritual opportunities for the transcendent joy of redemption, compromised only by the trauma of witnessing unspeakable human suffering. John Newton, the author of *Amazing Grace*, best represented the tortured soul of a slaver turned evangelical in the mid-to-late eighteenth century, wrestling with his conscience in a public confession that revealed much but never quite everything about the ugly business of the Trade.³

The radical declaration of 1789 offered a more forthright denunciation of slavery and a boost to abolition. Even the deeply Christian radical, Granville Sharp, the chairman of the London Abolition Society who had worked tirelessly to expose the evils of slavery and change the law and whose hope for change was millenarian, was elated by events across the Channel. Writing to General Lafayette in August 1789, he remarked: 'The wonderful Revolution, which has so unexpectedly taken place in France, demonstrates a peculiar Providence in favour of popular Right.' He commended the French abolition society, Les Amis des Noirs, for exposing the iniquity of the slave trade and also for reasserting the values of 'personal liberty and natural Right.'⁴ He looked forward to the time when it would combine with British associations to outlaw the slave trade and bring every other slaving nation in its train. 'A Kingdom of Righteousness' respecting human rights was imminent, so he thought.

In fact, things were never so easy. Nationalism complicated matters. Delegates to the French National Assembly championed liberty, equality and fraternity, but were ambivalent about abolishing the slave trade if it meant sacrificing French national interests. Patriots from slaving ports like Bordeaux and Nantes constantly reminded them of these dangers and mobilised petitions against abolition. When it came to the crunch Mirabeau, one of the leading supporters of abolition in France, discovered that only 300 of the 1,200 deputies in the National Assembly supported it, although another 500 considered doing so if Britain did the same.[5] In the circumstances Les Amis des Noirs decided their best immediate strategy would be to support the free blacks and mulattoes of St Domingue in their quest for full political and civic rights. This was consistent with the Declaration of Rights and with the policy of addressing the *cahiers des doléances* [petitions] that were inundating the assembly. And yet it further complicated abolition, because many prominent *gens de couleur* in St Domingue were themselves slave owners. They held roughly a third of all plantations on the island, principally the smaller ones producing coffee, cotton and indigo, and owned about 25 per cent of the slaves.[6] Consequently civil equality for mixed-race colonial proprietors did not easily mesh with abolition, let alone emancipation, since St Domingue's booming economy needed imported slaves. In fact, the year before the St Domingue insurrection, 1790, was a peak one for importing slaves, with Nantes sending 49 ships to Africa and the Caribbean.[7]

Abolition lost traction when violence erupted between colonial whites and free blacks in St Domingue, leading to a revolt by one of the leading delegates sent to France, Vincent Ogé, who was captured, tried and broken on the wheel in the square of Cap François in February 1791.[8] From then on St Domingue drifted in civil war, with each side of the planter divide mobilising slaves. Over time those slaves, about half a million, seized the initiative, generating a blood bath of race war and a liberation movement that ultimately ended in Haitian independence.

At the very beginning of the French Revolution Thomas Clarkson had travelled to France to liaise with Les Amis des Noirs and promote support for abolition and even emancipation in French territories. Clarkson gave the French the benefits of his own research. In his letters to Mirabeau he passed on information about the mortality and condition of slaves aboard ships and their heroic forms of resistance,

whether that meant suicide, food strikes or outright insurrection. He produced a version of the Brookes slave ship to
astonished Frenchmen. He relayed an account of an insurrection aboard a Bristol ship where the slaves broke thrown
the barricade, disarmed the sentries and momentarily took
possession of the ship. When they were finally suppressed
by sailors from the tops, Clarkson recounted, the slaves
'cast themselves into the Sea, with masks of Joy in their
Countenance, and of the most perfect Contempt for their
oppressors'. It was 'the wretchedness of their condition', he
concluded, which compelled them to prefer death to life.[9]
He pressed the French assembly to legislate abolition; to do
less would betray their revolutionary principles. 'I should
not be surprised', he wrote to London after passage of the
Declaration of the Rights of Man, 'if the French were to do
themselves the honour of voting away this diabolical traffic in a night.' When this did not transpire, he pushed the
French on their revolutionary credentials. 'France must
abolish the Slave-Trade whether any other Nation does it or
not – Her Honour and her Reputation are at Stake.' Clarkson predicted that the circulation of revolutionary ideas
would promote 'very serious revolutions' in the colonies.
'The French Revolution can never be kept from the Negroes',
he assured Bouvet de Cressé. 'The Efforts of Good Men ...
must unavoidably reach their Ears.'[10]

Thomas Cooper, the calico printer and active abolitionist who helped found the Manchester Constitutional
Society, was of the same opinion. Noting that the slaves in
St Domingue had 'in some measure recovered their native
rights', he wondered whether 'their brethren in other islands
may be influenced by their example and that the infamous
traffic, which has been so obstinately persisted in, may ter-
minate in the expulsion of the West Indian planters.' There
was a point, he reflected 'beyond which, liberty, like air,
cannot be compressed.'[11] Clarkson was never so audacious
in his endorsement of slave resistance, but he admired the

principles of the French Revolution and the precedents it might set. The British didn't have the revolutionary spirit to inspire such revolts, but they were 'ready to develop Scenes that would have their Influence on the hardest heart, and to shew that the Slave Trade, even in the tenderest Hands, must be a Trade unavoidably in its own Nature replete with Misery and Oppression.'[12]

Clarkson returned from his six-month sojourn in France disappointed at his progress, but nevertheless fired up with revolutionary promise, as were many radicals in Britain during the early years of the crisis, when it seemed that the dawn of a new era was breaking. As he resumed his travels around Britain campaigning for abolition, his political sympathies troubled some of his colleagues. This was not immediately evident amid the busy campaigning for the parliamentary motion to end the slave trade in April 1791, but after its defeat, Clarkson found consolation in the events in France and cherished the stone he had collected from the Bastille. In July 1791 he attended the second anniversary of the fall of the Bastille at the Crown and Anchor tavern on the Strand. It was a large gathering, with a thousand or so people raising their glasses to the Revolution in France, the Rights of Man, the Sovereignty of the People, the Liberty of the Press, Trial by Jury, among other toasts. There was some confusion on the Strand as to whether lights should be illuminated or not, but the meeting itself was peaceful and orderly; 'the enthusiasm of freedom' one newspaper remarked, 'perfectly unmixed with the rage of innovation.'[13] In the run-up to the meeting, however, there had been a lot of adverse publicity about its likely subversion, with reports of pillars being erected to the 'sacred memory of Wat Tyler and Jack Cade.'[14] Some noteworthy members of the Whig party like Charles James Fox and Richard Brinsley Sheridan stayed away. This did not stop James Gillray from including them in his caricature of the event. Very mischievously, in what was a dreamscape of conservative paranoia,

Gillray portrayed Sheridan grabbing the king by the ears, so that executioner Fox could chop off his head. Meanwhile, the Queen and Pitt dangled from lampposts in a sexually suggestive way, while John Horne Tooke, who had grabbed George by the legs, might be said to be buggering the monarch. In a previous print just prior to the meeting, Gillray had Fox drumming up a storm for a cadaverous Alecto, or classical Fury, replete with a cap of liberty and bonnet rouge. In the not-too-subtle spin of the day, Bastille anniversaries were fomenting revolution.[15]

Members of the government were troubled by Clarkson's presence at the meeting. Henry Dundas, having learned of the riots against the reformers celebrating the Fall of the Bastille in Birmingham, wrote to Wilberforce to ask 'What

9. James Gillray, *The Hopes of the Party Prior to July 14th*, 1791

business had your Friend Clarkson to attend the Crown
and Anchor last Thursday. He could not have done a more
mischievous thing to the Cause you love.' Wilberforce asked
Lord Muncaster to dissuade Clarkson from talking about
the French Revolution as he campaigned for abolition:
'it will be the ruin of our cause'.[16] He feared abolitionists
would be identified as 'Jacobins', as people who advocated
republicanism, revolution and social equality. Slave traders
had already begun to caricature abolitionists in this way.
In the view of 'Philo-Detector' in the *Morning Chronicle*,
abolitionists were exciting in the people 'a want of subordination ... the same anarchy and confusion' that was to be
found in France. Men who insist all males have equal rights,
the author claimed, 'poison the minds of the people with
metaphysical sophisms', an argument taken from Edmund
Burke's *Reflections on the Revolution in France*. As for Clarkson, he was regarded as a troublemaker who advocated
resistance to slavery, as indeed he had done in his *Essay on
the commerce of the human species*, a widely published tract
that went through three editions in two years.[17] In a smaller
tract which addressed the topical issue of insurrection in
St Domingue, Clarkson claimed that the real source of the
trouble was the slave trade, which poured into the sugar
colony thousands of Africans 'who have been fraudulently
and forcibly deprived of the Rights of Men'.[18]

Words like these were provocative, although they were
not intended to incite violence so much as vindicate human
rights. Two years before, when Clarkson had just returned
from Paris, he had received an unexpected visit from Vincent Ogé, a leading mixed-race planter who was trying to
return to St Domingue by way of a British and American
port to agitate for more political power to free men of
colour. Ogé was angry that the white planter lobby, the
Club Massiac, had frustrated his demand for full civic and
political rights in Paris. He was embittered by the colonial
assembly's refusal to grant even voting rights to free men

of colour, despite the fact that the National Assembly had
been disposed to do so. Clarkson was extremely wary of
creating any impression that he was conspiring with Ogé,
and when Ogé asked for help, he sparingly contributed to
his passage out of the port of London. He was keen that
Ogé leave the metropolis before rumours spread that he
was hatching some nefarious deal with the mulatto deputies and Les Amis des Noirs. He had fought off that rumour
in late 1789, when he was in Paris.[19] He didn't need a reprise.
Clarkson was never openly accused of organising an arms
deal in 1790, but later on Bryan Edwards wove some British
complicity into his analysis of the St Domingue insurrection. This accounts for the somewhat defensive tone of the
Clarkson's narrative of the meeting, written some 38 years
after the event.[20]

Voicing remarks about the 'Rights of Men' was nonetheless going to raise hackles in the deteriorating international
situation of 1792. In the fall of that year there was a bloody
purge of aristocrats and their hangers-on in Paris as France
moved rapidly towards a republic and a political trial of
Louis Capet. Amid the turmoil, Clarkson stayed the course.
'He makes little doubt but that ye Revolutionists viz. the
main body of the People will stand their ground: and that an
Excellent Republic will be established on ye Ruins of Des-
potisms & arbitrary Power.' So noted Elihu Robinson after
a visit from Clarkson in November 1792.[21] Yet as Britain
braced itself for war with its continental rival, Tom Paine
was convicted in absentia of seditious libel for writing the
Rights of Man; and the winter of 1792/3 saw the beginnings
of a loyalist backlash to French-inspired radicalism. Loyalist associations sprouted in many towns, large and small,
vowing to suppress seditious and treasonable literature
and rally the populace to King and Country. These were
accompanied by effigy-burnings of Tom Paine in town and
village; how many is impossible to say, but there were likely
400–500 such incidents across the country.[22]

The loyalist reaction was orchestrated from above, and there is some debate as to how far it elicited a genuinely popular response. Many Paine-burnings were subsidised by local gentry and farmers: the one at Mells in Somerset was subsidised by the squire of Mells Park; the elaborately staged procession and execution of Tom Paine's effigy at Batheaston cost £44 and was raised by a public subscription among the freeholders and wealthier inhabitants. The residue of the subscription would be distributed to the poor 'in such manner as Henry Walters, Esquire, our worthy magistrate of the quorum, shall think proper'.[23] Paine-burnings thus provided some festive cheer in a hard winter when prices soared and food riots broke out in the South West.[24] They also allowed loyalists to take over public space; they made it difficult for abolitionists to organise, especially the Quakers, a key group, whose pacifism jarred in a nation gearing for war.

In the South West, for which I have accurate information, there is a significant geographical correspondence between the towns that petitioned for abolition in 1792 and the loyalist activity of subsequent years.[25] All the major towns in Devon, Dorset, Somerset and Wiltshire petitioned in 1792, Salisbury and Bristol excepted, and all organised loyalist meetings or associations cracked down on political dissidence. In east Somerset and west Wiltshire, where petitions were thick on the ground, there is a high incidence of loyalist festival; in places like Bath, Trowbridge, Devizes, Corsham, Bradford, Shepton Mallet and Wells. In the latter, a cathedral town, an effigy of Paine in a green coat, nankeen breeches and bag wig, was paraded around the streets, and eventually hanged and burnt in the market place from a gallows thirty feet high.[26] There are also significant overlaps between loyalist junkets and petitions in the Exeter area; in Exeter itself and in the small textile towns and villages to the north. Indeed in Exeter Tom Paine had been burnt in effigy on the king's birthday 1792, but three months after the city's petition to the Commons.[27]

There is less overlap between abolitionist petitions and loyalist meetings in the rich plain from Taunton Deane to Blackmoor Vale. Yet Taunton, Wellington, Sherborne and Yeovil all had active loyalist associations dedicated to rooting out radicals. The Yeovil association expressly condemned the 'daily attempts to introduce equalizing and levelling principles among the lower orders of society'.[28] The Taunton association was chaired by Matthew Brickdale, the former Bristol MP who had tried to delay a consideration of Dolben's bill to regulate the transatlantic shipment of slaves. Here loyalism was opposed to abolition. That might not have been the case everywhere, although gestures towards human rights or the spiritual equality of all persons would likely raise fears of sedition by 1792. Loyalism discouraged abolitionist activity, if it did not disable it.

Loyalism descended like a fog on England in the winter of 1792–3. As many as 1,500 loyalist societies were created in a matter of months.[29] They didn't last. There were successive waves of loyalism as David Eastwood has shown, of which the Reeves' associations were but one.[30] But the loyalist backlash was enough to arrest the momentum of the abolition movement. To begin with, the campaign to abolish the slave trade had been a broadly based alliance in which social conservatives shelved differences with radicals in pursuit of a common goal. This became increasingly difficult in the highly-charged political climate of 1792–5, when all were under pressure to declare their allegiance to the state, when Britain mobilised for war, and when the government adopted repressive legislation to muzzle and outlaw political radicalism. Abolitionists quickly found themselves in different camps. Hannah More wrote simple tracts to try to keep the workers loyal, parading the virtues of British liberty and deference in contrast to the anarchy of rebellion in France. Her comments on the slave trade were framed within a quest for a national conservative regeneration. We must rid ourselves of the slave trade just as we should rid ourselves of radicals and 'reclaim the vicious'.[31]

In contrast, radical abolitionists ran foul of the state and were tried and jailed for sedition. Thomas Walker, the principal mobiliser of the Manchester petition, was heckled and harassed by church-and-king loyalists for not observing the king's birthday in 1792. Six months later, as a fresh wave of loyalist agitation deluged Manchester, his house was attacked, as was the printing office of the radical *Manchester Herald*.[32] Perhaps predictably, Walker was arrested on trumped-up treasonable charges. It took the expertise of Thomas Erskine and a lot of Walker's own money to acquit him. Thomas Hardy, the chairman of the London Corresponding Society, a man who declared that 'the rights of man are not confined to this small island but are extended to the whole human race, black and white, high or low, rich or poor',[33] suffered accordingly. Once again it was Erskine's skill that saved him.

Others were not so lucky. William Winterbotham, a Baptist preacher at How's Lane Chapel, Plymouth, told his congregation in November 1792 that the day of emancipation was nigh. 'The night of Slavery and Bondage is spent and the day of Universal Liberty is at hand', he declared; 'our African brethren teach us that men begin to understand each other's rights' and the day was not far off when men 'grown callous to the tender ties of nature will not be sufficient to withstand the generous exertions of the friends of mankind'.[34] For this radical sermon, with its French revolutionary inflections, he spent two years in prison.

So too, did Henry Redhead Yorke, a mixed-race Antiguan creole, the illegitimate son of a plantation manager who rose to planter status.[35] A friend of Tom Paine and a former member of a radical 'British Club' in revolutionary Paris, Yorke chaired a meeting in Sheffield calling for parliamentary reform and 'the total and unqualified abolition of negro slavery'.[36] He advocated armed rebellion in Britain

and elsewhere, anticipating the French government's decision to emancipate Caribbean slaves and mobilise them into
black armies. He told a crowd of metal workers to 'avenge
peacefully ages of wrongs done to our Negro Brethren' but
in his more rhetorical moments he urged the people of
Africa and Europe to retaliate if tyrants refused to 'expiate
their crimes'; 'let the People roll on them in a tempest of
fury, and compel them to expire in agonies'. The government nailed Yorke for conspiracy.

The French Revolution and the political repression it
generated in Britain arrested the abolition movement. So
too, eventually, did the situation in St Domingue. The blood
bath on the northern plains in the late summer of 1791 was
not always reported in macabre detail in the British newspapers; accounts sometimes alluded discreetly to 'the horrors
of intestinal commotion'. Even so, the estimate of a thousand
white killings and of women 'held in captivity' left little doubt
there had been a massive slave reprisal against masters.
What narratives leaked out suggested planters were being
paid in kind, pinned to the ground, tortured, their wives and
daughters violated, as had so many African women. A six-
penny pamphlet disclosed that the standard of rebels at the
Galifet plantation was of a white child impaled on a pike.
Women were raped in front of their husbands and fathers,
and in one case on a planter's dead body. One planter from
Petit-Goâve was crucified in the marketplace in Léogâne,
blinded, mutilated and his body parts fed to hogs. An 'opu-
lent proprietor' was tied to a ladder and whipped to death,
a humiliation that doubtless replicated a slave punishment
and signalled a world turned upside down.[37]

Dreadful as these accounts were, they did not immediately arrest the momentum of abolition. The reports of
atrocities did not inhibit petitions, most of which materi-
alised in the final weeks of March 1792, some months after
the revelations of racial rage broke in the press. Part of the
reason for this was that the disclosures emerged from the

speeches of white planters in Paris and were designed to discredit the abolitionists and their allies among the mixed-race planters. They could be dismissed as parti pris. This explains why some pro-abolitionist newspapers ignored them. The *Derby Mercury*, for example, which devoted a lot of space to the inquiries into the slave trade, allotted only one report to the violence of the Northern Plain. Prominent abolitionists like the Liverpudlian, William Roscoe, moreover, believed the violence a one-off affair. He insisted the root of the problem was the white planters' refusal to make any any concessions to the people of colour and deprecated the idea that slaves had been incited by abolitionist rhetoric, as the West Indian interest had claimed. If white planters and their coloured counterparts could resolve their differences, he maintained, then black insurrection would quickly peter out. On this issue he approvingly cited a speech from Louis Hardouin Tarbé, the French minister of finance, who concluded in February 1792 that the real danger of slave revolt had passed.[38] Even Pitt, who was momentarily troubled by the violence of St Domingue and the possibility of it spreading to the British Caribbean, did not believe it warranted a brake on abolition.

As the revolutionary crisis deepened, and the massacres in France became paired with those in St Domingue, abolitionists found it more difficult to brush off the charge of complicity. In their own responses to the violence, they did not indulge in schadenfreude; they certainly did not luxuriate in the white planters' distress. Yet some abolitionists adopted an 'I told you so' attitude, arguing that the savagery of the blacks echoed the savagery of their masters. William Roscoe, who thought the butchery lamentable, saw it as an understandable reprisal to the 'long continued injury' of slavery. 'Resistance is always justifiable when force is the substitution of right', he contended, 'nor is the commission of a civil crime possible in a state of slavery'.[39] Similarly, as we have already seen, Clarkson saw the insurrection as a vindication of the 'unalterable Rights of Men'.[40] In the eyes of slave-traders and not a few neutral observers, such remarks confirmed the reputation of abolitionists as mischief-makers and advocates of rebellion.[41] Amid the massive destruction of the richest sugar colony in the world, with losses estimated at £25 million, it became increasingly difficult for abolitionists to dissociate themselves from the charge that they were subversive. Abolitionists, claimed Philo-Detector, perpetrated 'the same want of subordination, the same spirit of anarchy and confusion', that prevailed in France and by extension, St Domingue. Rebellion, declared the *Whitehall Evening Post*, was the natural fruit of Les Amis des Noirs and of Wilberforce's 'wild visions respecting the emancipation of the negroes'.[42]

In parliament Lord Abingdon declared that abolitionist rhetoric was 'nothing more than liberty and equality' on a par with Paine's *Rights of Man*. He saw the correspondence between the London Abolition committee and Les Amis des Noirs as equivalent to the correspondence of the radical corresponding societies with the National Assembly; both potentially treasonous. And he accused the abolitionists of fomenting unrest in St Domingue, and facilitating massacres and race war. If liberty and equality triumphed in the Caribbean islands, he declared, we should have to bear the blight of unseemly miscegenation.[43]

Some abolitionists in the upper House such as Lord Stanhope wrote this off as alarmist waffle, but it proved difficult to extricate abolitionism from the tangled politics of the French Revolution. Robespierre added to the alarm. A member of Les Amis des Noirs, he declared he would rather sacrifice a colony than a revolutionary principle. As a friend wearily told Wilberforce, 'People connect democratical principles with the Abolition of the Slave Trade.'[44] In this respect the actions of the French National Assembly didn't help. In the summer of 1793, it offered honorary citizenship to five Englishmen: Jeremy Bentham, Joseph Priestley, Tom

Paine, Thomas Clarkson, and William Wilberforce. Clarkson revelled in the honour; Wilberforce reviled it. In response he joined a campaign to relieve French émigré clergymen. He preferred to be identified with counter-revolution. He recognised that Jacobins were the natural allies of abolition but felt the association was injurious to 'our cause'[45]

None of this boded well for Wilberforce's efforts to push abolition through the Commons. Although historians have sometimes noted the small majorities that defeated his motions after 1792, it is worth reminding ourselves that they occurred on second, not third, motions and before a pitifully small House.[46] On every motion from 1793 to 1796, whether it was leave to bring in a bill, to postpone one, or to ban the export of slaves to foreign countries, the attendance rate ranged from 11 to 26 per cent. MPs became increasingly disenchanted with Wilberforce's annual ritual of a motion to abolish the Trade. The *coup de grâce* came in February 1796 when Henry Dundas declared that a swift move to abolition was no longer propitious or feasible.[47] The international climate was simply too volatile to entertain motions for abolition, especially as the French general in the Caribbean, Victor Hugues, had invaded British territories with his black armies and was raising the tocsin of emancipation and revolution.[48] Security first, abolition later. Even William Pitt, who persisted in supporting his friend's advocacy of total abolition, was horribly compromised. Once war was declared with France in 1793, he poured troops into St Domingue to prop up white planter slavery and stem the contagion of rebellion. The price was terribly high. Of the 20,000 of the troops sent there, some 75 per cent died of sepsis or tropical diseases.[49]

By 1796 if not before, the first wave of abolition was over. It would require changes in the international situation and the eclipse of France as a naval power before abolition would regain momentum. It is difficult to argue otherwise.[50] The London committee abandoned its regular meeting-place in 1794 and met intermittently in the next three years. The revolution and the insurrection in St Domingue exposed divisions within abolitionist ranks. Its leaders found themselves at loggerheads over government policy. Wilberforce supported the 1795 gagging acts banning corresponding societies and restricting public assembly; his main ally in parliament, William Smith, did not. He sympathised with Christopher Wyvill's efforts to oppose the acts in York, where Wilberforce's friends had mustered in force.[51] In this polarised climate the London committee thought another public campaign for abolition inadvisable. 'We do no think the present juncture favourable to any further public measures & therefore we leave it to the serious consideration of every individual what measures to take in order to sap the foundation of this enormous mass of iniquity.'[52] Further campaigns were in any case rendered more difficult by Thomas Clarkson's retirement to the Lake District, where he tried to rehabilitate his health after journeying some 35,000 miles around Britain in seven years of hard campaigning.

And in Bristol?

In Bristol the slave trade declined dramatically after the declaration of war with France as the risks increased and bankruptcies among some of the major players like James Rogers took their toll. Thirteen ships sailed in 1793 compared to 48 the previous year, and while roughly the same number set out from the port in 1794 and 1795, only five or so ships sailed annually thereafter. There was a corresponding slump in the Jamaican trade as well.[53]

The sharp decline did not immediately weaken Bristol's commitment to slavery. In July 1796 a black runaway slave cum seaman named Harry Harper was detained on board the *Levant* and denied habeas corpus on the grounds he had 'freely' signed articles with Captain Alleyne under the Master and Servant Act. In fact, he had been summoned to the captain's cabin and forced to make his mark on the document when he was two days from the port. Walter Jacks, the owner of the vessel, Kimber's former partner and patron, a merchant who had recently acquired an interest in a Jamaica plantation, backed the detention on the grounds that Alleyne was liable to a hefty fine if he did not return Harper to Dominica.[54] His support for Alleyne meant that the Quaker abolitionist and lawyer, Harry Gandy, was unable to invoke the Mansfield ruling of 1772. As Gandy complained to Granville Sharp, the whole business was done 'under colour of Law' and he asked the more experienced Sharp how he might counter 'this act of oppression'. Nothing, it transpired, could be done for the runaway.

In the summer of 1795 the young poet Samuel Taylor Coleridge hoped to rally support for abolition in a lecture on the slave trade at the Assembly coffee house, not far from the docks. The tone of his lecture and its subsequent publication in the *Watchman* was pointedly angry. Coleridge chided Bristolians for their complicity in the slave trade as consumers. If they abandoned luxuries like sugar and rum, and even cotton and mahogany for homespun products like linen and oak, the slave trade would soon grind to a halt. Echoing Mary Wollstonecraft, who wrote that the miseries of slavery 'deserved more than tears ... and infantine sensibility',[55] Coleridge urged them to abandon fashionable sentimentalities in favour of a Christian benevolence that squarely addressed the atrocities of the trade. How would they like their family to be kidnapped and sent into slavery, disoriented, branded and whipped into submission? How was the brutal exploitation of bio-power, which sent millions of Africans to an early grave, compatible with Christianity?

Coleridge argued that the real African economy, what he saw as a viable peasant society of diverse petty producers, had been warped by the European slave trade. He cast the Trade as an aspect of a global economy that compelled workers to produce exports for the benefit of a luxury elite, whose taste for sugar, rum and fine furniture sustained it. He

rather fudged slavery's involvement in the industrial economy and the complexity of its interconnections, something
that has vitally interested historians since Eric Williams.[56]
To Coleridge, the slave trade was based on false needs; its
revenues helped consolidate Old Corruption. The 22-year-
old had little time for the equivocations of MPs about the
timeliness of abolition. Coleridge sardonically compared
Pitt's purported commitment to abolition to his enthusiasm
for the sedition and treason acts of 1795. He blamed Henry
Dundas for facilitating the postponement of abolition, and
with an impudent nod to Tom Paine, took the royal Duke of
Clarence to task for making a maiden speech in the Lords
in favour of the slave trade and slavery. Sugar and slavery
had brought the country to an international crisis. British soldiers were dying like flies in the tropics supporting
brutal labour regimes and luxury, while the French liberated
their slaves and produced black armies. If only the British
labouring classes recognised the extent to which they were
exploited; something the slaving interest was eager to admit
when defending plantation society. In its eyes slaves lived
more comfortably than British workers.

Coleridge's critique of the slave trade was unlikely to
win over new supporters and for some hard-liners simply
confirmed the linkages between abolition and radical
reform. To those in the know, the critique may well have
been blunted by the fact that Coleridge and his friend
Wordsworth were partially dependent on slave-trade
money for their livelihood. For it was through the auspices
of Azariah Pinney that Wordsworth and his wife were
allowed to live rent-free in Racedown Lodge, a three-storey
Georgian house in Dorset, to which Coleridge was a regular
visitor. Indeed, the young Coleridge fantasised that he and
his circle might create a Pantocracy on Nevis, the site of
the Pinney plantation, where they would receive sinecures
as phony 'negro-drivers' to cover their expenses for food
and 'necessary conveniences'.[57] No doubt this whimsical

idea was laden with irony, but it does suggest that budding Romantic poets in Bristol, circa 1795, found it difficult to attract patrons who were not in some way linked to the slave economy. The Pinneys, in fact, were business partners with James Tobin, who as we have seen, was a vociferous and vocal supporter of plantation slavery.

Robert Southey was another Romantic poet who engaged slavery, and his contribution probably struck a deeper chord in Bristol society than did Coleridge. A Bristolian by birth, the son of a linen draper with links to the gentry on his mother's side, Southey attended various local grammar schools and subsequently Oxford University where he fell under the spell of Coleridge, who was two years older. In one of his first poems Southey depicted the relationship between commerce and the slave trade in diabolical terms. 'For the pale fiend, cold-hearted Commerce there/Breathes his gold gender'd-pestilence afar/And calls, to share the prey, his kindred Daemon War.' In his fifth sonnet, the young poet exonerated the 'bold slave' who rears 'the sword of Vengeance ... in the cold bosom of his tyrant lord', sympathising by implication with the rebellions that were breaking out in the British Caribbean.[58] This was followed by one poem that admired the slave who endured the cruel punishments of stake and gibbet, who 'groans not, tho' the gorging Vulture tear/The quivering fibre!' In response to this grisly torture, Southey warned the planter that 'before the Eternal' the 'thunder-tongued' slave 'shall plead/Against the deep damnation of the deed.'[59]

In the following year, 1798, Southey changed his poetical venue from the South Atlantic to Bristol, the port of origin. The tone changed too, from devastation and defiance to white guilt and penitence.[60] Drawing on an incident brought to his attention by Joseph Cottle, a Bristol bookseller whose shops in Corn and Wine Street became a mecca for down-at-heel intellectuals, the story recalled the lamentations of a sailor who was found praying in a cow-house. The seaman told the minister who found him, very likely Dr John Estlin of the Lewin's Mead congregation, that he had joined a slave ship where he lost his 'innocence'. Among the 300 slaves on board, the captain took particular exception to one female who refused to eat, and ordered the seaman to beat her to within an inch of her life. The slave died the following day, but her shrieks, groans and whimpers continued to haunt the sailor. The minister urged him to pray to God for redemption; to 'call on him for whose dear sake/All sins shall be forgiven'. The seaman resolves never to enter the Trade again. In an amended version the poem ends with the hope that others who read 'this dreadful tale' would draw comfort from it.[61]

Some critics have suggested that Southey's poem was a response to Coleridge's *Rime of the Ancient Mariner*, which he felt was too enigmatic a tale of colonial guilt.[62] Whether this was true or not, Southey clearly hoped his poem would mobilise the conscience and humanity of seamen who were drawn to the Guinea trade. Initially abolitionists had emphasised the hazards of the trade, the extent to which it was a graveyard for seamen. As we have seen, Clarkson had great difficulty getting ordinary seamen to testify against the trade's iniquities. Generally speaking, he managed to solicit the help of ex-Guineamen who had gravitated to the protection of the Royal Navy, recognising the pressures which slave-ship sailors faced from captains and merchants in their home ports. Those pressures had surfaced very clearly in the Kimber trial. Indeed resonances from that particular trial were to be found in Southey's short poem: it featured an intractable female slave who refused to eat and was considered 'sulkier than the rest'; a merciless captain bent on making an example of such recalcitrance; and a reluctant seaman forced to participate in the flogging ritual, who in his nightmares sees her 'twisting everywhere'.[63] The comparison should not be pushed too far, but we do know that Southey was aware of the Kimber affair. Doubtless readers of his poem, which was quickly redistributed as a penny chap-book, would have been reminded of the celebrated case five years previous; especially since the flogging of the girl was depicted on the front page. In the wake of the naval mutiny of 1797, 23-year-old Southey no doubt hoped that slave-ship sailors would confront their ordeal with more courage and Christian fortitude. In his conversations with Coleridge, his friend had openly praised the 'intrepid humanity which characterizes the English Tar.'[64]

Southey and Coleridge were still minority voices in Bristol in the 1790s when war encouraged a postponement of abolition and its marginalisation in the political sphere. This was very evident in the 1796 election when caucus politics once more came to the fore. Henry Somerset, the son and heir to the Beaufort estate, decided to run for Gloucestershire, and so with the assent of the Tory White Lion Club, he was replaced by another Beaufort man, Charles Bragge, a local lawyer who had been the Recorder and MP for Monmouth.[65] John Baker Holroyd, Lord Sheffield, continued to stand for the other seat with the backing of the Union Club, much to the displeasure of more progressive sectors of the Whig party. It was not a popular choice. 'Bristol, Mirabile Dictu,' quipped the *Telegraph*, 'has chosen Lord Sheffield because he gave himself out to be a Whig!'[66] Foxite Whigs would have preferred Benjamin Hobhouse, a local merchant and banker who had boosted his financial fortunes by marrying the daughter of a wealthy Wiltshire textile manufacturer. He advocated peace, parliamentary reform, religious tolerance and abolition, and when he finally entered parliament became a regular speaker for the Whig opposition to Pitt. But he was unsuccessful in 1796. Put up by a dissident Whig group just four days before the election, he secured just over 100 votes before quickly conceding to the two dominant factions in Bristol.[67] The city was thus deprived of an advocate for abolition in the Commons and its 5,500 voters once

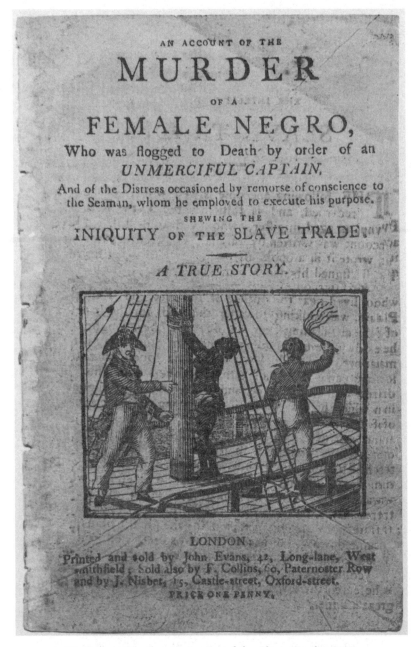

AN ACCOUNT OF THE

MURDER

OF A

FEMALE NEGRO,

Who was flogged to Death by order of an
UNMERCIFUL CAPTAIN,
And of the Distress occasioned by remorse of conscience to
the Seaman, whom he employed to execute his purpose.
SHEWING THE
INIQUITY OF THE SLAVE TRADE.

A TRUE STORY.

LONDON:
Printed and sold by John Evans, 42, Long-lane, West
smithfield; Sold also by F. Collins, 60, Paternoster Row
and by J. Nisbet, 15, Castle-street, Oxford-street.
PRICE ONE PENNY.

10. Robert Southey, Iniquity of the Slave Trade, 1800,
© The British Library Board

again bore the dubious privilege of having Bristol's mercantile elite settle the constituency for them.

And so what was Captain Kimber and company doing all the while? Surgeon Thomas Dowling had gone into compulsory exile in America after his discharge from jail in September 1793. Stephen Devereux acquired a berth on a ship to Sierra Leone, thanks to Thomas Clarkson.[68] And Kimber resumed his slaving ways. In November 1792 he boarded the *Levant*, a 210-ton ship owned by Walter Jacks and John Gordon junior. It arrived at Cape Coast Castle in early January 1793 and then sailed on to buy slaves in New Calabar, Kimber's old trading ground. This time Kimber's crew was older than those of the *Recovery*. Forty-four per cent were under 25 as opposed to 67; 31 per cent were under 20 as opposed to 46. The crew was also marginally more experienced, with 12 [37.5 per cent] having been at sea for ten years or more, the average rising to 7.7 years. Roughly half hailed from the South West and Wales as before, but this time two crew members came from outside the British Isles. Ordinary seaman John Williams, age 25, reputedly hailed from Germany, although given his Welsh name it is likely that he simply worked out of the German Baltic ports. Muster rolls are sometimes ambiguous in this respect, because their second columns flipped from 'usual places of abode' to 'where born' and we don't know whether masters always respected the difference. Williams was joined by an American, Matthew Christie, aged 17, who was one of three 'boys' on board.[69] Two seamen from the *Recovery* joined Kimber again, despite his controversial captaincy. They were Harry Watkins, the cook, who had been reluctant to prosecute his captain when the matter had been discussed at the Chepstow Boathouse; and Evan Richards, who had given evidence on behalf of Kimber before Mayor John Noble in Bristol, and was expected to do so in the perjury trial of Stephen Devereux, although he was at sea when the court convened.[70]

It took eighth months for Captain Kimber to reach Africa, buy his slaves from the Niger delta and the Gulf of Guinea islands, and deliver them to Montego Bay, Jamaica. In a voyage that was longer than his previous one, he lost 24 of his 348 slaves on the Middle Passage, 7 per cent of the total.[71] How he treated his slaves is unclear, but once again he ran into trouble with his crew. Some of the less experienced sailors died of fevers, including the surgeon's mate, William Porter, of Bristol. The other victims included the cooper, the Welshman Philip Thomas, who had two years' experience at sea, and a boy from Cowbridge, Lewis Jones, an eighteen year-old newcomer. None of these men were 'seasoned' to withstand malaria and other tropical diseases. By the time the ship reached Jamaica, one of the oldest members of the crew joined them as well: the 38-year-old William Salter from Bristol, who had been at sea since the age of thirteen; and also the surgeon, John Wood, aged 25, from Monmouth-shire, who died from a fever on 25 July 1793.[72]

More ominously, eleven members of Kimber's 31-man crew deserted ship once the *Levant* reached Montego Bay in the summer of 1793. These included some officers and experienced men: James Ferguson, the boatswain from Glasgow, with fifteen years' experience under his belt; John Freeborne from Scotland, aged 30, a sailor for 20 years; John Rogers, an ordinary seaman from London aged 23, who first went to sea at age eight. All three seventeen-year-olds in the crew took flight as well, as did the two 'foreigners' Williams and Christie, and significantly Evan Richards, one of Kimber's former supporters. What happened? Why did men steal away in the course of a few weeks? Did Kimber deliberately drive some off, since slave captains were keen to reduce the size of their crews once slaves had been dis-embarked and sold? I rather suspect there was some fallout earlier, since officers were involved, and faithful mariners like Richards. Kimber may have been unhappy he was losing so many slaves, and took it out on his men. If this was the case, he was running true to form. As late as 1797 British traders on the slave coast were calling him out for his intemperance and cruelty. A white middleman named Graham, resident at Cape Mesurado, a slave trading post in what is now Liberia, reflected: 'He has seen many bad men on the Coast during a residence of ten years, but he had never seen such savage ferocity as marked Kimber's conduct towards his men on the most trivial occasions. One has only to witness his behaviour on board his own ship to feel convinced that he is capable of anything.' These comments were made when Kimber was captaining the *Defiance* in 1797, on his way to trade at Cape Lahou on the borders of the Windward and Ivory Coast.[73] They suggest Kimber was a captain whose brutality remained unaffected by his trial.

Kimber went on three more slaving voyages before he retired from the trade three months short of his fiftieth birthday. Two of them were on the *Defiance*, a vessel registered in Whitehaven but sailing out of London. The owners were William Parry and the brothers Peter and Thomas Mallett, warehousemen and merchants in Aldermanbury, London.[74] They insured their ship with the Sun Fire Office in May and September 1797, but they took a risk not arming their 267-ton vessel at a time when the war in the Caribbean was heating up, especially in the Windward Islands where the *Defiance* planned to sell slaves. Fortunately for the owners, both voyages were successfully completed without capture by enemy shipping. In the first voyage Kimber was away just over a year, trading on the Lamo river and Cape Coast Castle. His time on the Middle Passage was short, just 37 days, and 399 of his 401 slaves on board survived. The second voyage, to the Gold Coast and then Barbados, was also successful, with a high rate of survival among the 409 slaves, only one fatality. Whatever Kimber's reputation as a hard taskmaster, he delivered for his employers.

Kimber's final slave voyage was on the *Hinde*, which was owned by a consortium of wealthy Liverpool and London merchants. They included Thomas and Alexander Hughan, men originally from Kirkcudbright, Scotland, who had previously acted as agents and factors in Jamaica before settling in Liverpool; and the Taylor brothers who were well established in London and Jamaica, where Simon Taylor was a member of the colonial assembly. The *Hinde* was a vessel geared for war. She was no bigger than the *Defiance* but she had 22 guns, allowing her to venture into privateering had the occasion been right. The vessel left Liverpool in August 1799, called at São Tomé, and then tacked back to trade in the Bight of Benin before heading for Kingston, Jamaica. The *Hinde* was away a year and three months and nine of the original 45-man crew, some 20 per cent, died. Eight per cent of the slaves died as well, on a par with Kimber's previous two ventures. The ship was sold in the Americas once the slaves were disembarked, although she did sail back to Britain, arriving in London in June 1801.

After 1801 Kimber's trail grows cold. I cannot track him down in city directories or sailing news. I don't know what happened to him after the summer of 1801, but several intriguing possibilities do surface. The first concerns the 1802 will of John Kimber, a gentleman of Winterbourne, just outside of Bristol. This John Kimber was childless at the time of his death. He assigned the profits and assets of his estate to his wife, Mary, during her lifetime and then to his nephew John Tozer, likely the son of a hat manufacturer or tinplate-worker in the city.[75] The two trustees to this will were George Gay, an ironmonger in Bridge Street, and John Barrow, a merchant of College Green. The latter subsequently achieved mayoral and aldermanic status in Bristol and became Master of the Merchant Venturers in 1824. If this is our Captain Kimber, then he retained some influential connections in Bristol despite his notoriety and saved something from his slaving ventures. After five slaving voyages he had enough money to retire to the country, although the wealth he accrued from the Trade was by no means exceptional.[76] He died within a few years of his final voyage. When his will was proved in April 1803, he would have been 51 years of age. One of his cousins married a Brownlow, who just might be the master of the slave-ship *Hope*, bound for Africa and Madeira in 1802.[77]

Two other whimsical possibilities open up in 1807. In newspapers of the South West there is a reference to a marriage by special licence of the eldest daughter of John Kimber, Esquire, of Fowey, the Collector of the Customs there. The groom was Captain Graham Eden Hammond, of the *Lively* frigate, the only son of Sir Andrew Hammond.[78] Could this be the notorious Captain Kimber and his daughter? Did he manage to land himself a cushy job in Cornwall through his mercantile connections? And see his daughter marry well in an Austen-like way? I seriously doubt it. This John Kimber was older. He is found swearing affidavits in Fowey in late 1767 when the Bideford Kimber was just sixteen.[79] He or his son seem to have been the deputy steward of the Duchy Manor of West Antony, responsible in part for the administration of Fowey's manorial court. In 1780 this Kimber could not fulfil his responsibilities because of gout.[80]

I have always imagined the notorious John Kimber as a bit of a loner, a sea captain who continued to ply the seas to the Guinea coast for the highest bidder, whether from Bristol, Liverpool or London.[81] By 1807, of course, Kimber had to find other options, for in March of that year the abolition of the slave trade finally entered the statute books. And so in April 1807, we learn of a collier called the *Friendship*, commanded by a certain Captain Kimber.[82] The vessel was captured by the French sailing back from London to Newcastle. The same Kimber? He would then be in his mid-fifties, still capable of a six-week trip along the North Sea coast, weather permitting. If he was the infamous captain, I wonder what the French would have made of him.

6

Afterthoughts

———◆———

Micro-histories zoom into the historical canvas. They focus intensely on particular events or places in order to capture the texture and social dynamic of human relationships and assess, as neatly as possible, the creative agency of ordinary people. Keith Wrightson, on a more cautious register, has recently described micro-history as 'a way of observing and trying to comprehend the network of relationships and webs of meaning in which [the chosen individuals or groups] lived their lives.'[1] In some measure the popularity of micro-history grew as historians became dissatisfied with serial history and the dangers of ignoring the jagged edges of human experience in favour of homogenised patterns of human behaviour popularised by the social sciences.[2] Some micro-historians adopted a highly nominalist stance in which clues, anecdotes andtrifles unlocked hidden worlds of human endeavour, lost or barely visible, in the records of the past.Carlo Ginzburg's *The Cheese and the Worms*, for example, is a brilliant account of how a Fruilian miller imagined Creation, how he 'misread' the Bible, what books influenced him, and what his interrogation by the Inquisition might tell us about peasant radicalism in sixteenth-century Italy. Ginzburg's work expresses a critical impatience with the then dominant school of European social history, the French Annales, whose majestic vistas and penchant for 'histoire immobile' overlooked, in his eyes, a great deal of unorthodox behaviour.[3] And yet other micro-historians have seen the construction of historical series as a valuable context for situating a particular event or place. David Levine and Keith Wrightson did this in their study of Terling, a grain-growing parish in Essex.[4] Working from a backbone of historical demography over several centuries, and combining this with legal records of parochial disputes and conflicts, they were able to test the solidarity of local social structures and, by identifying the rise of a middling sort in the village, identify critical changes in the tempo and nature of parish life in the seventeenth and eighteenth centuries.

My debt to serial history should be obvious. A lot of vital information about transatlantic shipping, and of Bristol ships and their crews in particular, would not have been at my fingertips had it not been for the work of David Eltis, David Richardson and company, whose slave voyage database allowed me to identify the ships John Kimber captained, who owned them, when they sailed, and in the most basic terms what happened on their voyages. By extension, that database and Richardson's earlier reconstruction of Bristol slave voyages for the Bristol Record Society, offered a quick entry into the nature of the crews Kimber led, and some very valuable information about the other people who worked on Bristol vessels and were prepared to give evidence before the various inquiries into the slave trade. This was all essential to building the story, although its fine details rested with a reconstruction of the available court records, manuscript and printed; the perjury trials, in particular, because the evidence offered there related back to the initial affidavits taken before Mayor John Noble, and to conversations in Bristol about the killing of No-name. It is here that the social drama of John Kimber begins to unfold.

Some historians might consider this story not to be a micro-historical venture at all, since it spread out rapidly into the Georgian public sphere. The accusations against Kimber were at the centre of the battle for abolition, were first brought to public life by its leading advocate in the Commons, William Wilberforce, and were very widely reported in the press. If your taste is for the Italian version of micro-history, with its emphasis on the 'exceptional-normal', how a bizarre event could reveal broader norms or tensions in local life, then the Kimber affair fits awkwardly. Yes, the trial itself was exceptional, but it lacked the uncanny quality central to *microstoria*. It is not an event that dramatically alerts you to the strangeness of the past.[5] Given the publicity and political controversy, the media attention that the trial attracted, the Kimber case looks more like a modern event as defined by Pierre Nora; that is to say, an expansive event that generates others, radiates out of itself to explore wider frames of reference.[6] From this perspective three strands of the story require deeper scrutiny.

The first pertains to the legal personality of slaves on board ship. Why did the slave lobby not offer substantive reasons *against* the prosecution of Captain Kimber for the murder of a slave? After all, legislation on the slave trade tended to regard slaves as cargo. In 1677 the Solicitor General, Sir Francis Winnington, claimed 'Negroes ought to be esteemed goods and commodities within the Acts of Trade and Navigation', and subsequent legislation in the eighteenth century did little to dislodge this view.[7] In a 1732 act for recovering debts in colonial America, 'houses, lands, negroes, and other hereditaments and real estates' could be demanded to redeem them. In 1750, in an act for reorganising the African trade, commanders or masters who took on board 'negroes or natives' by fraud and force and 'committed any violence' on them were subject to a £100 fine, half of which went to the prosecutor and the other half to the maintenance of the forts.[8] Nothing was explicitly said about criminal liability. Because of this legislation and the heavy significance of the Zong affair in the legal history of slavery, some historians have assumed that Kimber's trial for murder was ultra vires; he could kill a slave without a criminal penalty.[9]

Yet slavery did not confer an unqualified property right on owners, let alone ship commanders, who were technically

trustees for the vessel's investors. European writers such as
Hugo Grotius and Samuel von Pufendorf recognised that
owners had no right to take the lives of slaves unless in
self-defence.

As John Locke had argued, the right to life was inaliena-
ble.[10] In 1706, Lord Chief Justice Holt pushed the argument
further. In the case of Smith v. Gould, he declared a man
might have a special property in his captive in order to get
a ransom, or in the case of a slave entering England, some
claim to his services, but he could not therefore wantonly
'Wound or Mahame [Maim] him'.[11]

The issue of what power a captain had over the slaves
in his charge emerged in a case before the vice-admiralty
court of Boston in 1736, where the captain and former mate
of the *Defiance*, John Barnes, was accused of brutally beating and murdering a black cabin boy. His defence counsel
cited the Roman jurist Justinian in maintaining that slaves
were to all intents and purposes prisoners of war over whom
their owners had the power of life or death.[12] This argument was not entertained by the advocate general, William
Shirley, who cited Grotius' limitations on the proprietary
nature of slavery and also biblical precedent. He believed
the malicious death of anyone came within the 'original law
universally received by all Civilized Nations of the world'
and invoked Genesis 9:5–6,'Whoso Sheddeth man's blood
by man shall his Blood be shed.'[13] Barnes was consequently
found guilty, although the commissioners, no doubt anxious
about setting precedents that might disrupt the authoritar-
ian regimes of the slave trade, respited the sentence to allow
him time to seek a pardon from London. Barnes escaped
from Boston prison before a favourable judgment travelled
back across the Atlantic.[14]

Slaves on board ship might be regarded as merchandise,
but they still had residual rights to some legal protection.
They occupied a liminal position between property and personhood. Justice Buller recognised this when he ruled out

the possibility of murder in the Zong case, which was treated purely as a matter of marine insurance. 'The argument drawn from the law respecting indictments for murder did not apply', he declared.[15] He didn't say it didn't exist. Indeed, subsequent insurance cases highlighted the contradiction between slaves as chattels and persons and prepared the groundwork for an inclusive definition of human rights.[16] Even so, progress towards that goal was slow.[17] Slaves liberated from foreign ships after the abolition of the slave trade, for example, were only technically free. They were actually considered the 'property' of the Crown as prize negroes, capable of being 'apprenticed', enlisted in the armed forces, or compelled to work for the colonial authorities.

In the heyday of the slave trade abolitionists certainly tried to augment the humanity of slaves to protect their persons from arbitrary mistreatment. In his appeal to the Admiralty to prosecute the crew of the *Zong* for murdering the slaves thrown overboard, Granville Sharp argued that while the slaves were 'unhappily considered as goods and chattels ... yet that still they are men; that their existence in *human nature* and their actual rights as men, nay as brothers, still remain'. Casting them into the sea was an offence against God and mankind, and the common law 'ought to be deemed competent to find a remedy in all cases of violence and injustice'. As Sharp had argued a decade earlier, a slave had 'a superior right and title in his own person', a claim of 'natural property in himself which is estimable'.[18] This human right, with its condition of personal autonomy, trumped any propertied right that a master might claim. This sense of autonomy made headway in the public sphere through activities like novel reading, particularly those which focused on the psychology and bodily integrity of their heroines, such as Samuel Richardson's *Pamela* (1740) and *Clarissa* (1748). It is perhaps not coincidental that within decades of their publication a captain was tried for murdering a slave child thrown overboard.[19]

Sharp does not appear to have known of that case; at least he did not cite it in his memorandum to the Admiralty. But he was certainly aware of the 1536 act bringing Admiralty law closer to common law jurisdiction and making a felony on the high seas an offence without benefit of clergy; that is to say, without making concessions to criminals literate enough to read passages from the bible.[20] The burden of proof for murder, however, remained extremely high, especially for murdering slaves. Commanders were regarded as sovereigns of their ships; long gone were the laws of Oléron when captains 'chaired' their crews. Captains had wide discretionary powers on what actions should be taken for a crew's survival and welfare, and a slave ship was always one that was potentially insurrectionary. Slave revolts were frequent; roughly one in ten voyages experienced one, with probably two revolts on British slavers every year of the eighteenth century. 'Seldom a year passes but we hear of one or more such catastrophes', remarked John Newton, and 'it is always taken for granted that they [the slaves] will attempt to gain their liberty if possible'. One 'unguarded hour or minute is sufficient to give the slaves the opportunity they are waiting for', risings that brought on 'instantaneous and horrid war'.[21]

Consequently many brutal acts by officers could be justified on grounds of 'necessity'. In the Boston case of 1736, defendant John Barnes contended that the cabin boy's nightmares, which so irritated him that he threw the ten-year-old around the deck and smashed in his face, might have been a diversion for risings in the hold. The court rejected the explanation and deemed the so-called provocation slight. Barnes had the reputation of being a brute of a mate who had killed one of the crew's seamen as well as the boy. Witnesses reminded the court he showed no remorse killing Bawow, the name of the cabin boy, and did not bother to call on the services of a surgeon. Barnes' defence was simply incredible. Did he seriously think a ten-year-old's

nightmares threatened the safety of the ship? Yet the government in London ultimately gave Barnes the benefit of the
doubt and pardoned him. We can't have black cabin boys
disrupting slave ships.

Moreover, for murder, malicious intent had to be proven.
There was no secondary offence of manslaughter until 1799
in the Admiralty courts. So when it came to culpability for
a shipboard death, it was all or nothing. The issue arose in
1770 when another captain, David Ferguson of the Virginia
snow *Betsey*, was indicted for murdering three of his crew
at the High Court of Admiralty in London.[22] Ferguson had
been previously arraigned in Williamsburg for fatally beating his cabin boy slave, Caesar, as well as the three members
of his crew on the homeward run from Antigua to Virginia.
The case of Caesar was considered cognizable in the General
Court of Virginia because it occurred in the Hampton Road
rather than on the high seas, but without a commission
from the government the other men would have to stand
trial in London.[23] The governor, Lord Botetourt, applied to
try their cases in Williamsburg, but the government, already
at odds with the Virginians over the contentious Townshend
duties, the import taxes on items such as paper, lead and
tea, decided it was best to transfer the case to London.
There Captain Ferguson was found guilty of killing his boy
Jack, whipping him with a rope, stomping on his chest, and
exposing him to the harsh weather by binding him on the
windward side of the open boat for over half and hour.[24]

Ferguson seems to have believed he would be acquitted
on the grounds that his harsh treatment of the men was necessary to sail his vessel through winter gales, so severe that
snow and ice ripped through the sails. Indeed, the captain
maintained that the sudden change in weather had been
responsible for the seamen's deaths, not their 'correction',
two of them suffering from frostbite as the vessel approached
Cape Charles. He was so confident of this that he refused
to marshal medical evidence in his own defence. Having

been acquitted of murdering Caesar, he no doubt thought his chances of acquittal in the other cases were good, especially since he had helped save the vessel in which he was sent to London in a storm off the Sussex coast. One of the passengers on that trip, Major Watson, commended him as 'modest, well-behaved man' whose seamanship had been a great asset in getting them safely to port. In the light of this compliment his counsel, Arthur Murphy, thought there were enough extenuating circumstances to merit an acquittal.[25] Yet despite the fact that one of the key prosecuting witnesses, the mate James Arnold, had absconded, Ferguson was found guilty. The brutality of his beatings, and the medical evidence that the boy had suffered an internal haemorrhage, counted against him. All Murphy could achieve was a week respite of Ferguson's sentence, and in early January 1770, the 26-year-old captain was hanged at Execution dock and gibbeted in chains in the marshes down river.[26]

Ferguson had argued that his harsh treatment of the crew was necessary to get it to attend to the *Betsey* in gale-force winds. In this exceptional case the evidence worked against him. Normally captains received the benefit of the doubt on such grounds, emphasising they were the proper and sole judges of what was necessary for the safety of the ship. Even when manslaughter was introduced as a secondary option to murder in 1799, it proved very difficult to incriminate captains who pummelled crew members to death. In 1807 seamen on the Liverpool-based slave ship *Cleopatra* alleged that their captain, John Butman, the supercargo Mr Lawson, and the mate Daniel Saunders, had killed three crewmen and maimed others with firebrands, hammers and dogs. Inquest juries brought in a verdict of death by 'cruel and ill-treatment', but at the trial the captain claimed he had to whip the men into shape because he needed an efficient workforce to counter the threat of a slave revolt.[27] 'Coercive measures were necessarily resorted to', ran the rationale, 'to compel the seamen to do their duty, and that the wounds and bruises which they said had been inflicted on them by their officers, were the effect of disease.' Despite the fact that manslaughter was now on the books, the three officers were acquitted.[28]

If the manslaughter of sailors was difficult to prove, it was doubly difficult to prove of slaves, whose legal identity was more ambiguous and whose fellow captives, potential witnesses to such violence, could not always give testimony in courts of law. This meant that the legal bar was often too high to have sea captains successfully indicted for killing them. Yet at the height of the abolition campaign, the slave lobby could not afford to be nonchalant about the death of slaves on the Middle Passage. What had changed people's minds?

One crucial factor was that the War of American Independence had brought the issue of slavery squarely on the political agenda, with both sides accusing the other of libertarian hypocrisy; that is to say, trumpeting liberty while tolerating slavery. After 1783, slavery, and the campaign to abolish the slave trade in particular, could be seen in Britain as part of a campaign for national regeneration, a propitious step to assuage the pangs of defeat and move forward.[29] Indeed, a few years before the war began there were signs of a growing uneasiness about the violence inflicted on slaves and their loss of freedom. In the Somerset case of 1772, Lord Mansfield declared slavery was 'so odious' and contrary to natural law that it could only be justified by 'positive law'. Despite this moral condemnation of slavery, the terms on which Mansfield freed James Somerset were actually narrow and technical; it rested on his entitlement to habeas corpus and the inability of his former master to restrain him. The judgment did not abolish slavery in England or even create a slave-free zone, because masters could still use master and servant law to control and restrain their slaves.[30]

The ruling was sometimes openly flouted in the slave ports. Hannah More was horrified to hear a Bristol crier offering a reward for a runaway slave as late as 1790, and wrote 'To my great grief and indignation, the poor trembling wretch was dragged out of a hole in the top of the house, where she had hid herself, and forced on board ship.' Fortunately the girl escaped and found her way to the Quakers, who obtained a warrant to protect her.[31] The same was not true of a black female servant two years later. After many years of service she was sold for £80 Jamaica currency and shipped back to that island. A bystander saw her depart from Lamplighter's Hall on the river Avon; 'her tears flowed down her face', he observed, 'like a shower of rain'.[32]

Still, the rhetorical terms in which Mansfield condemned slavery were interpreted more capaciously outside the courtroom and in America. The liberal *Bristol Gazette* asserted that Lord Mansfield's decision meant 'every slave brought into the country ought to be free, and that no master had a right to sell them here'. Blacks openly welcomed the decision in the courtroom and celebrated it at a dinner and dance in Westminster at which glasses were raised to the Lord Chancellor for what was considered a breakthrough judgment. The exhilaration that greeted Mansfield's decision was such that some alarmists feared the judgment might denude the Americas of slaves.[33] Misleading as these sentiments were, they raised expectations and prepared the ground for abolition. In Scotland a series of court cases resulted in a ban on slave holding north of the border. Black poets like Phillis Wheatley attracted new audiences.[34] Advertisements for runaway slaves fell away in Britain; and efforts to re-enslave free blacks faltered. However cautious and reluctant Mansfield might have been in rendering a judgment on Somerset, he came down hard on a Liverpool captain who tried to sell a black sailor into slavery, awarding the plaintiff £500 in damages.[35]

As Christopher Brown rightly notes, the Somerset case did not immediately generate an anti-slavery or abolition movement.[36] It did, however, put diehard slavers on the defensive, as did the Zong case of 1783. The atrocity did not receive a lot of coverage in the newspapers. When the story first surfaced in March 1782, it was described in a matter of fact manner, as the regrettable decision of the captain of a distressed ship. The *London Courant*, for example, reported that Captain Collingwood was 'reduced to the greatest distress imaginable for want of water and provisions' so that 132 slaves, 'which consisted of choice Gold Coast Negroes, were obliged to be thrown overboard for the preservation of crew and remainder'.[37] It was only a year later, in the wake of the insurance suit, that the *Morning Chronicle* revealed the horrors of the story. It was the only newspaper to do so, but the scandal was picked up in various pamphlets, some of them widely circulated like Thomas Cooper's *Letters on the Slave Trade*. This made the Zong one of the staple narratives of abolition literature.[38] Most accounts expatiated on the moral outrage of throwing sick slaves overboard and the cynicism of the insurance claim, but matters of personhood did surface. They were voiced by Granville Sharp in his letter to the Admiralty and elsewhere. In the insurers' submission on the Zong case, Mr Heywood pretentiously claimed his team appeared 'as Council for millions of Mankind and the Cause of Humanity in general'. Barrister Arthur Pigott [who later defended Kimber] argued that 'as long as any water remained to be divided, these men [Africans] were as much entitled to their share as the captain, or any other man whatever'. He did not see on what grounds Captain Collingwood could have justified throwing the slaves overboard. 'The Life of one Man is like the life of another Man whatever the complexion is, whatever the colour'.[39]

The slave lobby would never accept such an argument, yet within a decade its supporters took steps to recodify the legal status of slaves in the colonies and inhibit the malicious murder of Africans.[40] In the wake of abolition agitation, colonial legislatures tried to regularise the punishments of slaves and subject them to judicial review. They eliminated the policy of allowing slave-owners to claim compensation

for dead slaves, a practice that had encouraged the abandon-
ment, even death, of old labourers on the plantations. The
Jamaican slave code of 1789 also made the wanton killing of
slaves a capital offence, for owners as well as others.[41]

At the same time benefit of clergy facilitated verdicts of
manslaughter if trials were ever held. This meant that planters and their agents would likely be fined or imprisoned for
mutilating slaves, their sentences determined by JPs who
were often planters themselves.[42] In the Leeward Islands, the
murder of slaves by masters was not considered a common
law offence under colonial law until 1797; although technically, as the slave apologist Gordon Turnbull contended in
1786, British law prevailed in the absence of such legislation.[43] So when the *Bath Journal* assured its readers in 1792
that in the Caribbean 'the life of a slave is held as sacred as
that of a white person', it was very wide of the mark. So was
the statement that 'any Master occasioning the death of a
slave' was guilty of a capital felony without benefit of clergy.[44]
Such conditions only prevailed in the United States, and
there they were hedged with all manner of qualifications. In
North Carolina, the distinction between murdering a white
and a black was erased in 1791, but caveats were added that
still made slaves highly vulnerable to violent punishment,
without redress. In other southern states, white liability for
killing slaves was also expanded to include death by wilful,
malicious and excessive whippings; although again, such
deaths were decriminalised in the case of slave insurrections
or resistance; and 'resistance' was defined very broadly to
include striking a master or overseer, even in retaliation.[45]

Much of this legislation should be seen as tokenism.
Slaves could not give testimony against whites, and whites
rarely broke rank in societies where they were conspicuous
minorities.[46] Drewry Ottley, the chief justice of St Vincent,
admitted before the Commons committee that 'the difficulty
of legally establishing facts is so great that white men are in a
manner put beyond the reach of the law'.[47] He cited a number

of instances where whites killed blacks in the presence of slaves and evaded justice because slave testimony was disallowed.[48] Yet however ineffectual the legislation, it did signal that slaves could not simply be regarded as property. If the slave lobby was to make the case for planter paternalism, and it began to do so in earnest once the abolition campaign heated up, it had to show there was legal machinery acknowledging the humanity of slaves and the possibility of some reciprocity between them and their masters.

This issue came to the fore when the Reverend James Ramsay published his reflections on slavery in 1784. A former preacher and slave owner in St Kitts, Ramsay argued there was no moral bond in colonial slavery: 'the larger part of the community [the slaves] is literally sacrificed to the less [the masters]; their time, their feelings, their persons are subject to the interest, the caprice, the spite of masters and their substitutes, without remedy, without recompense, without prospects.'[49] James Tobin, a Bristol merchant who countered Ramsay's bleak image of slave society, was thus forced to come up with some examples of legal redress for slaves. He claimed before the Commons inquiry that he knew of two instances before 1785 where whites had been prosecuted for the murder of slaves on the small island of Nevis, albeit under British rather than colonial law. One failed through lack of evidence and the other resulted in verdict of manslaughter against an overseer for excessively whipping a slave to death. He was sentenced to one year's imprisonment.[50] Similarly, Sir Ashton Warner Byam, the Attorney General of Grenada after Arthur Pigott, assured the Commons committee in 1790 that the severe punishment of slaves was actionable in law. He cited a case in the mid-seventies where a white man had been tried and executed for the murder of a slave. All efforts to have the judgment arrested failed.[51]

In the politically charged era of abolition, slave traders and their supporters openly acknowledged that slaves were entitled to some kind of protection, on the plantation and on board ship.[52] Some pro-slavery MPs contended that the existing laws were more than sufficient to punish murders on the high seas because the Dolben Act of 1788 specified that surgeons should report all mortalities and their causes.[53] Although a few cavilled that this regulation undermined a captain's authority, they did insist it offered slaves some kind of protection against their wanton destruction. In the case of John Kimber, they argued that had Thomas Dowling done his duty in accurately reporting No-name's death, the captain would have been committed to stand trial at the Caribbean port of call, in this case Grenada.[54]

In reality the chances of this happening were remote: first, because surgeons and sailors took a chance defying captains about deaths on board ship; and second, because island magistrates tended to support captains in disputes with their crews. Prosecutions would have also raised the question of whether 'global humanitarianism' was really enforceable, especially on islands where murdering slaves was normally not regarded as a capital offence. A liberal cosmopolitan notion of human rights faltered in the face of legal pluralism.

Many contemporaries thought pro-slavers were simply hiding behind the technicalities of the law by suggesting the Dolben Act was sufficient to indict Kimber, ignoring the social fields of force in which the law operated. Interestingly, a clause in the 1792 bill to abolish the trade demanded exemplary punishments of any British subjects who 'shall be guilty of any outrage, violence, or malpractice against any native of Africa' whether 'in the country, the coast, or on board ships owned or navigated by British subjects.'[55] Although slave traders and their supporters continually argued that the maltreatment of slaves was never in the interests of captains and owners because of the profits that could be made from their sale,[56] abolitionists clearly thought the existing laws were insufficient to control the abuse. They needed a boost.

Just prior to the exposé of Kimber, a case surfaced in which an American captain was charged with murdering a female slave. The incident involved James D'Wolf, a prominent Rhode Island captain and owner of the slave ship *Polly*. When his vessel returned from a slaving expedition to the Gold Coast via Havana in May 1791, rumours quickly spread that D'Wolf had deliberately isolated a female slave with smallpox by hoisting her up to the main top. Two or three days later he dumped her alive into the ocean. None of the crew willingly co-operated with the captain in carrying out this deed, and in the end D'Wolf had to order an English boy named Thomas Gorton to help him gag, mask and tie the woman to a chair and lower her down on the larboard side of the vessel. One newspaper account suggested she 'swam a little way' but was soon engulfed by the waves, although she was likely sentenced to a watery grave lashed to the chair.[57]

Captain D'Wolf probably thought he could get away with the killing on the grounds that the African's disease threatened the safety and well being of the ship. Smallpox was one of the most contagious diseases encountered on board ship and could decimate slave 'cargoes'.[58] Yet public revulsion in Rhode Island ran high. One gentleman reported that the captain's 'barbarous transaction' had 'excited in the people of this state more aversion to the traffic than any event which has ever occurred, and will probably awaken their attention to a more accurate enquiry into the general state of the odious commerce'.[59] Under public pressure a Newport grand jury requested depositions from the crew, and on the testimony of James Cranston, D'Wolf was charged with murder. He quickly skipped town, on another run to the Gold Coast. When tempers cooled, he arranged for two members of the *Polly*, Isaac Stockman and Henry Clannen, to offer their version of the incident; not in America though, but at Statia or St Eustatius, the Dutch free port. They argued that smallpox had threatened the safety of the crew, one of who, the cooper, had contracted the disease. Had the whole crew been infected, they continued, the sailors would have been unable to handle the unruly body of Coromantee captives, men 'famed for Insurrection'.[60] The old card of 'necessity' was played, and almost four years after the indictment, a judge on the Dutch island of St Thomas ruled that James D'Wolf was innocent of the charges against him. Although this decision was made outside American jurisdiction, D'Wolf was not prosecuted in the United States and continued to prosper as a merchant and leading light on Rhode Island. He went on to build Mount Hope, a grand mansion in New England; and having served as a state legislator for 25 years, he became Rhode Island's federal senator.

Nonetheless the 1791 incident was a sign of the times.[61] Slave captains could not kill their captives with impunity without risking public censure and possible prosecution. Predictably, the D'Wolf affair attracted attention in Britain. Both the *Star* and the *World* covered the story and Wilberforce likely knew of it from the newspapers or from abolition networks in America.[62] It possibly emboldened the British crusader to propel Kimber into the limelight.

Wilberforce's exposé had zoned in on the flogging of a girl. It did so at a time when the whipping of women at the cart's tail was being phased out in Britain and when new vagrant legislation banned female flogging. In fact, after 1787 the whipping of women for property offences in jails and houses of correction declined considerably, although the public whipping of women was not officially banned until 1817.[63] Whipping a naked or near-naked woman in all manner of postures, in effect taunting and tormenting her, was bound to offend Evangelical sensibilities in the late eighteenth century; especially in the terms Cruikshank represented it in the Kimber affair. Here it constituted a form of 'pornotroping' in which the 'captive body' became 'a source of irresistible, destructive sensuality'.[64]

In the late eighteenth century, the treatment of women increasingly became one of the criteria by which one measured 'civilisation'.[65] In this context the sugar colonies fared badly. Commentators were surprised that some of the most vicious and capricious whippings of slaves were supervised by plantation mistresses who abandoned all sense of decorum in the pursuit of petty revenge; particularly on female domestic servants who broke plates and teacups or were suspected of forced liaisons with their husbands. They could expect harsh whippings or the humiliation of having their ears nailed to posts and fences. 'Instead of gentleness and compassion, modesty and meekness,' observed Theophilus Houlbrooke, 'women of rank have inflicted some of the most severe punishments upon slaves.' He cited the testimony of Captain Lloyd, who noted that slaves 'are often punished as caprice and passion dictates, and to such lengths do people go, whose minds are depraved by the exercise of unlimited power.'[66] To Britons the depravity of slavery was keenly exemplified by the whipping of women, especially pregnant women, for whom holes were dug in the ground to accomodate their distended bellies. The miscarriages such whippings inflicted, the sexual humiliations and violations that preceded them, meant Caribbean society was characterised as a site of barbaric decadence and the slave ship as a degrading rite of passage to it. And in this discussion of what it meant to be 'civilised', the spectacle of suffering and the depraved voyeurism it encouraged, among planters, merchants and their hangers-on, was as corrosive as the act itself.[67]

In broad terms, the whipping of slaves was an iconic act. As Mary Wollstonecraft tersely observed: 'the lash resounds on the slave's naked sides'.[68] Flogging underscored the brutal cruelty of slavery and its capricious power. On board ship slaves were whipped to keep them in shape and force them to eat. On the plantation they were whipped to perform unremitting labour; from sunup to sundown, they were always vulnerable to the overseers' lash. If slaves were late for duty, remarked James Towne, who visited plantations in Barbados and Antigua, there were 'a number of drivers with whips on purpose to flog them.'[69] The same was true of urban slaves who failed to run errands or the assigned tasks of their masters and mistresses, often tavern or brothel-keepers. Captain Alexander Scott, a naval commander who had served in Senegal and various Caribbean ports, was astonished to see a slave hoisted up in Kingston, and stretched with weights so that the lashes would more easily lacerate his body, simply for failing to run an errand on time. Captain Cook of the 89th Regiment of Foot who served in the Leeward Islands, recalled the mistreatment of Rachel Lawder's slave, who was suspected of cheating her mistress of the profits of prostitution. Bawd Lawder beat the slave's head with the heel of a shoe until it was 'almost of a jelly' and then tried to immerse it in the privy. The slave would have suffocated in a pool of excrement had not people intervened.[70] The vicious brutality of the act astounded this army officer, a man accustomed to policing slave societies in Barbados and elsewhere, just as the ubiquity of flogging stirred the conscience of Mark Cook, a former clerk, schoolmaster and small-time planter. 'I constantly heard the whip going,' he recalled; 'slaves were treated as beasts.'[71]

The slave lobby's answer to these revelations was twofold. First, the evidence mustered by the abolitionists was sensational and selective. It was as if one mobilised the most grisly scenarios in the Old Bailey Proceedings to typify British domestic relations. The fact that monsters like Elizabeth Brownrigg beat, starved and tortured to death a fourteen-year-old pauper apprentice girl named Mary Clifford could not stand as a synecdoche for employer–servant relations.[72] And neither could the atrocities raked up the abolitionists. Second, whipping was endemic in eighteenth-century society; it wasn't confined to slaves alone. Schoolboys were birched; apprentices and servants were beaten; wives were corrected with canes. In the early nineteenth century, almost a thousand petty offenders were whipped every year, a third of them publicly rather than within institutions like the house of correction or the penitentiary; 35 per cent of them were under 20 years of age.[73]

Moreover, flogging in the army and navy was legion. Thomas Wilson, who sailed as a teenager on a merchant ship to the Baltic, recalled that 'not behaving as he should', he 'was fourteen times lashed till Raw, and then salted, and was six times hung up by the heels'. In the Royal Navy flogging was routine. In the first seven months of 1804, 105 of the 800 complement on Nelson's *Victory* were subjected to a lashing: that is, 13 per cent of the crew, all of whom would witness at least fifteen floggings a month, or on average one every other day. During the Seven Years' War, a private in the British army might watch a flogging of 50–100 lashes every day or two, and a more severe lashing once or twice a week.[74] Indeed, several spokesmen for the slavers said flogging in the army, in particular, was more severe than that practised upon slaves. Tobago planter Gilbert Franklyn thought slaves were punished more leniently than soldiers for equivalent offences, such as theft.[75]

It is difficult to capture the pain and suffering of a flogging in any quarter, but two accounts give some sense of it. Samuel Leech, an American sailor who served on *HMS Macedonian* in 1811, zoned in on the humiliation of punishment, a common feature in military accounts. He recalled one seaman before the grating: 'his flesh creeps, the sufferer groans, lash follows lash'. After two dozen strokes of the cat, 'the lacerated back looks inhuman; it resembles roasted meat burnt nearly black before a scorching fire'. At four dozen strokes, Leech continued, the cat had 'cut up his flesh and robbed him of all self-respect; there he hangs, a pitied, self-despised, bleeding wretch'.[76]

The second account comes from Alexander Somerville, who was stationed with the Scots Greys in Birmingham during the Reform Bill riots of 1832. Openly critical of the role the military played in those disturbances and troubled

by the order to repress the Birmingham Political Union if
it staged a march to London, he was court martialed on a
trumped up charge of insubordination and sentenced to
200 lashes. In his autobiography he remembered the terror
and pain of the ordeal. The regimental sergeant major stood
behind him, book in hand, and meticulously recorded the
strokes. He ordered Farrier Simpson 'to do his duty':

> The manner of doing that duty is to swing the 'cat' twice
> round the head, give a stroke, draw the tails of the 'cat'
> through the fingers of the left hand to rid them of skin, or
> flesh, or blood; again swing the instrument twice around
> the head slowly, and come on and so forth.

> Simpson took the 'cat' as ordered ... I did not see him,
> but I felt an astounding sensation between the shoulders,
> under my neck, which sent to my toe nails in one direc-
> tion, my finger nails in another and stung me to the heart,
> as if a knife had gone through my body. The sergeant-ma-
> jor called in a loud voice, 'One.' I felt as if it would be
> kind of Simpson not to strike me in the same place again.
> He came on a second time a few inches lower, and then
> I thought the former stroke was sweet and agreeable
> compared to that one. The sergeant-major counted 'two.'
> The 'cat' was swung around the farrier's head again and
> he came on somewhere about the right shoulder blade,
> and the loud voice of the reckoner counted 'three.' The
> shoulder blade was as sensitive as any other part of the
> body, and when he came again on the left shoulder and
> the voice cried 'four' I felt my flesh quiver in every nerve,
> from the scalp of my head to my toenails. The time
> between each stroke seemed so long as to be agonizing,
> and yet the next came on soon. It was lower down, and
> felt to be the severest. The word 'five' made me betake
> myself to mental arithmetic, this thought I, is only the
> fortieth part of what I am to get.[77]

At 25 lashes, a trumpeter was exchanged for the farrier
to perform the next round of floggings. After fifty lashes

Somerville's face started to turn black and he spat blood, either from biting his tongue or from an internal injury. The hospital sergeant offered him water at this point, but the lashings continued. Only at one hundred did the commanding officer call a stop to the punishment.

By any standards this was staggeringly cruel, but it does give us some sense of what a sustained flogging felt like with a cat o' nine tails. The wonder is so many soldiers survived, for one hundred lashes was a customary punishment in army courts martial, often remitted from some higher number. A study of two British regiments during the American war found that 47 per cent of those found guilty by a court martial actually received 100 lashes, 14 per cent received 250–300 lashes and 12 per cent over 300. In the Royal Berkshire Militia, stationed at Chelmsford and Dublin during the years 1798–1799, the range of punishment was a little wider in that some militiamen received twenty lashes. But proportionately the figures were much the same. 45 per cent received between 98–140 lashes and 23 per cent two hundred or more.[78] Severe punishments were rendered for quite trivial offences. William Gunn was sentenced to 200 lashes for selling his shirt while drunk and then sent to the black hole until he could pay for two more. Thomas Smith of the Grenadiers was sentenced to 300 lashes on suspicion of stealing a watch. In fact the watch ended up in his possession after a hard night's drinking with two other soldiers. There is good evidence he intended to return it only he could not remember the private's name. His sentence was reduced to 160 lashes, not much of a reduction in the circumstances.[79]

Whippings were intended to keep 'riff-raff' soldiers in line. Lord Palmerston declared: 'from the classes from amongst which the British army was composed, it was impossible to preserve discipline but by some coercive measures'.[80] This view was widely supported by commanders such as Wellington and the Duke of York, Clarence's brother. Mercy was offered sparingly, normally because of good character references from a superior. Two thirds of the soldiers sentenced to 100 lashes or more in Boston during the American war received the full sentence; overall 59 per cent. The sentencing patterns of two other regiments during the American war, one stationed in Canada and the other in Scotland, were more lenient, especially among the South Fencibles north of the Tweed, where a quarter received the full sentence and 40 per cent had sentences which were partially remitted.[81] Much depended on the disposition of the officers and their calculations as to how many bloody matinees were necessary to instil fear and terror in their regiments.

Among the regiments in Boston about a third of the troops were subject to a court martial, and around 30 per cent of all privates received the lash since the acquittal rate was marginal, a mere 4 per cent. In general terms discipline in the army was more extensive and more brutal than in the British navy, where sailors customarily received twelve lashes for drunkenness and insubordination, and where the proportion formally flogged was smaller. On the 73 vessels at the Leeward Island station between 1784 and 1815, 9 per cent of the crews were flogged and in 60 per cent of all cases the culprits received twelve lashes or less.[82] On the longer, more arduous journeys of discovery to the Pacific, the proportion whipped reached one in five, and spiked at 45 per cent on Vancouver's *Discovery*. Once again most received twelve lashes.[83] Discipline in the navy very likely increased in the late eighteenth century as the threat of rebellion and mutiny loomed; more floggings were ordered for drunkenness and insolence as lower-deck deference declined. In North American waters, only 36 per cent of recorded punishments involved twelve lashes or less; 63 per cent involved eighteen lashes or more, and 56 per cent twenty-four or more.[84]

For mutiny and desertion, sailors were subjected to more spectacular punishments. As befitted a regime of judicial terror, they were hanged from the yardarm. Alternatively, they were flogged around the fleet in circumstances akin to army punishments, with surgeons in attendance to ensure that victims were not irreparably disabled by the ordeal, at least while the punishment was conducted. This could also occur for violent disruptive behaviour. The chaplain of HMS *Gloucester* remembered a man who was sentenced to 150 lashes for drawing a knife on another seaman and flogged around the fleet by the boatswain's mates of each ship. 'When he arrived at the *Gloucester*,' the chaplain recalled, 'he was very faint and bloody; and before he returned to the *Valiant*, must have endured what, to me, appeared [a fate] worse than death.'[85] Indeed, William Spavens recalled that one sailor sentenced to 600 lashes through the fleet requested he be hanged rather than face the punishment.[86]

In addition to these punishments, sailors were subjected to informal forms of correction by boatswains and others. Petty officers would chivvy seamen into working the ship by striking them with pieces of rope or whatever came to hand. Jacob Nagle remembered that on HMS *Prudent*, 'The moment the boatswain blew his call, there must be a full run till the tackle was ablock, and every officer thrashing away, even the captain himself with his cane when he took the notion.' Charles Pemberton recalled how as a seventeen-year-old he learnt

> to come at a whistle and run at a blow ... to watch continually in avoidance of abuse and beating and watch in vain – to be scourged by ropes by brutes who were charmed with delight at the sound of the heavy dense blows which they dealt around in sheer wantonness ... whose best sport was in watching and smiting at and prolonging the suppressed cries and writhing of their victims.[87]

This quotidian form of punishment was called 'starting' and was never recorded in the logbooks. We have little idea how frequently or tyrannically it was exercised. Some 'men's backs have often been so bad from the effects of the starting system,' remarked William Robinson, 'that they have not been able to bear their jackets on for several days.'[88] As Pemberton's comments reveal, starting was hated for its arbitrariness and potential sadism. It surfaced as a smouldering grievance in the naval mutinies of 1797, alongside complaints that naval officers had acted as 'tartars', that is, as martinets who flouted the conventional exercise of seaborne discipline by flogging arbitrarily and erratically. This abuse resulted in the ejection of petty officers from select ships at Spithead.[89] After an incident on HMS *Nereide* in 1809, when seamen were beaten beyond endurance and mutinied, starting was banned from the navy. How effectively this ban was enforced remains unclear. It probably took years to rein in commanders who saw themselves as sovereigns of their ships and responsible for those under them.

Where does this leave us with respect to the flogging of slaves? It is not at all clear, and the problem is compounded by the fact that a straightforward cliometric analysis does not really get to the root of the problem, because punishment is essentially a strategy of rule; its severe or discretionary implementation depend upon the micro-politics of each ship, each regiment, each plantation. But here I shall hazard a few observations. A lot of plantation punishment was equivalent to starting; it involved coercing people to labour.[90] 'I never saw a gang of Negroes at work', observed one lieutenant in the marines, 'without one or more tormentors snapping their whips and threatening every moment to make them feel them.'[91] The difference lay in the power relations. Slaves could not openly resist. To do so would run the risk of severer punishment, mutilation or even death. Masters might conceivably be a check upon sadistic overseers, but too often they were absentees, nominal owners of heavily indebted plantations, under pressure from creditors, and unwilling to experiment with more lenient regimes or tinker with the local autonomy of the overseer and his drivers. Even owners who rented out their slaves sometimes had little control over their punishment. Boston King, for example, who served an apprenticeship to a carpenter in colonial South Carolina, was subject to such savage beatings by his employer that he was laid up for weeks on end. There was little his owner could do other than transfer Boston to another master.[92]

Seamen, by contrast, could very occasionally obtain legal redress for punishments they thought to be unfairly inflicted. Three privateersmen took a naval captain to court for intervening in their capture of a French prize and flogging them for their impudence. The captain involved, Policarpus Taylor of HMS *Fowey*, protested that whipping 'was a common correction for drunkenness and petty faults on board men of warr, Indiamen and Turkeymen, and that he had used the sea nineteen years.'[93] This did not absolve him from paying out £80 to each of the injured sailors as a result of an action at the Lancaster Assizes; a 'monstrous verdict', thought the Admiralty Solicitor, which should be appealed at King's Bench. Admittedly this was an unusual case, but there were others where seamen under the direct jurisdiction of the Royal Navy sought redress for arbitrary punishment. In Barbados in 1743, a quarter gunner named James Man refused an order to heave to and was beaten severely with a rattan by the master of the vessel, George Gill. Man took Gill to court and sued for £100 in damages, on the grounds that only the captain could serve him this way. The Admiralty Solicitor, Francis Winnington, admitted that James Man, who was said to be 'Lazy, Drunken', and 'Mutinous', was technically in the right. And indeed the jury did not hesitate to bring in a verdict for the plaintiff.[94]

In most cases seamen did not have much protection from the actions of petty officers, although paternalist captains did sometimes intervene to curb glaring excesses. Collectively seamen could exercise some informal resistance to very abusive behaviour; they could make their grievances known in nightly conversations and murmurings at the forecastle, and very occasionally they conducted reprisals against abusive petty officers once the ship was in port. In October 1748 some seamen from a man of war cornered the lieutenant and the master of the ship on Tower Hill, London, and beat them 'very severely'. When asked why, they answered 'they had been remarkable for Tale-bearing, Lying, and taking Pleasure in seeing Men whipt'.[95]

When it came to spectacular punishments, there was a debate amongst contemporaries about the severity of floggings in servitude and in the army. Superficially, army floggings seemed harsher because they inflicted higher quotas of the lash. By 1792 a few slave islands had instituted a 39-lash rule, although this ceiling was easily evaded by separating each session by an intermission in the stocks. Sometimes the 39-lash rule was quite openly flouted in front of JPs. In 1810, during the period of so-called 'amelioration' after the abolition of the slave trade, Nevis planter Edward Huggins had thirty slaves whipped in the marketplace over the course of two to three hours. The average number of lashes inflicted on men was calculated at 141, on women 110, with two of each sex receiving more than 200 lashes. Only toward the end of this brutal matinee did JPs think it necessary to intervene, and some were clearly reluctant to do so, for under cross-examination they insisted that the punishment matched the crime, which concerned a truculent gang of slaves who sought to 'try it on' with their new owners.[96] Indeed, some justices clearly bristled at the 39-lash law, believing exemplary punishments and planter discretion were necessary to dampen signs of rebellion. Nevertheless, Huggins' punishment was condemned in the local assembly and he was charged with violating the recent Leeward Islands Amelioration Act. He was acquitted, partly no doubt because the magistrates supported him, but also one suspects because those same magistrates took the trouble to inspect the slaves a week later, reporting that while a number had been disabled from working only one died, allegedly from 'pleurisy'.[97] A later pamphlet suggested that the lenient

verdict had been dictated by planter fears of a wave of insubordination among the slaves and the 'then unsettled state of
the black population in the French islands'.[98]

Even allowing for cumulative punishments and gro-
tesque floggings such as those ordered by Huggins, slaves
do not appear to have normally received a hundred or more
lashes, unless it was for running away.[99] We cannot be sure,
because slave floggings were rarely recorded in the same way
as regimental. We have to rely on the testimony of plantation
owners such as Gilbert Franklyn, who thought 20–40 lashes
were customary for offences like stealing rum and breaking
into stores.[100] And yet if slaves received fewer lashes, they
were flogged more frequently. Thomas Thistlewood, the
overseer of the Egypt plantation, Jamaica, between 1751 and
1759, whipped a slave more than once a week on average and
physically punished virtually all of them in the course of one
year, forcing some slaves to defecate on others and subject-
ing others to agonising insect invasions by pouring molasses
all over them. The use of the whip declined a little after
abolition, but it still remained fundamental to discipline on
Caribbean estates. The number of recorded punishments
per slave per year in Demerara in the late 1820s was 0.31
compared to 0.41 at Egypt. In other words, the chances of
being flogged every year in Demerara was one in three; in
Egypt, Jamaica, two in five. By the 1840s, things were no
better on the Louisiana cotton plantation of Bennet Barrow,
although Barrow was not as perverse as Thistlewood.[101] Here
75 per cent of the field hands were flogged in the course of
two years, and over half of them were flogged more than
once, with little distinguishing male from female save that a
slightly higher percentage of females [30 per cent] received
no punishment at all.

The limited evidence we have suggests that slaves were
flogged more frequently than soldiers and sailors, and that if
they endured fewer lashes, the damage inflicted might well
have been higher. Certainly General Tottenham thought so,

as did Doctor Harrison, a surgeon with experience of military and slave floggings in Jamaica and America. He thought 'The punishments of soldiers (which he has often witnessed) were generally mild compared to the whipping of slaves in gaol or round the town.'[102] This was because slaves were more likely to be punished with bull or horse whips made of cow hide, six feet or so long, which cut deeper into the back than a cat o'nine tails. Harrison remembered that after one severe flogging in jail he could 'lay two or three fingers in the cavity of the wounds'. Clarkson was told that 'the whip generally takes out a piece of flesh at every stroke.'[103] This was especially the case if the lashings were inflicted by 'jumpers', expert floggers who could be hired to exercise their craft with diabolical exactness, to a point of lodging the tip of the whip under the skin from six to eight feet.[104] This brutal torture was frequently followed up by floggings with ebony switches, which drew blood from bruised skin.

Cowhide floggings drew flesh not simply skin; they cut deeper from the beginning. James Towne, a carpenter on HMS *Syren* who had served on two slaving voyages in the 1760s, said many slaves had conspicuous scars on their backs, crisscross lacerations that stood out like elongated fingers from the surrounding skin.[105] Many slaves were permanently marked. Thomas Woolrich, a West Indian merchant usually resident in Tortola, but sometimes at Barbados, Antigua and St Kitts, said slave backs were often 'one undistinguished mass of lumps, holes, and furrows.'[106] This was not necessarily true of soldiers and sailors. And to these sickening and disabling punishments, one might add the devilment of contrived tortures for rebellious slaves, who were mutilated, slowly burnt to death, gibbetted alive, or even skewered and hoisted up on the gallows, as William Blake so grippingly illustrated in John Stedman's narrative of his time in Surinam. Gruesome as these punishments were, they are often elaborations of the European panoply of judicial punishment and torture.[107]

Slave punishments represented their victims' sickening abjection; they had no legal redress. It was not until 1811 that a plantation owner was brought to justice for brutally killing his slaves, one Arthur Hodge of Tortola. In the post-1807 era, he was considered by imperial officials to be beyond the pale, having tortured and disfigured at least a dozen slaves and killed at least three. And yet many locals thought Hodge unfairly victimised, since the punishments occurred three years previous to the trial. His friend and lawyer William Musgrave allegedly declared it was 'no greater offence in law for his owner to kill [a slave] than it would be to kill his dog'.[108] The weight of island feeling and the belief that local feuding over prizes in the vice-admiralty court had fuelled the charge against Hodge led the jury to recommend mercy. Even so, Governor-General Hugh Elliot thought Hodge an incorrigible offender who had ordered a superlatively harsh flogging of a slave named Prosper for simply stealing a mango; a whipping so severe that the slave never walked again and died soon afterwards. In the wake of the Huggins case, he ordered a special commission to try Arthur Hodge, and once he was found guilty of murder, advised London that the sentence should take place to check the dispositions of other planters who did not consider the mortal whipping of a slave to be 'a heinous and atrocious murder' in the eyes of the law. As a safeguard against any attempt to rescue Hodge, Elliot declared martial law and mobilised the militia during the execution and its aftermath.[109]

———◇———

And so we return from the legal personality of slaves, to their whipping, to the story itself. Because it is a seemingly accessible story it has become a signature event for repossessing, or trying to repossess, the trauma of the Middle Passage. In her autobiographical travelogue of her time in Ghana, retracing the journey of the Atlantic slave route, African-American writer Saidiya Hartman uses the Kimber story to try to recapture the horror of the Middle Passage for the slave. Although this is technically the story of a young woman from the Niger Delta, likely Igbo or Ibibio, possibly sold at one of the monthly fairs at Bende or Uburu and sent to New Calabar to be shipped to Grenada, Hartman appropriates the story to address the wounded legacies of slavery in America today.

Hartman finds the task a daunting one. The girl has no name, and but for the trial she would be lost. 'Exceptional circumstances prevented her from simply vanishing into the heap of obscure lives scattered along the ocean's floor.'[110]

Utilising the four printed versions of the trial, she mimes the records and 'fabulates'; that is, fictionalises around them.[111] Hartman tries to imagine what might have happened to the girl, not so much to recover her voice, which she regards as impossible, as to explore 'a realm of experience between social and corporeal death.'[112] Here she declares her allegiance to Orlando Patterson's notion of social death,[113] which emphasises the disruption and alienation of slavery, the inability of slaves to hold on to their memories and heritage, first in the sodden, clammy, sewer-like holds of the slave ship.

Hartman does this with eloquence and panache. We get slightly different versions of No-name's predicament, depending on her decrepitude or defiance. In the latter condition some aggravated punishments are added to make her eat: the speculum oris to force-feed her, thumbscrews to make her submit.[114] Hartman sees Kimber's decision to suspend and flog No-name as an exemplary punishment to keep the other slaves in line and perhaps 'stave off an insurrection'. She writes: 'It only took one bad seed to plant the idea of rebellion, so you had to destroy it quickly, before it took root and spread.'[115] Hartman's sense of 'social death' is clearly not absolute. Slaves are not catatonic but offer various forms of resistance to their forced captivity.

Yet other aspects of the story go awry. Hartman constructs No-name as a lone, abject victim, confronted with a wall of white indifference. The seamen on the *Recovery* were complicit to the murderous flogging. 'Everyone knew that murder was part of "work at sea".'[116] Wilberforce exploited the girl; indeed Hartman suggests 'she was more useful dead than alive' to him. She offered a salutary lesson to the Commons about the miseries of the slave ship. 'He wanted the members of Parliament to squirm in their seats, to flinch before her battered body, to recoil with every lash that cut the girl's flesh.'[117] The whole exercise made Wilberforce feel good and elevated his saintliness. And if MPs were not appalled by the depiction, they could 'pornotrope' with Cruikshank, whose print could be read as mocking Wilberforce's moral conceits.[118]

The problem with this interpretation is that it ignores key elements of the story and glosses the politics of abolition. The critical window into the reactions of the crew comes from the perjury trial of Stephen Devereux, which Hartman did not read. This reveals that some members of the crew were far from happy with No-name's flogging and pondered how they might bring Kimber to justice. Their conversations became common knowledge on the quays of Bristol and prompted Kimber's supporters to corral as many members of the crew as they could to contain or counter the allegations. The strategy almost succeeded. The sailors lacked the resources or courage to pursue the suit. It only surfaced when Dowling and Devereux casually mentioned the flogging to Clarkson and then Wilberforce.

So the reaction of the crew was not unanimously indifferent. And Wilberforce's decision to expose the flogging before the Commons was not simply prompted by his decision to shame the House; he knew that a graphic incident like this might be grounds for a legal prosecution. He did not dwell on the other murders Kimber committed because he was aware that *mens rea* had to be established at law.

Others recognised the problem as well. While Dowling and Devereux were initially summoned to give evidence about the deaths of two additional slaves, namely Venus and O'Keibra, the grand jury excluded them from the indictment. The writ charged Kimber with two accounts of murder, first for brutally whipping No-name, and second, for whipping and suspending her from the mizzen stay. *Pace* Hartman, Venus was never part of the indictment.[119] The reason why Wilberforce zoned in on No-name had to do with the legal possibilities of the exposé, of a woman visibly hoisted up and whipped unmercifully. The punishment had legal legibility. And Wilberforce was far from 'desperate' in making his case before the House of Commons.[120] He had more petitions behind him than any other politician in British history. Thousands deplored the trade in over 500 petitions, the largest number submitted on one issue since parliament began. This public dimension, the waves of protest against the trade, impressive in 1789 but momentous in 1792, never enters Hartman's account. It would have muddied the waters of her interpretation, which centres on racial polarisation and is fuelled by American identity politics.

Nevertheless Hartman's chapter in *Lose Your Mother* and her subsequent essay on Venus do raise the issue of what we can really know about slaves in the European, in this case, British archive. Like Hartman, many literary scholars who have ventured into the slavery and abolition archive with the aim of recovering African voices, recoil at its intransigence. Marcus Wood talks of a 'white archive' in which African subjectivity is indelibly entangled and emasculated.[121] Others follow Foucault in defining the archive as a citadel of surveillance and governmentality, perhaps with a Derridean twist as in Ann Laura Stoler's *Against the Archival Grain*, in which the archive appears as a series of sequestered sites of uncertainty.[122] From these perspectives what is recoverable about slaves is their ruined health and abject condition, their function in the calculus of marine insurance and capital; or, if one is dealing with the sexual politics of slavery, with the slipperiness of hybridised classifications and the indissoluble difficulty of reconciling the brute life of a slave with his or her humanity; or again, with the contradictory tensions inherent in plantation paternalism where masters were never sure what their slaves were doing on their nocturnal revels and were perpetually troubled by the prospect of slave revolt. The last perspective at least offers some recognition of slave agency, although many literary scholars, in particular, continue to believe the archive emasculates it. Marisa Fuentes, confronted with the parliamentary inquiries into the slave trade, finds them impenetrable, fixated on the horror of slavery at the expense of the slave's suffering and subjectivity. In her view the slave's cries and groans become the only punctum, the only arresting note, that draw our attention back to the slave's humanity.[123]

These perspectives are too bleak and too frequently top down. They privilege victimhood over agency, the administrative gaze over the tactics of the oppressed. For example, Fuentes ignores the evidence of surgeons like James Arnold and Alexander Falconbridge who both testified that female slaves sometimes resisted their servitude by refusing to eat and suicide. They also confirmed that slaves could only be made to dance under the cat.[124] This resistance was reproduced in newspapers like the *Derby Mercury*, which claimed that slaves 'often hang, kill and starve themselves, or jump overboard'. One witness recalled female slaves who were repeatedly flogged and force fed, to no avail. 'In the very act of chastisement they have looked up at the flogger *with a smile*, and in their own language have said, *presently we shall be no more*.'[125] This journalistic disclosure came from the evidence submitted by surgeon Isaac Wilson to the Commons committee. It was a striking departure from the 'melancholy realism' of many abolitionist accounts, revealing a politics of witnessing that stressed defiance, not abjection. Thomas Clarkson captured some of it in his history of abolition.[126]

The agency of slaves, then, is not occluded from the archive. Nor is the archive as monolithic or Kafkaesque as it might appear. In fact the abolition archive is an on-going enterprise in which new databases are being created that enhance our knowledge of the Middle Passage and the ethnic clusters at slave destinations.[127] The slave voyages database, in particular, has greatly increased our understanding of the trade, its routes and its risks. Parliamentary inquiries also provide a welter of information about the slave trade, and because they were conducted in a politically charged context that prompted hesitations, elisions, and evasions to the questions directed at witnesses, it is possible to read against grain and tease out, for marginal groups, what Antoinette Burton has called 'the fragmented and fugitive traces of historical subjectivity'.[128] These insights can be supplemented by the observations of the few literate blacks, like Cugoano and Equiano, who acted as cultural brokers and interlocutors in the abolition debate. They served as surrogates for the thousands who could not speak of the horrors of the Middle Passage and the transition to slavery; although it is important to consider how politics and the memories of their capture and enslavement, recalled many years later, affected their self-presentations. This is particularly the case with Olaudah Equiano, the self-styled 'African', who at times claimed he was from Carolina, and whose spiritual autobiography is fashioned towards a redemptive freedom, capped by a Methodist conversion, that appealed to white readers.[129]

Certainly one cannot fully recapture a slave's experience, particularly a female slave's experience. We simply do not know where No-name came from, what gods or ancestors she invoked as she underwent the horror of capture and enslavement, and what her relationship was to the other slaves. One version of the trial transcript suggested they shunned her, but for what reason? Because of her medical condition, as Sir William Scott suggested?[130] There is a sense

in which her brief appearance in the records of the past illustrates the limits of history. She does not speak; she groans,
she suffers. Europeans, in this case sailors and abolitionists,
speak for her. Here lies the frustration of many literary historians whose expectations of recuperating a slave's 'voice'
seem impossibly high.

One might be tempted to take a postcolonial tack and
suggest that No-name's historical plight is typical: she is
encased in an imperial archive, an object of inquiry whose
subjectivity is governed by metropolitan imperatives. There
is an aporia or lack of alignment between No-name's subjectivity and her place in the history of atrocity.[131] Yet while
acknowledging some of this I do think it possible to make
reasoned assessments about slave predicaments in the
most general terms, to capture their courage and self-respect in the adverse circumstances of the Middle Passage.
In the logbook of the *Black Prince*, for example, the captain
recounts anxiously that slaves were ready to die and willing
to take their lives during the Middle Passage. Captain Miller
noted the case of a sickly slave who tried to jump overboard
and he bemoaned the female slaves who were prepared to
starve themselves to death. In March 1763 he wrote, amid
the thunder and the swell of the ocean, 'Our women is very
bad. Many of them with purgings and some falls away not
eateing.'[132] In the end Miller cannot reconcile his disposition
to regard slaves as commodities with their humanity.

On the agency of slaves we can go further. Shipboard
revolts were subject to insurance claims and make possible a re-evaluation of shipboard resistance and its regional
incidence. One can build up a series that offers a window to
slave revolt and by extension to the role women played as
accessories to insurrection; for their greater freedom [and
sexual exploitation] aboard ship gave females the opportunity to collect nails and other tools to unlock chains and
manacles.[133] John Atkins remembered a woman who acted
as a lookout for rebellious slaves off Sierra Leone, alerted

them to the number of sailors on deck, and provided them with a hammer to attack seamen in the forecastle. She paid for her intervention with her life. She was 'hoisted up by the thumbs', Atkins recalled, and made an example; 'whipp'd, and slash'd with knives before the other slaves, until she died'.[134]

Court records can also provide us with fleeting evidence of direct interventions. They can act as a useful counterpoint to the scenes of subjection that proliferate in abolition testimony, where agency might only surface as a lone hunger strike or as an overboard suicide, actions that fell short of collective resistance. In 1783, for example, women tried to topple Captain Richard Bowen from the quarterdeck of the *Wasp* and subsequently participated in a failed insurrection in which rebellious slaves deliberately jumped over board and took their own lives. We know all this from a disputed insurance claim that came before the court of King's Bench in 1785.[135]

Many of the problems recovering the lives of slaves pertain to any subaltern group. We encounter them in conflict with authority; we read them through the eyes of their superiors; we need to be attentive to 'language' in its broadest sense, to the signifiers of dissent and dejection in action and song, to the social dramas so skilfully recreated by the Australian historian, Greg Dening.[136] As in contact history, there is a significant barrier of culture and language to overcome. But recovering the life of a slave is historically more intractable. European explorers usually had a disposition to understand the indigenous groups they encountered, for their own security and survival; even to the point of kidnapping some as putative intermediaries and trying to understand their language, customs and outlook.[137] Transatlantic slaves were mobile, disposable labour. They were there to be exploited, not understood. Across that sea of death that was the Atlantic, they were essentially cargo, biopower for plantation regimes, expendable labour whose rate of survival was often less than ten years in the British Caribbean. No-name was a young vulnerable woman who was either incapable or unwilling to adhere to the regimen of the ship. We don't know which. She died for it at the hands of a brutal captain. Her tragedy, several hundred miles from Grenada, reverberated back to Britain and became part of the abolition battle and its collective memory.

In 1805 the pro-slaver Robert Bisset expatiated on the trial of Captain Kimber. The alleged 'bloody deed was the subject of numberless declamations in the public papers, pamphlets, tabernacles and other common scenes of inflammatory misrepresentation' he railed. Democratic journalists imputed the murder to Kimber and to 'the existing establishments of polity and commerce' and 'predicted that such barbarities would prevail until the Africans were placed on a footing with civilised Europeans'; indeed, 'until all ranks and distinctions were levelled and universal equality established'.[138]

Bisset was paranoid and anti-Jacobin. He feared that scandals like the Kimber flogging would open the sluice gates of abolition and democracy. After 1807 the tone of remembrance changes and so too does the visibility of No-name. One early history of the trade reiterated the voyeuristic interpretation of the whipping in which No-name is dangled in revealing postures as a spectacle to the crew. This was followed by another slave-trade rebuttal of Kimber's prosecution and maltreatment of the girl. Here Thomas Clarkson, who brought the flogging to Wilberforce's attention, was accused of using 'revengeful seamen' to trash Kimber, notably Dowling, who was prosecuted for it.[139] Clarkson may have taken this kind of accusation to heart, because in his own account of the abolition campaign, he cites Kimber's participation in the bombardment of New Calabar, but ignores the whipping. In his reiteration of Wilberforce's speech before the Commons on the night of 2 April, he omits No-name's torment at the hands of the captain.[140]

Did Clarkson do this in deference to Wilberforce? Was he troubled by the hasty way in which the evidence against Kimber had been collected, to which he was a party? In the aftermath of the Kimber trial, abolitionists like William Rathbone of Liverpool felt the Kimber exposé had been clumsily executed, with the result that people 'would not come forward with any facts but those which would be substantiated in the clearest manner'.[141] Perhaps Thomas Clarkson wanted to smooth out the prickly episodes of the abolition campaign. He certainly wanted to convey the impression of the forward march of righteousness; yet Kimber's acquittal by a London jury allowed his opponents to arrogate to themselves the rights of the freeborn Englishman at a critical ideological juncture. The verdict became entangled in the contest between British liberty and the French Terror. Although the trial was a miscarriage of justice, the acquittal of Kimber could be seen as blemishing the rectitude of the prosecution. Whatever the reason for the amnesia or disregard, Captain Kimber became associated with the bombardment of New Calabar in Clarkson's *History*, not with the fatal flogging of No-name on the Middle Passage.[142] In the end, the Kimber murder trial lacked the staying power of the Zong as a synecdoche and haunting spectacle of slave-trade brutality. Perhaps this was because the Zong affair was so categorically about money and the heartless logic of finance capital, whereas the Kimber trial became enmeshed in debates about the ubiquity of punishment in the eighteenth century and could not entirely extricate itself from the pressures and foibles of abolitionist inquiry. Whatever the reason, Kimber's fatal flogging of a defenceless African girl fades from view and did not live on, as did the Zong, most conspicuously in J. M. W. Turner's memorable painting of floundering slaves in a stormy sea.[143] Unless, of course, you are aware of Cruikshank's memorable print.

APPENDIX

Newspaper advertisements for the trials of Captain John Kimber and Stephen Devereux 1792–3

1) *The Whole of the Proceedings of the Sessions of the Admiralty held at the Old Bailey, 7–8 June 1792* – official transcript shorthand E. Hodgson, printed by F. and C. Rivington, St Paul's Churchyard 1s. [*London Chronicle*, 12–14 June 1792; *Public Advertiser*, 14 June 1792] with the addition of an appendix containing the substance of the depositions before the Mayor of Bristol [*Morning Chronicle*, 16 June 1792]

1a) *The Whole Proceedings on the Admiralty Session at the Old Bailey* [By permission of the Judge] [*St James Chronicle*, 9–12 June 1792, *London Chronicle*, 16–19 June 1792. 1 and 1a both advertised in *Morning Herald*, 18 June 1792, but without appendix.]

1b) *Trial of Captain Kimber for the murder of a Negro girl.* By authority of the court, taken down by Hodgson, F. and C. Rivington, printers. After headline, *The Whole of the Proceedings*. Price 1s., noting appendix with depositions [*Public Advertiser*, 16 June 1792, *Morning Chronicle*, 18 June 1792]

2) *The Trial of Captain John Kimber, Commander of the African Slave Ship ... the Recovery, for the willful murder of a Negro Girl ...* taken in short hand by a student of the Temple, Charles Stalker, 4 Stationer's Court, Ludgate Street, 1s. [*Morning Herald*, 11 June 1792]

2a) *Trial of Captain John Kimber for the murder of two female slaves.* Shorthand by a student of the Temple, C. Stalker Ludgate St. [ECSTC]

3) *Trial of Captain Kimber for the murder of a Negro girl, with some observations on the extraordinary conduct of the Duke of Clarence*, London H. D. Symonds [Schomberg Center for Research in Black Culture, Sc Rare 343.1-K; New York Historical Society; Sawyer Library, Williams College, MA] [*Morning Herald*, 16 June 1792]

3a) *The Trial at large of Captain Kimber*, Henry D. Symonds, Pater Noster Row, taken in shorthand by a student of the Temple price 1s 6d [*Morning Herald*, 11 June 1792]

3b) *The Trial of Capt Kimber for the Murder of a Slave with observations ... on Clarence* H. D. Symonds, price 1s. 'The public are requested to be particular in ordering that printed for Symonds.'[*Morning Chronicle*, 20 June 1792.]

4) *Trial of Captain Kimber for the supposed murder of an African girl*, William Lane, Leadenhall Street. 'The Public will be careful to enquire for this Edition.' [*Morning Herald*, 11 June 1792]

4a) 2nd edition: *Genuine statement of facts. Trial of Captain Kimber* ... William Lane with appendix

4b) *Captain Kimber's Trial, the Genuine Edition* price 1s with the real, true and particular depositions by John George first mate, John Hamly carpenter, Joseph Hart cooper, Robert Mills, mariner, Charles Hayhurst mariner, James Corrick 2nd mate, Elias Mansfield armourer, John Barfitt, steward, Evan Richards mariner, John Donavan mariner. 'The public are requested to order the Bookseller to send Lane's Edition, and not any mutilated or abridged copy to answer particular Purposes.' price 1s. [*Morning Herald*, 20 June 1792]

4c) *The Genuine Trial of Captain James Kimber*, Lane's edition, not lengthened or abridged 'to answer one party.' [*Star*, 23 June 1792]

4d) *Observations in the particular case of Captain John Kimber, who was most honourably acquitted ...* Given gratis by William Lane at the Minerva Leadenhall St. [*Star*, 23 June 1792] Also an appendix to *Genuine State of Facts*.

5) *Whole of the proceedings and trial of Captain John Kimber for the willful murder of a Negro girl*, held at the Old Bailey ... Edinburgh printed for John Elder and J Watson, 1792 [New York Public Library]

6) *The trial of Captain Kimber for murder*. 1s. Printed for the publishers at Pater Noster Row [*Morning Herald*, 30 March 1793.]

Devereux's trial for perjury, 1793

1) J. Marsom and W. Ramsay, *Trials at Law and Pleadings of Counsel: The King v. Stephen Devereux* (London, 1793).

2) *The correct copy of the trial and acquittal of Stephen Devereux on the prosecution of the said John Kimber*, 20 February 1793, taken in short hand by Marsom and Ramsay, soon to be published, 'NB This trial comprised the Evidence of Captain Kimber's treatment of the Negro Girl.' [*Star*, 26 Feb. 1793]

2a) *The Trial of Stephen Devereux for Perjury, before Lord Kenyon and a Special Jury, by whom he was honourably acquitted at the Guildhall, London, 20th February 1793.* Price 1s. Taken in shorthand by Marsom and Ramsay. [*Morning Chronicle*, 19 March 1793]

3) Extract of the trial *King v. Stephen Devereux* in *The Diary, or Woodfall's Register*, 2 March 1792. It filled two columns. On 7 March 1792 *The Diary* devoted another column to the trial, saying 'several very imperfect accounts of the following interesting trial having appeared in the different Papers' it

laid before the public a statement extracted from the notes of the shorthand writers.

4) Extensive reports of the trial in the *Derby Mercury*, 28 March 1793, *Chester Chronicle*, 29 March 1793, *Cumberland Pacquet*, 2 April 1793 and the *Sheffield Register*, 19 April 1793.

Notes

◄━━◆━━►

Preface

1   BM, 1868, 0808, 6179. 'The Abolition of the Slave Trade'.
2   For example: Barbara Bush, *Slave Women in Caribbean Society 1650–1838* (Kingston, Jamaica, 1990); Clare Midgley, *Women Against Slavery. The British Campaigns, 1780–1870* (London and New York, 1992); J. R. Oldfield, *Popular Politics and British Anti-Slavery* (Manchester and New York, 1995); Hugh Thomas, *The Slave Trade* (London, 1997); Quobna Ottobah Cugoano, *Thoughts and Sentiments on the Evils of Slavery*, ed. Vincent Carretta (London and New York, 1999); Marcus Rediker, *The Slave Ship* (New York, 2007); Carol Bolton, *Writing the Empire* (London, 2007); Douglas Hamilton and Robert J. Blyth, eds *Representing Slavery* (London, 2007).
3   Srividhya Swaminathan, 'Reporting Atrocities: A Comparison of the *Zong* and the Trial of Captain John Kimber', *Slavery and Abolition*, 31/4 (Dec. 2010), 483–99; Brycchan Carey, *British Abolitionism and the Rhetoric of Sensibility. Writing, Sentiment and Slavery, 1760–1807* (London, 2005), pp. 144–85.

Chapter 1: Ship shape, Bristol fashion

1   BM, 1868, 0808, 6179. Isaac Cruikshank, *The Abolition of the Slave Trade*, 10 April 1792.
2   Cobbett's Parliamentary History, 29 (1792), 1070.
3   Alexander Pope, *Works*, 10 vols (London, 1806), 10:12.
4   Edward Daniel Clarke, *A tour through the south of England* (London, 1793), p. 148.
5   Kenneth Morgan, ed., *The Bright-Meyler Papers: A Bristol-West Indian Connection, 1732–1837* (New York, 2007) pp. 3–4.
6   David Eltis and David Richardson, 'Productivity in the Slave Trade', *Explorations in Economic History*, 32/4 (1995), 471–2.
7   *Bristol, Africa and the Eighteenth-Century Slave Trade to America. Volume 3, The Years of Decline, 1746–1769*, ed. David Richardson (Bristol Record Society, vol. 42, 1991) [hereafter BRS 42], pp. vii–xxxi.

8   On the importance of first-hand experience and 'factual writing' in the campaign against the slave trade, see Jeffrey Glover, 'Witnessing African War: Slavery, the Laws of War and Anglo-American Abolitionism', *William and Mary Quarterly*, 74/3 (2017), 506–7.

9   Thomas Clarkson, *The Substance of the Evidence of Sundry Persons on the Slave Trade* (London, 1789), p. iii.

10 The initiative for a Privy Council inquiry came from William Pitt, but some abolitionists in Parliament such as Charles James Fox were dubious about its potential benefits, perhaps because the committee was chaired by a slave owner, Lord Hawkesbury. Fox pushed for a Commons inquiry, which began in 1790 after the defeat of the first motion to abolish the slave trade in April 1789. On Fox's attitude to the Privy Council inquiry, see the Commons debate on 9 May 1788, reported in the *General Evening Post* and *Whitehall Evening Post*, 8–10 May 1788.

11 OED. A lawyer who prepares documents for the conveyancing of property and investigates title.

12 Thomas Clarkson, *The history of the rise, progress and accomplishment of the abolition of the slave trade by the British Parliament*, 2 vols (London, 1808), 1:296.

13 There is a substantial debate about the ways in which humanitarianism and class interest shaped the abolition movement. See the useful collection of essays in *The Antislavery Debate. Capitalism and Abolitionism as a Problem of Historical Interpretation*, ed. Thomas Bender (Berkeley and Los Angeles, 1992).

14 Bristol Archives, [hereafter BA] SMV/9/3/1/9, Muster rolls, 1786–7, no. 146; Clarkson, *History*, 1:297–300. My figures for the mortality of the crew are somewhat larger than Richardson's: *Bristol, Africa and the Eighteenth-Century Slave Trade to America. Volume 4, The Final Years, 1770–1807*, ed. David Richardson (BRS, vol. 47, 1996) [hereafter BRS 47], *Brothers* 1785/5, p. 101. See also Slave Voyages Database, [hereafter SV] nos 17950, 17985, to be found at http://www.slavevoyages.org.

15 BRS 47, *Brothers* 1787/5 p. 119; *Brothers* 1789/6, p. 148, where the captain is David Williams; SV 17985 & 18037.

16 Clarkson, *History*, 1: 365.

17 Randy J. Sparks, 'Two Princes of Calabar: An Atlantic Odyssey from Slavery to Freedom', *William and Mary Quarterly*, 59/3 (2002), 555–84; see also his *The Two Princes of Calabar: An Eighteenth-Century Atlantic Odyssey* (Cambridge, MA, 2004); for King's Bench depositions on the incident, see Clarkson, *Substance of the Evidence*, pp. 4–11.

18 Ruth Paley, 'After Somerset: Mansfield, Slavery and the Law in Eng-
    land, 1772–1830', in *Law, Crime and English Society 1660–1830, ed.*
    Norma Landau (Cambridge, 2002), pp. 167–84.

19 *Arminian Magazine*, 6 (1783), 98–99, 151–3, 211–12. Floyd's vessel
    was the *Indian Queen*, see BRS 42, *Indian Queen* 1767/11, p. 210; BA,
    SMV/9/3/1/5, Muster rolls, 1767–8, no. 214. Richardson notes that 12
    of the original 42 crew died at Calabar or at sea, some possibly as a
    result of the massacre; SV 17671.

20 Clarkson, *Substance of the Evidence*, pp. iii–iv.

21 Clarkson, *History*, 1:334–41.

22 Clarkson, *History*, 1:323.

23 BA, SMV/9/3/1/9, 1787–8, no 27. Charles Osler is registered as hav-
    ing died on 8 Dec. 1786. Thomas Dixon and Matthew Pike were from
    Bristol. Four sailors were brought on at Bonny, all Liverpudlians, and
    a further four, this time from London, entered in Jamaica. Two of the
    original 27-man crew [Captain Robe excluded] deserted in Jamaica.

24 See Simon Schama, *Rough Crossings. Britain, the Slaves and the
    American Revolution* (London, 2005). There is something of a debate
    about the origins of the colony and whether it amounted to repatria-
    tion or deportation. For the latter view, see Peter Fryer, *Staying Pow-
    er. The History of Black People in Britain* (London, 1985), pp. 195–201.

25 Alexander Falconbridge, *An account of the slave trade on the coast of
    Africa* (London, 1788), pp. 52–3.

26 Clarkson, *History*, 1:359–60

27 Ibid, 1:361

28 Ibid, 1:359–64, 427–34.

29 See Steve Poole and Nicholas Rogers, *Bristol From Below* (Wood-
    bridge, 2017), pp. 289–94; Mark Harrison, *Crowds and History*
    (Cambridge, 1988), pp. 281–6; Wilson Armistead, *A Cloud of witness-
    es against slavery and oppression* (London, 1853), pp. 53–4.

30 Clarkson, *History*, 1:400.

31 Ellen Gibson Wilson, *Thomas Clarkson: A Biography* (Basingstoke,
    1989), p. 35.

32 SV 83978 [1785–6] see also TNA, BT 98/47, 218. Green is entered on
    the muster roll as having 'died' 19 Sept. 1786. For Alexander Robe and
    his voyage on the *Sally*, see BA, SMV/9/3/1/9, Muster rolls, 1786–7,
    no. 28. Seven men died on Robe's vessel; two deserted. On the *Vul-
    ture*, of the original crew of 49, 15 died and one deserted. Fourteen
    new men were entered in Jamaica.

33 Clarkson, *History*, 1:400–6.

34 Ibid, 1:406.

35 Ibid, 1:407.

36 Ibid, 1:409–10.

37 The ship is reported landing about 600 slaves in either Barbados or Jamaica in late 1788 or early 1789. See *Morning Chronicle*, 7 Feb. 1789 and *Whitehall Evening Post*, 17–19 Feb. 1789. See also SV 83980. On this voyage six of the 52 seamen died, and 55 of the 657 slaves.

38 Clarkson expended a great deal of money on securing witnesses and housing them during the campaign. Wilberforce arranged for a private subscription of £1500 but only £500 was subscribed. Josiah Wedgwood, who profited handsomely from manufacturing and marketing the medallion of the kneeling slave, offered only £50; Wilberforce £100. See Earl Leslie Griggs, *Thomas Clarkson. The Friend of Slaves* (London, 1936), pp. 75–7.

39 Clarkson, *History*, 1:438–9.

40 *Journal of the House of Commons*, 44 (1789), 352–4, 12 May 1789.

41 For the list of Bristolians, see University College of London, Legacies of Slave Ownership, http://www.ucl.ac.uk/lbs.

42 John Latimer, *Annals of Bristol*, 3 vols (Bristol 1893, Bath reprint 1970), 2:482.

43 *Felix Farley's Bristol Journal* [hereafter *FFBJ*], 11 August 1787, 5 April 1788. On the play, see Madge Dresser, *Slavery Obscured. The Social History of the Slave Trade in an English Provincial Port* (London and New York, 2001), pp. 150–2, and Peter Hulme, *Colonial Encounters. Europe and the Native Caribbean 1492–1797* (London and New York, 1986), ch. 6.

44 University of Bristol archives, Pinney Letter Book 1788–92, John Pinney to William Croker, 9 Feb. 1788, cited by Peter Marshall, 'The Anti–Slave Trade Movement in Bristol', in *Bristol in the Eighteenth Century*, ed. Patrick McGrath (Newton Abbot, 1972), p. 195.

45 James Ramsay was a former naval surgeon who took holy orders in 1761 and spent sixteen years in St Kitts as a parson and a doctor. As a result he had an intimate knowledge of plantation society. Upon leaving the Caribbean he re-joined the navy, settled into a benefice in Kent owned by the Controller of the Navy, Sir Charles Middleton, and in 1784 wrote *An Essay on the Treatment and Conversion of African Slaves in the British Sugar Colonies*.

46 Marshall, 'Anti-Slave Trade Movement', pp. 195–6, Pinney Letter Book, 1788–92: Pinney and Tobin to Ulysses Lynch, 25 April 1788.

47 I comment on the particular terms of the act in the next chapter.

48 *Cobbett's Parliamentary History*, 27 (1988), col. 576, 579. James W. LoGerfo, 'Sir William Dolben and "The Cause of Humanity": The Passage of the Slave Trade Regulation Act of 1788', *Eighteenth-Century Studies*, 6/4 (Summer, 1973), 440, mistakenly believed Brickdale seconded the bill rather than the motion to postpone it for three months.

49   John Baker Holroyd, Lord Sheffield, *Observations on the project for abolishing the slave trade* (London, 1790), advertised in *The World*, 2 April 1790.

50   Holroyd, *Observations*, p. 34.

51   Ibid, pp. 44–5.

52   Ibid, p. 18.

53   Ibid, p. 51.

54   Cf. Clare Midgley, *Women Against Slavery. The British Campaigns, 1780–1870* (London and New York, 1992), p. 34, who suggests Edward Protheroe ran on an anti-slave trade platform in 1788. There was no election in 1788. While Edward Protheroe Snr ran in 1818, it is his son who ran on an anti-slavery platform in 1830. The campaign poster, *The Negro Mother's Petition to the Ladies of Bristol*, cited by Midgley, is now associated with that election. See PortCities Bristol website, www.discoveringbristol.org.uk and Latimer, *Annals of Bristol*, 3:137–8.

55   David Lewis, *A letter to the Reverend Edward Barry*, MD (Bristol 1790), pp. 1–7.

56   *General Evening Post*, 15–17 June 1790.

57   Whitehall Evening Post, 19-22 June 1970

58   David Lewis, *A letter to Barry*, pp. 4–6.

59   *Bath Journal*, 2, 9 May 1791.

60   The votes were 254 to 162 and 88 to 163.

61   *World*, 22 April 1791; *Star*, 25 April 1791.

62   *Bath Chronicle*, 28 April 1791; Adam Hochschild, *Bury the Chains* (Boston, 2005), p. 190.

Chapter 2: The accusation

1   See Dror Wahrman, 'Virtual Representation: Parliamentary Reporting and the Language of Class in the 1790s', *Past and Present*, 136 (1992), 83–113.

2   *Diary, or Woodfall's Register*, 3 April 1792.

3   The debate on 2 April 1792 began at 6 pm and lasted until 6:30 or 7 am.

4   *Lloyd's Evening Post*, 2–4 April 1792. Some newspapers claimed the bombardment went on intermittently for the better part of the day. See *Bath Chronicle*, 5 April 1792.

5   *The debate on a motion for the abolition of the slave trade ... the second of April 1792, reported in detail* (London, 1792), p. 28. All the captains found new berths, although William Hutcheson switched Bristol ships and owners.

6   John Newton, *Thoughts Upon the Slave Trade* (London, 1788), p. 14.

7   *Lloyd's Evening Post*, 2–4 April 1792; *Evening Mail*, 2–4 April 1792.

8   These figures are derived from the Slaves Voyages database, www. slavevoyages.org.

9   The Philadelphia abolitionist Anthony Benezet claimed that if six of ten slaves survived the seasoning it was 'looked upon as a gaining purchase'. Anthony Benezet, *Some historical account of Guinea* (London, 1772), p. 92.

10 James Walvin, *The Zong. A Massacre, the Law and the End of Slavery* (New Haven, 2011).

11 *Morning Chronicle*, 15 July 1788, cited in Ottobah Cugoano, *Thoughts and Sentiments on the Evil of Slavery*, ed. Vincent Carretta (London, 1787; Penguin ed. 1999), p. 191; Walvin, *The Zong*, p. 175.

12 28 George III, c. 54. See also James W. LoGerfo, 'Sir William Dolben and "The Cause of Humanity": The Passage of the Slave Trade Regulation Act of 1788', *Eighteenth-Century Studies*, 6/4 (Summer, 1973), 431–51.

13 Olaudah Equiano, *The Interesting Narrative*, ed. Vincent Carretta (New York, 1995), pp. 337–8, open letter to the British Senate, published in the *Public Advertiser*, 19 June 1788.

14 Thomas Clarkson, *An essay on the comparative efficiency of regulation or abolition, as applied to the slave trade* (London, 1789), pp. 14–16, 54–6.

15 For the historical debate on whether there was a decline in mortality after Dolben, see Herbert S. Klein, *The Middle Passage. Comparative Studies in the Atlantic Slave Trade* (Princeton, 1969); David Eltis, 'Mortality and Voyage in the Middle Passage: New Evidence from the Nineteenth Century', *Journal of Economic History*, 44/2 (1984), 301–8; Raymond Cohen, 'Deaths of Slaves in the Middle Passage', *Journal of Economic History*, 45/3 (1985), 685–92.

16 *The debate on a motion for the abolition of the slave trade ....second of April 1792*, p. 26.

17 *Diary, or Woodfall's Register*, 3 April 1792, of which the London Abolition Committee purchased 3,000 unstamped copies. See BL, Add. Ms. 21 255, minutes of the Abolition Committee, 5 April 1792.

18 David Geggus comments on the late pubescence of African women, noting that in his sample of sugar estates in St Domingue, only one African female had a child before the age of 20. He attributes late menstruation to poor nutrition. David P. Geggus, 'Sugar and Coffee in Saint Domingue', in *Cultivation and Culture. Labor and the Shaping of Slave Life in the Americas*, eds Ira Berlin and Philip D. Morgan (Charlottesville and London, 1993), p. 79.

19 *Evening Mail*, 2–4, 9–11 April 1792; *Bath Journal*, 9 April 1792; *Senator, or Parliamentary Chronicle* (1792), p. 510. Mary Favret

has interpreted the phrase to mean that the girl was pregnant. See Mary Favret, 'Flogging: The Anti-Slavery Movement Writes Pornography', in *Essays and Studies 1998: Romanticism and Gender*, ed. Anne Janowitz (Cambridge, 1998), p. 19. Similarly, Paula Byrne, *Belle. The Slave Daughter and the Lord Chief Justice* (New York, 2014), p. 42.

20   *The debate on a motion*, p. 31; *World*, 10 April 1792; *Public Advertiser*, 11 April 1792.

21   There were some frank statements that plantation slaves were forced to have sex with overseers or bookkeepers under the threat of a whipping. See Sheila Lambert, ed., *House of Commons Sessional Papers of the Eighteenth Century*, 175 vols. (Wilmington, DE, 1975), 82:157, 195.

22   The *Substance of the Evidence of Sundry Persons in the Slave Trade* (London, 1789), passim.

23   Alexander Falconbridge, *An account of the slave trade on the coast of Africa* (London, 1788), pp. 23–4; George F. Dow, *Slave Ships and Slaving* (New York, 2002), p. 81.

24   Thomas Cooper, *Letters on the Slave Trade* (Manchester, 1787), p. 13; and his *Considerations on the slave trade and the consumption of West Indian Produce* (London, 1791), p. 8; John Newton, *Thoughts Upon the Slave Trade*, pp. 11, 20.

25   *General Evening Post*, 3–5 April 1792; also in *Derby Mercury*, 12 April 1792.

26   Cf. Mary A. Favret, 'Flogging: The Antislavery Movement Writes Pornography', pp. 24–5. Favret's argument works as effects, but not as intentions. She claims 'abolitionists aimed to arouse the strong passions of the gentlemen of the House, and scenes of flogging served as the crucial means of arousal'. On 'The Birch', see the *Bath Chronicle*, 5 June 1792.

27   See Ian Baucom, *Specters of the Atlantic. Finance Capital, Slavery and the Philosophy of History* (Durham, NC and London, 2005), pp. 213–21, who probes the different genres of history telling in the eighteenth century and situates the abolition stories, specifically the Zong, within them.

28   *Salem Gazette*, 3 July 1792. Among the provincial papers which featured the Kimber exposé are *Leeds Mercury*, 7 April 1792, *Newcastle Chronicle*, 7 April 1792; *Bath Journal*, 9 April, 1792.

29   For a general discussion of the jurisdictional problems of enforcing law in the wider Atlantic, see Eliga H. Gould, 'Zones of Law, Zones of Violence: The Legal Geography of the British Atlantic, circa 1772', *William and Mary Quarterly*, 60/3 (2003), 471–510.

30   23 George II, c 31, s. 29; on slavery and unjust wars, see Jeffrey Glover, 'Witnessing African War', 503–32. The idea that slave trading was

piratical was ultimately rejected by the courts. See Lauren Benton, 'Abolition and Imperial Law 1790–1820', *Journal of Imperial and Commonwealth History*, 39/3 (Sept. 2011), p. 357.

31   The phrase 'violators of human liberty' is Clarkson's. See Thomas Clarkson, *An essay on the comparative efficiency of regulation or abolition, as applied to the slave trade* (London, 1788), p. 17. For the 1724 case see TNA, Adm 1/3671, ff. 261–263. Richard Fuller thought the relevant statute was 33 Henry 8, c. 2.

32   *The Proceedings on His Majesty's Commission of Oyer and Terminer and Gaol Delivery for the High Court of Admiralty, 9 March 1759* (London, 1759), pp. 43–4. *Gazetteer*, 12 March 59; *London Evening Post*, 15 March 1759; *Lloyds Evening Post*, 16–19 March 1759. See also TNA, HCA 1/21 ff. 5, 14 for the calendar of prisoners tried and the indictment itself and SV 17391.

33   Ten of the slaves jumped overboard rather than be thrown into the sea.

34   Lambert, 67:281–3.

35   Thomas Clarkson, *Substance of the Evidence* , p. 20; *An abstract of the evidence delivered before a Select Committee of the House of Commons … 1790 and 1791* (London 1791), p. 43. The committee cited an example from George Millar, a seaman on the *Canterbury*, Captain Sparkes [actually Nonus Parke]. This uncooperative female was also hoisted to the mizzen spar when whipped. See also SV 77918. The *Canterbury* sailed from London to the Bight of Biafra and the Guinea islands, delivering 260 slaves to Puerto Rico. The mortality of slaves on this voyage was very high, 47 per cent.

36   Clarkson, *Substance of the evidence*, p. 13.

37   *Diary, or Woodfall's Register*, 5 Feb. 1791, reporting a debate in the Commons.

38   Seymour Drescher, 'Public Opinion and Parliament in the Abolition of the British Slave Trade', *Parliamentary History*, 26 supplement (2007), 54.

39   R. I. & S. Wilberforce, *The Life of William Wilberforce*, 2 vols (London, 1838), 1:333.

40   Ibid, 1:334–7.

41   BL, Add Ms. 21 255, f. 44, MS. Proceedings of the Committee for the Abolition of the Slave Trade, 29 July 1788; also found in David Brion Davis, *The Problem of Slavery in the Age of Revolution, 1770–1823* (Ithaca, NY and London, 1975), p. 404.

42   *Bath Journal*, 16 April 1792.

43   *Berrow's Worcester Journal*, 19 April 1792; *Bath Chronicle*, 19 April 1792.

44 Clarkson, *History ... slave trade*, 2:352–3. Historians rightly empha-
    sise the important role of Quakers in anti-slavery movements, but
    Methodists became increasingly important. See David Hempton,
    'Popular Evangelicalism and the Shaping of British Moral Sensibil-
    ities, 1770–1840', in *British Abolitionism and the Question of Moral
    Progress in History*, ed. Donald A. Yerxa (Columbia, SC, 2012), pp.
    58–80.
45 Seymour Drescher, *Capitalism and Anti-Slavery* (London, 1986), p.
    80; J. R. Oldfield, *Popular Politics and British Anti-Slavery* (London,
    1998), pp. 60–1, 114.
46 *Newcastle Courant*, 3 March 1792, cited in Midgley, *Women Against
    Slavery*, p. 24.
47 *Derby Mercury*, 1 September 1791.
48 Thomas Clarkson, *Letters on the slave trade ... written at Paris in
    December 1789 and January 1790* (London, 1791), pp. 72–6; E. P.
    Thompson, *The Making of the English Working Class* (London, 1980
    ed.) pp. 378–9, for Cooper's reflections on the manufacturing system.
49 E. P. Thompson, 'Time, Work-Discipline and Industrial Capitalism',
    Past and Present, no. 50 (1971), 76–136, reproduced in *Customs in
    Common* (London and New York, 1991), pp. 352–403; for the testi-
    mony, Lambert, 82:178–9; for its reproduction in a small tract, The-
    ophilus Houlbrooke, *A short address to the people of Scotland on the
    subject of the slave trade* (Edinburgh 1792), p. 18.
50 For example, Thomas Bender, ed., *The Antislavery Debate. Cap-
    italism and Abolitionism as a Problem of Historical Interpretation*
    (Berkeley & Los Angeles, 1992).
51 Cited by Drescher, 'Public Opinion and Parliament', p. 55; Midgley,
    Women Against Slavery, pp. 35–40.
52 *Diary, or Woodfall's Register*, 3 Feb. 1791; *St James's Chronicle*, 4 Feb.
    1792.
53 Clarkson, *History ... slave trade*, 2:192.
54 Ibid, 2:111.
55 Ibid, 2:189–91.
56 For an extended commentary, see Brycchan Carey, *British Abolition-
    ism and the Rhetoric of Sensibility. Writing, Sentiment and Slavery,
    1760–1807* (London, 2005), pp. 100–2.
57 Hannah More, *Slavery, a Poem* (London, 1788), lines 95–104.
58 *Derby Mercury*, 5 April 1792.
59 Cf. Mary Favret, 'Flogging', p. 27, who argues that the discourse of
    'sympathy' did not inform the anti-slavery movement until the 1830s
    and 1840s. Favret focuses instead on the flayed body of the girl, sug-
    gesting it played into the flagellation fantasies of the MPs. Perhaps,
    but in fact the 'flayed' body is not emphasised in accounts of the

torture. It can only be inferred from the scourges in Cruikshank's cartoon

60 Lambert, 73:121–3.

61 Houlbrooke, *A short address to the people of Scotland*, p. 11; *London Chronicle*, 19–21 April 1792. The story was also to be raised in the 1792 debate by an MP denied the opportunity to speak. See *Substance of a speech intended to have been made on Mr. Wilberforce's motion …* (2nd ed., London, 1792), p. 49n.

62 William Wilberforce, *A letter on the abolition of the slave trade* (London, 1807), p. 177.

63 This has now been rectified by Paula Dumas in *Proslavery Britain. Fighting for Slavery in an Era of Abolition* (Basingstoke, 2016), although she devotes more time to the parliamentary debates than to the official inquiries.

64 Davis, *The Problem of Slavery*, p. 423.

65 Abolitionists also enlisted the support of naval captains sympathetic to their cause. See Lambert, 73:3–18, the testimony of Captain Thomas Wilson, RN.

66 On the prestige of slave trade witnesses, see Stephen Fuller's letter of 7 April 1790, printed in the *Diary, or Woodfall's Register*, 12 August 1790. On the witnesses and a defence of slavery and the slave trade, see, for example, the *Bath Chronicle*, 19 April 1792.

67 As early as April 1788 Stephen Fuller complained of the 'many misrepresentations that have been industriously propagated to the prejudice of the planters in the Sugar Islands … the press has for some time teemed with pamphlets that are printed at no small Expense and distributed gratis all over the Kingdom.' See TNA, PRO/30/8/349, ff. 138–139. For distribution, see *Star*, 5 October 1791. For extracts of the inquiries, see *Derby Mercury*, 20 October and 17 November 1791.

68 Roger Anstey, *The Atlantic Slave Trade and British Abolition 1760–1810* (London, 1975), pp. 294–5; Clarkson, *History*, 2:209–10.

69 Sir Clifford N. Morgan, 'Surgery and Surgeons in Eighteenth-Century London', *Annals of the Royal College of Surgeons of England* (1967), 17–18.

70 John Ranby, *Observations on the evidence given before the committee of the Privy Council and the House of Commons* (London, 1791), p. 267.

71 *London Chronicle*, 19–21 April 1792; [Sir George Thomas], *An Appeal to the Candour of both Houses of Parliament with a recapitulation of the facts respecting the abolition of the slave trade* (London, 1793), p. 25.

72 Lambert, 69:119–20. For Norris' voyages see SV 91567–70, 92002,
    92729. Norris was also the owner of ships that sailed between 1774
    and 1776. See SV 91969, 91970, 92002.

73 On the use of human pawns as collateral for credit, see the next
    chapter.

74 For Fraser's evidence before the Commons Select Committee, Janu-
    ary 1790, see Lambert, 71:3–58.

75 Clarkson, 1:350.

76 See [Thomas], *An Appeal to the Candour*, pp. 23–4; *Bath Journal*,
    25 Feb. 1793, reporting the perjury trial of Thomas Dowling, where
    Wilberforce gave evidence.

77 *Cobbett's Parliamentary History*, 29:1157.

78 Ibid, 29:1097.

79 Ibid, 29:1236–92.

80 *Sussex Weekly Advertiser*, 30 April 1792; *Newcastle Courant*, 14 April
    1792.

81 *Derby Mercury*, 5 April 1792.

82 BL, Add Ms. 4126 A, f. 82, 27 April 1792.

83 The offer of freedom after five successful births was the idea of
    Charles Jenkinson.

84 Lambert, 72:94–5; *Kingston Daily Advertiser*, 14 June 1791.

85 M. W. McCahill, *The Correspondence of Stephen Fuller, 1788–1795:
    Jamaica, the West India Interest at Westminster and the Campaign to
    Preserve the Slave Trade* (London, 2014), pp. 229–33, appendix 1.

86 Seymour Drescher, *Econocide. British Slavery in the Era of Abolition*
    (Durham, NC, 2010), pp. 45, 56–7. Table 12 suggests the British West
    Indies accounted for 25 per cent of British cotton imports, but the
    British West Indies also imported cotton from the other Caribbean
    islands in return for slaves.

87 Douglas Hall, 'Absentee Proprietorship in the West Indies, to about
    1850', *Jamaican Historical Review*, 4 (1964), 15–35; Richard Sheridan,
    'The Commercial and Financial Organization of the British Slave
    Trade, 1750–1807', *Economic History Review*, 11 (1958–9), 249–63; Ja-
    cob Price, 'Credit in the Slave Trade and Plantation Economies', in
    Barbara L. Soltow, ed., *Slavery and the Rise of the Atlantic System*
    (Cambridge, 1991), pp. 313–17. Stanley Engerman calculated that over
    a third of Britain's total commercial and industrial investment was
    bound up in some way with the slave trade. See his 'The Slave Trade
    and British Capital Formation in the Eighteenth Century', *Business
    History Review*, 46 (1972), 430–43.

88 Michael Duffy, 'The French Revolution and British Attitudes to the
    West Indian Colonies', in *A Turbulent Time. The French Revolution*

and the Greater Caribbean, eds D. B. Gaspar and D.P. Geggus (Bloomington, IN, 1997), pp. 81–2.

89   *Diary, or Woodfall's Register*, 15 March 1792; on Dominica, see *General Evening Post*, 19–22 March 1791; *World*, 19 March 1791; *Public Advertiser*, 21 March 1791; on the pernicious influence of abolitionist sentiment in St Domingue, see *Ipswich Journal*, 25 Feb. 1792; *Morning Chronicle*, 12 March 1792.

90   David Geggus, 'The French and Haitian Revolutions and Resistance to Slavery in the New World: An Overview', *Revue Française d'Histoire d'Outre-Mer*, 282/3 (1989) 102–24; David Geggus, 'Slavery, War, and Revolution in the Great Caribbean, 1789–1815', in *A Turbulent Time*, pp. 1–50; David P. Geggus, 'The Causation of Slave Rebellions: An Overview', in *Haitian Revolutionary Studies* (Bloomington and Indianapolis, 2002), pp. 62, 66; Laurent Dubois, *Avengers of the New World. The Story of the Haitian Revolution* (Cambridge, MA, 2004), pp. 106–7.

91   Michael Craton, *Testing the Chains: Resistance to Slavery in the British West Indies* (Ithaca, NY 1982), pp. 224–7; Bernard A. Marshall, 'Maronage in Slave Plantation Societies: A Case Study of Dominica 1785–1815', *Caribbean Quarterly*, 54/4 (2008), 103–10; Lennox Honychurch, *In the Forests of Freedom. The Fighting Maroons of Dominica* (London, 2017), pp. 96–120.

92   *Report of the Jamaican House of Assembly*, 8 Nov. 1792, p. 9. Clarkson's witnesses offered two demographically viable estates, Sir William Young's in Tobago and a Mr Blizzard's in Antigua. Clarkson, *Substance of Evidence*, p. 129. Clarkson found 26 among the British, French and Dutch islands. See his *Essay on the Impolicy of the African slave trade* (London, 1788), pp. 82–9. For an historical assessment, see Richard Sheridan, 'Slave Demography in the British West Indies and the Abolition of the Slave Trade', in *The Abolition of the Atlantic Slave Trade*, eds David Eltis and James Walvin (Madison, WI, 1981), 259–85 and his *Doctors and Slaves* (London and New York, 1985), ch. 8.

93   *Two Reports of the Committee of the Assembly in Jamaica on the Slave Trade* (London, 1789) p. 9; David Eltis, *The Rise of African Slavery in the Americas* (Cambridge, 2000), table 4.2, p. 95; David Eltis and Stanley L. Engerman, 'Was the Slave Trade Dominated by Men?', *Journal of Interdisciplinary History*, 23/2 (1992), 237–57. The Upper Guinea coast appears to be the only region where the rising proportion of male slaves did not occur. See figure 2, p. 251.

94   Benezet, *Some historical account of Guinea*, p. 92. For mortality on the Worthy Park estate, see Michael Craton and James Walvin, *A Jamaican Plantation. The History of Worthy Park 1670–1970* (Toronto,

1970), pp. 129–35. Ward calculated that the depletion rate, the excess of crude deaths over births, ran at 30 per 1000 in Jamaica in the first half of the eighteenth century and 25 per 1000 in the second. Depletion rates in Barbados were higher: 49 per 1000 from 1701 to 1725, 36 from 1726 to 1750, 37 from 1751 to 1775. See J. R. Ward, *British West Indian Slavery 1750–1834* (Oxford, 1988), pp. 120–1. Fogel and Engerman calculated that on a demographically sustainable US plantation in 1850 the mortality rate for first-year infants was 180 per 1000. They argue that it was not until a slave reached 26 years that planters made a profit from their labour. See Robert William Fogel and Stanley L. Engerman, *Time on the Cross. The Economics of American Negro Slavery* (Boston, 1974), pp. 123, 153. These figures suggest that even allowing for the extra policing on Caribbean plantations, the abolition of the slave trade would cut into a planter's profit margin.

95 Lambert, 82:90; see also 82:222–3, 224–5.

96 *Diary, or Woodfall's Register*, 6 June 1789; *London Chronicle*, 15 March 1792; Davis, *The Problem of Slavery*, p. 424n.; John Pinfold, ed., *The Slave Trade Debate contemporary writings for and against* (Oxford, 2007), pp. 362–3. In 1788 the slave trade employed roughly 14,000 seamen in 689 ships. See also Robin Blackburn, *The American Crucible. Slavery, Emancipation and Human Rights* (London, 2011), p. 168, where he perceptively claims this phase of abolition failed to overcome three ideological supports: property rights, racial fear and concern for the national interest.

97 Simon Schama, *Rough Crossings. Britain, the Slaves and the American Revolution* (New York, 2005), part 2; Suzanne Schwarz, 'Commerce, Civilization and Christianity: The Development of the Sierra Leone Company', in *Liverpool and Transatlantic Slavery*, eds David Richardson et al. (Liverpool, 2007), pp. 252–76; Padraic X. Scanlan, *Freedoms Debtors. British Antislavery in Sierra Leone in the Age of Revolution* (New Haven, 2017), pp. 28–39.

98 *Diary, or Woodfall's Register*, 8 April 6 June 1789; *London Chronicle*, 9–12 May, 1789, *St James's Chronicle*, 3–5 Sept. 1789; *Morning Star*, 14 Sept. 1789.

99 Drescher, *Econocide*, pp. 48–9.

100 Cited in the *Derby Mercury*, 24 Nov. 1791.

101 Davis, *The Problem of Slavery*, pp. 348–85, 427–37. See also Seymour Drescher, 'History's Engines: British Mobilization in an Age of Revolution', *William and Mary Quarterly*, 66/4 (Oct. 2009), 746, who makes gradual abolition a pivotal event in the abolition campaign, although as a signifier of popular pressure upon parliament.

102 Karl Marx, *Manifesto of the Communist Party*, in *The Revolutions of 1848. Political Writings I*, ed. David Fernbach (Harmondsworth, 1973), in section 'Bourgeois and Proletarians', p. 70.

Chapter 3: The man and his crew

1 SV 18115. Cf. Dale H. Porter, *The Abolition of the Slave Trade in England 1784–1807* (Ann Arbor, MI, 1970), p. 90, who misleadingly cites Kimber as the master of a Liverpool ship.

2 John Kimber was christened on 15 Sept. 1791. His parents were George and Elizabeth Kimber. See Stephen D. Behrendt, 'The Captains in the British Slave Trade from 1785 to 1807', *Trans. Historical Society of Lancashire and Cheshire*, 140 (1991), 126.

3 Basil Greenhill and Michael Nix, 'North Devon Shipping, Trade and Ports 1786–1939' in *The New Maritime History of Devon*, eds Michael Duffy et al. (London, 1994), vol. 2, pp. 48–59.

4 Michael Nix, 'The Maritime History of the Ports of Bideford and Barnstaple, 1786–1841', (unpublished PhD thesis, University of Leicester, 1991), p. 83, table 3.1.

5 N. A. M. Rodger, 'Devon and the Royal Navy, 1689–1815' in *New Maritime History of Devon*, eds Duffy et al., vol. 1, pp. 209–15.

6 BA, SMV/9/3/1/7, Muster roll, 1772/3 no. 164, 1773/4, no. 155.

7 BA, SMV/9/3/1/8, Muster roll, 1777/8, no. 70, which shows he was the only seaman to enter the vessel in Africa. See also SV 17883 (*Sally*), 117892 (*Constantine*).

8 BA, SMV/9/3/1/8, Muster roll, 1779–80, no. 91. SV 17897.

9 Privateering was an accepted form of warfare until the mid-nineteenth century, and many long-haul mercantile ships switched to this predatory activity in time of war.

10 J. W. Damer Powell, *Bristol Privateers and Ships of War* (Bristol, 1930), pp. vii, 240, 253, 266.

11 David J. Starkey, *British Privateering Enterprise in the Eighteenth Century* (Exeter, 1990), ch. 3. Private men-of-war were paid entirely from prizes. A letter of marque, or admiralty-licensed privateer, normally paid their crews a monthly wage.

12 BA, SMV/9/3/1/8, Muster roll, Sept. 1780–Sept. 1781, no. 25

13 TNA, Adm 1/314, f. 92; Damer Powell, *Bristol Privateers*, pp. 266–7, which shows that two Barbadian privateers were also involved in the Surinam venture.

14 TNA, Adm 1/314, f. 49. In Pensacola, West Florida, at the same time, naval officers complained that they were deprived of the legitimate confiscation of a Spanish sloop, first taken by an unauthorised sloop from Jamaica, see TNA, Adm 1/1709 (Robert Deans), 15 Feb. 1781,

and journal of the prize court proceedings, 13 Jan. 1781. The episode revealed the fractious and litigious manner in which prizes were claimed.

15   TNA, Adm 1/314, f. 80.

16   TNA, HCA 26/55, 3 Jan. 1781, f. 130; Adm 1/314, f. 129; Sir William Laird Clowes, *The Royal Navy*, 6 vols (London, 1897–1903), 4:62–3; Robert Beatson, *Naval and Military Memoirs of Great Britain from 1727 to 1783*, 6 vols (London, 1790), 5:173. The *Bellona*, Patrick Driscoll, and the *Mercury*, Robert Craggs, also had letters of marque TNA, HCA 26/55, ff. 8v, 101v.

17   TNA, Adm 1/314, ff. 90v–91, f. 103; *Lloyds Evening Post*, 20–23 April 1781; the annual produce of Demerara and Essiquibo was estimated at 10,000 hogsheads of sugar, 5 m lbs of coffee, 800,000 lbs cotton, plus unspecified quantities of rum cocoa and indigo.

18   TNA, Adm 1/314, ff. 78, 80v.

19   TNA, Adm 1/314, f. 181.

20   TNA, CO 111/1, ff. 2, 6.

21   *FFBJ*, 2 March 1782

22   *FFBJ*, 14 Dec. 1782, 11 Jan. 1783; *London Chronicle*, 17–19 Dec. 1792. He may even have taken another vessel, *Les Trois Soeurs* bound from France from St Domingue, which was originally taken by the *Sally*, Langdon, retaken by an American privateer, and then repossessed by Kimber in the *Hornet*. It is possible *Les Trois Frères* and *Les Trois Soeurs* are the same vessel.

23   *FFBJ*, 18 Jan., 1 Feb. 1783

24   BA, 45933/8, articles of agreement on the *Hornet*, 13 April 1780.

25   For variations see Starkey, *British Privateering Enterprise*, ch. 3.

26   See Walter Minchinton, *Letters of Marque Declarations against America, 1777–1782* (BAAS Series Booklet, no. 25, Bristol, 1980). Minchinton's introduction to the series shows that Bristol was the third privateering port during the American war, after London and Liverpool, with 9.4 per cent of all licences issued. The average Bristol ship was 175 tons, the average voyage seven months. The *Hornet* was 300–350 tons, and voyaged for two years. See Damer Powell, *Bristol Privateers*, pp. 253, 266–7 and TNA, HCA 26/55, 3 Jan. 1781, f. 130. For the *Hornet's* letters of marque against the French and Spanish, dated 13 March 1780, see TNA, HCA 26/39, f. 87v, and HCA 26/48, f. 37v.

27   *Leeds Mercury*, 21 April 1792.

28   For the physical description of Kimber, see the Home Office criminal register, TNA, HO 26/1, 9 April 1792, no. 10; *St James's Chronicle*, 7–10 April 1792.

29 *Leeds Mercury,* 21 April 1792; Thomas Chatterton, *The Squire in his Chariot* (London, 1775); see also Poole and Rogers, *Bristol from Below,* ch. 9. *FFBJ,* 13 April 1782 announced that a Mrs Kimber, a milliner in Clare Street Bristol, would 'decline business' on 16 April 1782. Could this be Kimber's wife, preparing to retire?

30 North Devon RO, BBT/A1.b/Bundle 21.

31 *Public Advertiser,* 3 July 1786; no Bristol muster roll has been found for this vessel.

32 *FFBJ,* 16 Aug. 1783, 8 May 1784, 30 Aug. 1787; Kenneth Morgan, 'Bristol West India Merchants in the Eighteenth Century', *Trans. Royal Historical Society,* 3 (1993), 193–4, 207.

33 *FFBJ,* 26 July 1788.

34 Jerry Bannister, *The Rule of the Admirals: Law, Custom and Naval Government in Newfoundland, 1699–1832* (Toronto, 2003), pp. 47–9; *The committee appointed to enquire into the state of the trade to Newfoundland* (London, 1793), appendix 16.

35 *London Gazette,* 28 April–2 May 1789; *FFBJ,* 26 July 1788, 4 April 1789.

36 28 Geo III, c. 54, clause 11. The Dolben Act, commonly known for regulating the number of slaves on a ship, also tried to ensure that vessels were commanded by seamen with some experience in the slave trade.

37 Behrendt, 'The Captains in the British Slave Trade from 1785 to 1807', 124–7.

38 For Falconbridge's comments as surgeon on McTaggart's *Alexander,* see Lambert, 72:304–9.

39 Stephen D. Behrendt, 'The Annual Volume and Regional Distribution of the British Slave Trade, 1780–1807', *Journal of African History,* 38 (1997), 189, table 1.

40 David Richardson, 'Consuming Goods, Consuming People. Reflections on the Transatlantic Slave Trade', in *The Rise and Demise of Slavery and the Slave Trade in the Atlantic World,* eds Philip Misevich and Kristin Mann (Rochester, 2016), p. 37. Richard Sheridan's figures for Jamaica are more modest, although they are *average* prices: £46 in 1793–4, £58.5 by 1798. See Sheridan, 'Slave Demography in the British West Indies', p. 277, table 14.5. Slaves sold by Watt and Allardyce in 1775–6 in Jamaica ranged from an average of £62 to £39, which suggests considerable volatility in sales in wartime. Those sold by Barrett and Parkinson, 1789–1791 appear more stable, averaging £47.25, but rising to £57.5–£59.5 in 1792. See *Proceedings of the Hon. House of Assembly of Jamaica on the sugar and slave-trade* (London, 1793), appendices 3–5, pp. 21–3.

41   David Richardson, 'Slavery and Bristol's "Golden Age"', *Slavery and Abolition*, 26/1 (April 2005), 35–54 and Kenneth Morgan, *A Short History of Transatlantic Slavery* (London, 2016), pp. 53–5. Richardson and Morgan's figures vary slightly, but they are very comparable to one another. The prominent slave trader in Liverpool, William Davenport, made an average of 11 per cent on his 110 voyages between 1757 and 1785. See Anthony Tibbles, *Liverpool and the Slave Trade* (Liverpool, 2018), p. 65.

42   Lambert, 72:349–50.

43   Behrendt, 'The Captains in the British Slave Trade from 1785 to 1807', 93–4; see also https://www.hsic.org.uk/wp-content/uploads/140-5-Behrendt.pdf, accessed 12 March 2018; Genuine Dicky Sam, *Liverpool and Slavery. An historical account of the Liverpool-African slave trade* (Liverpool, 1884), p. 39; Merseyside Maritime Museum, D/Earle/1/4 which notes the commission given to Captain William Young of the *Enterprize*, March 1794.

44   Sam, *Liverpool and Slavery*, p. 109.

45   Charles Davenant, *Reflections upon the constitution and management of the trade to Africa* (London, 1709), p. 39.

46   See Figure 3 in chapter 1.

47   James A Rawley [with Stephen D Behrendt] *The Transatlantic Slave Trade* (Lincoln and London, 2005), p. 235; Paul E. Lovejoy and David Richardson, 'African Agency and the Liverpool Slave Trade', in *Liverpool and Transatlantic Slavery*, eds David Richardson et al. (Liverpool, 2007), pp. 43–65. The decay of the forts and the decline in trade by the late 1770s is tracked in TNA, BT 6/3.

48   Lambert, 72:299.

49   Paul E. Lovejoy and David Richardson, '"This Horrid Hole": Royal Authority, Commerce and Credit at Bonny, 1690–1840', *Journal of African History*, 45 (2004), 377; Paul E. Lovejoy and David Richardson, 'Trust, Pawnship and Atlantic History: The Institutional Foundations of the Old Calabar Slave Trade', *American Historical* Review, 104/2 (1999), 333–55; Paul Lovejoy, 'Pawnship, Debt and "Freedom" in Atlantic Africa During the Era of the Slave Trade: A Re-assessment', *Journal of African History*, 55 (2014), 55–78.

50   BA, 45933/4, logbook of the *Black Prince*, 31 December 1764.

51   TNA, Adm 1/2289 (Thomas Pye), 19 March 1750.

52   Lambert, 69:54. This story emerged from the testimony of surgeon James Arnold.

53   Lambert, 69:54; see also Dow, *Slave Ships and Slaving*, pp. 169–72.

54   Lovejoy and Richardson, 'Trust, Pawnship and Atlantic History', 347–9; Lovejoy, 'Pawnship, Debt, and "Freedom"', 67–70.

55 *The Diary of Antera Duke*, eds Stephen D Behrendt, J. H. Latham and David Northrup (Oxford 2010), pp 56–7.

56 Lambert, 82:10.

57 Lambert, 69:203.

58 Anon., *A country gentleman's reasons for voting against Mr. Wilberforce's motion for a bill to prohibit the importation of African negroes into the colonies* (London, 1792), p. 33.

59 Merseyside Maritime Museum, D/EARLE/1/1, dated 22 May 1751, retrieved from the Adam Matthews microfilm collection, *Abolition and Emancipation*.

60 Duke University, Thomas Leyland's *Christopher* logbook, 1791–2, reproduced in Adam Matthew, *Abolition and Emancipation* collection, reel 105; SV 80834. See also the instructions given to Captain William Young of the *Enterprize*, March 1794, Maritime Mersey Museum, D/Earle/1/4; SV 8195.

61 BA, SMV/9/3/1/9, Muster rolls, 1786–7, no. 146; SV 17950. Hard drinking at the coast was customary, and probably necessary given the dangers and disagreeable business of collecting and embarking slaves. The crew of the *Antelope* lost patience with their captain in 1750 because he deprived them of their rum, and when he decided to linger on the coast to search for more slaves, they mutinied. See TNA, HCA 1/58, ff. 3–11.

62 Lambert, 69:115.

63 I thank my family physician, Dr Harvey Kaplovitch, and my friend Professor Dickson Eyoh, an Africanist at the University of Toronto, for enlightening me about this disease.

64 BA, SMV 9/3/3/1 nos 4 and 6. See also petitions 7 and 8.

65 Lambert, 72:312.

66 These figures are derived from *Bristol, Africa and the Eighteenth-Century Slave Trade to America. Vol. 4, The Final Years 1770–1807*, ed. David Richardson (BRS, 47, 1996) [hereafter BRS 47]. For the 1784 figures, see Lambert, 69:148. The corresponding figure for 88 slave voyages from Liverpool in 1787–8 was just over 20 per cent. See Lambert, 69:145–6.

67 *General Evening Post*, 7–10 May 1791; *London Chronicle*, 7–10 May 1791; *Oracle*, 9 May 1791.

68 The exception is Herbert Klein who produced histograms showing staggered rates of mortality for the period 1791–9. He showed that at least 50 per cent of voyages had mortality ratios of 6 per cent or under. Averages were inflated by exceptional incidents of mortality. See Klein, *The Middle Passage*, graph 3, p. 232.

69 Thomas Clarkson, *Substance of the Evidence of Sundry Persons in the Slave Trade*, pp. 16, 20, 24, 27, 38, 47, 56, 66, 78, 82, 85, 121, 123, 129, 133; see also Dow, *Slave Ships and Slaving*, p. 157.

70 Lambert, 73:162, 82:26–7; see also Marcus Rediker, *The Slave Ship. A Human History* (New York, 2007), pp. 225–30.

71 Clarkson, *History*, 1:313, 349–50; Lambert, 72:310.

72 BA, SMV 9/3/1/9, Muster rolls, 1787–8, no. 27.

73 Richardson, BRS 47, p. 158, entry for the *Thomas*, 1789/26; BA, SMV/9/3/1/10, Muster rolls, 1790–1, no. 97; SV 18057.

74 Lambert, 82:294.

75 Clarkson, *History*, 1: 296; Richardson, BRS 47, p. 101, entry for *Brothers*, 1785/5; BA, SMV/9/3/1/9, Muster rolls, 1786–7, no. 146; SV 17950.

76 On advance money, Rediker, *Slave Ship*, p. 228. In Bristol two months advance was typical. See BA, SMV/9/3/1/10, Muster rolls for the *Active*, 1790–1, no. 82; the *Hector*, 1790–1, no. 197; the *Royal Charlotte*, 1791–2, no. 88.

77 BA, SMV/9/3/1/6, Muster rolls, 1768–9, no. 27. The roll lists last vessel and using David Richardson's registers of slave ships it is possible to ascertain which vessels were slavers.

78 BA, SMV/9/3/1/9, Muster rolls, 1786–7, no. 146; SV 17950. Unknowns and men on their first voyage amounted to two-thirds of the crew on the *Brothers*.

79 Lambert, 73:135.

80 Lambert, 72:124–5.

81 Falconbridge, *An account of the slave trade*, p. 25.

82 Stephen D. Behrendt, 'Human Capital in the British Slave Trade', in *Liverpool and Transatlantic Slavery*, eds David Richardson et al. (Liverpool, 2007), pp. 86–7.

83 BA, SMV/9/3/1/10, Muster rolls, *Recovery* 1791–2, no. 246. The following details are derived from this source and others in the rolls. See also SV 18115.

84 N. A. M. Rodger, *The Wooden World* (London, 1988), app. 7. The age profile of the *Recovery* approximated that of ordinary seamen and landsmen. If able seamen and petty officers are included, it had a younger profile. On HMS *Prudent*, 21 per cent of the crew were under 20, and 56 per cent were in their twenties. See TNA, Adm 36/9365, Muster book, August–September 1780.

85 For a ship of 189 tons, Liverpool vessels should have had a crew of 32, not 28 including the captain. See Klein, *Middle Passage*, p. 166.

86 Dowling said the voyage was his first, see *The Trial of Captain John Kimber for the murder of two female slaves* (London, 1792), p. 16.

87 Mike Breward, 'Crewing the Slave Trade: The Bristol Ships' Muster Rolls, 1790–1795', in *A City Built Upon the Water. Maritime Bristol*,

ed. Steve Poole (Bristol, 2013), pp. 101–2; Behrendt, 'Human Capital in the British Slave Trade', table 3.4, pp. 78–9. Cf. Peter Linebaugh and Marcus Rediker, *The Many Headed Hydra* (Boston, MA, 2001), p. 311, and Nicholas Rogers, *The Press Gang* (London, 2007), pp. 93–4. Rediker continues to insist that 'Slave-trade sailors were a "motley crew" from "all over the globe."' *The Slave Ship*, p. 229.

88 BA, SMV/9/3/1/10, Muster rolls, 1791–2, no. 204; Richardson, BRS 47, p. 160, entry for *Albion* 1790–2. See also SV 18060.

89 Emma Christopher, *Slave Ship Sailors and their Captive Cargoes 1730–1807* (Cambridge, 2006), ch. 2.

90 Breward, 'Crewing the Slave Trade', pp. 101–2; Behrendt, 'Human Capital in the British Slave Trade', table 3.5, p. 80.

91 BA, 45933/8. These articles of agreement list crewmen so a comparison with the muster rolls of the *Recovery* is possible.

92 See Adrian Randall, *Before the Luddites* (Cambridge, 1991), pp. 80–3; R. S. Neale, *Bath, 1660–1850: A Social History* (London, 1981), p. 326.

93 J. R. Holman, 'Orphans in Pre-Industrial Towns – The Case of Bristol in the Late Seventeenth Century', *Local Population Studies*, 15 (Autumn 1975), 42–4. There were complaints about 'irregular marriages' in the poor law reports of the nineteenth century, which can be interpreted as markers of sexual nonconformity and the fragility of two-parent families.

94 Mary E. Fissell, 'The "Sick and Drooping Poor" in Eighteenth-Century Bristol and its Region', *Social History of Medicine*, 2/1 (1989), 40, table 1.

95 The final figures are to be found in Lambert, 69: 175, 184. The others are taken from the Bristol muster rolls, BA, SMV/9/3/1/9 & 10. *Thomas*, no. 247, *Crescent*, no. 190; and from the articles of agreement on the *Hornet*, BA, 45933/8.

96 R. S. Schofield, 'Dimensions of Illiteracy, 1750–1850', *Explorations in Economic History*, 10 (1973), 450, table 1, Illiteracy by Occupational Group, 1754–1844.

97 This observation is based on the muster rolls of the *Recovery*, the *Thomas* and the *Wasp*, the three Bristol ships that bombarded New Calabar in August 1791. See BA, SMV/9/3/1/10, Muster rolls, 1791–2, nos 178, 246, 247,

98 Gerald Francis Lorentz, 'Bristol Fashion: The Maritime Culture of Bristol 1650–1700' (unpublished PhD dissertation, University of Toronto, 1997), pp. 118–20, 139–50; *An alphabetical list of the freeholders and burgesses ... of the city and county of Bristol who polled at the election in the year 1734* (London, 1734).

99 George St Lo, *England's safety* (London, 1693), p. 15, cited in Lorentz, 'Bristol Fashion', pp. 123–4.

100 BA, DC EP/J/4/18, probate inventories dated 25 Jan .1721, 17 Feb. 1721, 30 Sept. 1721. It is noteworthy that the probate inventories published by the Bristol Record Society take no account of cases where there are no material household goods, which stacks the deck in favour of middling people.

101 *Abridgment of the minutes of evidence, 1791* (London, 1791), pp. 13–14; Lambert, 82:27. As happened on the *Peggy*, Cuthbert Davis, sailing out of Liverpool in the mid-1760s. This voyage is not found in the slave voyages database.

102 Lovejoy and Richardson, "'This Horrid Hole'", 363–92.

103 Lambert, 69:39. Old Calabar and the Cameroons delivered 7,000 slaves p.a., less than half of those from New Calabar and Bonny. For recent assessments of the slaves exported from the Bight of Biafra, see Lovejoy and Richardson, 'Trust, Pawnship and Atlantic History', 337.

104 *The whole of the proceedings and trial of Captain John Kimber* (Edinburgh, 1792), pp. 34–5. Lovejoy and Richardson note that the death of a king in 1792 disrupted trading arrangements in Bonny, but they offer no explanation for the slowing of trade in New Calabar [Elem Kalabari] the year before. See Lovejoy and Richardson, "'This Horrid Hole'", 388.

105 *Public Advertiser*, 11 April 1792.

106 Clarkson, *History of Abolition*, 1 307; Lambert, 69:20.

107 Lambert, 69:20; Theophilus Houlbrooke, *A short address originally written to the people of Scotland* (Shrewsbury, 1792), pp. 6–8.

108 *An abstract of the evidence delivered before a select committee of the House of Commons*, p. 27; see also Lambert, 82:9 and *Abridgment of the minutes of evidence 1791*, p. 4.

109 *Morning Herald*, 3 April 1792.

110 *Morning Chronicle*, 24 April 1792; *Star*, 24 April 1792; *Ipswich Journal*, 14 April 1792; *Bath Chronicle*, 12 April 1792; *Norfolk Chronicle*, 14 April 1792; *Caledonian Mercury*, 14 April 1792.

111 *World*, 10 April 1792; *Public Advertiser*, 11 April 1792; *Stamford Mercury*, 13 April 1792.

112 SV 80517, 80518, 82492, 82493, 80210, 80600.

113 J. Marsom and W. Ramsay, *Trials at Law and Pleadings of Counsel: The King v. Stephen Devereux*, (London, 1793) p. 54.

114 *World*, 10 April 1792; *An accurate account of that horrible and inhuman traffic, the Slave Trade* (London, 1816), p. 9; *Connecticut Courant*, 8 June 1792, which asserts that all surgeons were sent in to assess the damage.

115 Klein offers an average of 100 days, see Klein, *The Middle Passage*, table 7.8, p. 157.

116 These reports were required under the Dolben Act of 1788. They
       were submitted to the customs officer at the port of delivery and
       copies were then sent on to London.

117 The formula was five slaves for every three tons in a vessel of under
       201 tons.

118 See SV 80210 (*Amacree*), 80517 (*Betsy*), 82492 (*Martha*), 18115 (*Re-
       covery*), 18123 (*Thomas*), 18126 (*Wasp*). The mortality ratio of the
       Thomas was 4 per cent. The average length of the Middle Passage is
       taken from the slave trade database for 1770–90. See www.slavevoy-
       ages.org, summary statistics, 1770–90. The average mortality of ships
       from the Bight of Benin in the 1790s was 4–5 per cent. See Sheridan,
       Doctors and Slaves, pp. 122–3.

119 *Whole of the proceedings*, p. 31; Phillips captained the following: SV
       17923, 17939, 18010, 18031, 18057.

120 Richardson, BRS 47, p. 193; BA, SMV/9/3/1/10, Muster rolls, *Recovery*
       1791–2, no. 246.

121 For details of sailing schedules, see the relevant entries listed in notes
       97 and 118.

122 *The Trial of Captain John Kimber for the supposed murder of an Afri-
       can girl* (London: 2nd ed., 1792), pp. 26–8; TNA, HCA 1/61, f. 168.

123 TNA, HO 26/1, criminal register, 18 June 1793, no. 11.

124 Stephen Behrendt suggests owners tried to hire one crewman for
       8–10 slaves. See Behrendt, 'Human Capital in the British Slave Trade',
       p. 70.

125 Under the articles of agreement after the Dolben Act, masters of
       slave ships were officially bound to supply their crews with 'good and
       wholesome Victuals, and a portion of wine and spirits'. See the agree-
       ment of the *Thomas*, Captain Phillips, BA SMV/9/3/1/10, Muster
       rolls, 1791–2, no. 247.

126 *King v. Devereux*, p. 46; Lambert, 82:67.

127 TNA, HCA 1/61, f. 170v.

128 BA, SMV/9/3/1/10, Muster rolls, 1791–2, no. 246; *King v. Devereux*, p.
       36.

129 Lambert, 69:135; see also Daniel P. Mannix, with Malcolm Cowley,
       Black Cargoes. A History of the Atlantic Slave Trade 1518–1865 (New
       York, 1962), pp. 144–5.

130 Lambert, 69:129–30; Richardson, BRS 47, p, 132; BA, SMV/9/3/1/9,
       Muster roll, 1788–9, no. 7.

131 Klein, *Middle Passage*, p. 157, table 7.8. Klein calculated that of the 113
       ships leaving the Bight of Biafra for Jamaica in the years 1791–8, the
       average stay on the coast was 100 days. Kimber's ship the *Recovery*
       arrived in New Calabar in early June and completed the buying of
       slaves at the end of August. TNA, HCA 1/61, f. 166.

132 See the case of Jones v Small in *The Times*, 1 July 1785.

133 *World*, 10 April 1792; *Public Advertiser*, 11 April 1792.

134 *The trial of Captain Kimber for the murder of two female slaves* (London, 1792), p. 29.

135 *The trial of Captain John Kimber for the supposed murder of an African Girl*, pp. 31–2; *Genuine State of Facts. The trial … for the supposed murder of an African Girl*, appendix p. 3. *The Whole of the Proceedings*, p. 25 and the *Trial of Captain Kimber for the murder of a Negro girl*, pp. 19–20, suggests Venus was brought on board by Jackamacree, but the other accounts suggest Jackamacree's girl was someone else, as testified by the crew.

136 *King v. Devereux, pp.* 39–40; *World*, 10 April, 1792; *Public Advertiser*, 11 April 1792; *Caledonian Mercury*, 14 April 1792.

137 TNA, HCA 1/25, part 1, f. 207. See also TNA, HO 26/1, criminal register, 9 April 1792, no. 10. It is sometimes argued that Kimber was indicted for the murder of two slaves, often on the basis of the trial pamphlet that claimed this in the title. See note 134 above, and Benton, 'Abolition and Imperial Law 1790–1820', 364.

138 *King v. Devereux*, p. 32. Edward Williams thought she was between 16 and 17 years of age.

139 TNA, HCA 1/61, f. 169. The clap was the common term for gonorrhoea, used by Dowling in his testimony.

140 Katrina Dyonne Thompson, *Ring Shout, Wheel About. The Racial Politics of Music and Dance in North American Slavery* (Urbana, Chicago, Springfield, 2014), p. 42, claims Dowling raped the girl, but I have found no evidence for this in the testimony.

141 *The Whole of the proceedings*, appendix, p. 3.

142 TNA, HCA 1/61, f. 166v. For hunger strikes, see Rediker, *The Slave Ship*, pp. 288–91; For Devereux's claim that No-name had the flux, see *Trial of Captain Kimber for the murder of a Negro Girl*, p. 24.

143 *King v. Devereux*, p. 33.

144 TNA, HCA 1/61, f. 166v.

145 Kimber appears to have used a coachman's whip, with a large handle of 3 feet and a strap of 6 feet. One account suggests the strap was 4 feet long with a handle of two feet. See *Trial of Captain Kimber for the murder of a Negro girl*, p. 14; *General Evening Post*, 7 June 1792; TNA, HCA 1/61, f. 166v. For Devereux's testimony on the suspensions, see HCA 1/61, ff. 169v–170.

146 TNA, HCA 1/61, f. 167.

147 TNA, HCA 1/61, f. 170–170v; *The Whole of the proceedings*, p. 27.

148 Seymour Drescher, 'The Atlantic Slave Trade and the Holocaust: A Comparative Analysis', in *Is the Holocaust Unique? Perspectives on*

Comparative Genocide, ed. Alan S. Rosenbaum (New York, 1969), 65–85; Newton, *Thoughts upon the African Slave Trade*, p. 14.
149   *King v. Devereux*, p. 18.

Chapter 4: The trial

1   Paul Finkelman suggests the complaint was lodged by the London Committee to Abolish the Slave Trade, and presumably does so on the basis that Dowling gave evidence to them [actually, to Clarkson and Phillips and then Wilberforce]; see Paul Finkelman, *Slavery in the Court Room. An annotated bibliography of American Cases* (Washington DC, 1985), pp. 278, 283. In fact, given the line-up in court, this looks to be a state prosecution, prompted by Wilberforce's exposure in the Commons. Wilberforce was not a member of the London Committee at the time. I have found no evidence in the London Committee minutes that it initiated the prosecution.

2   SV 17391, the *Hope* (1756); *The Proceedings of Oyer and Terminer and Gaol Delivery for the High Court of Admiralty*, 9 *March 1759*, pp. 43–4; *Gazetteer*, 12 March 1759; *London Evening Post*, 15 March 1759; Elizabeth Donnan, ed., *Documents Illustrative of the slave trade*, 4 vols (Washington, 1931), 4:338; TNA, HCA 1/21, ff. 5, 14.

3   *Bath Journal*, 16 April 1792. The possibility that West Indian merchants encouraged Kimber to turn himself in comes from the *Northampton Mercury*, 14 April 1792. It also claimed the West India merchants were determined to get to the bottom of the case and presented them as disinterested parties. The *Bath Herald*, 14 April 1792, contended that three special messengers arrived on the Saturday to arrest Kimber and had him in custody by the end of the day, but most newspapers opt for a Sunday arrest.

4   On the runners, see J. M. Beattie, *The First English Detectives. The Bow Street Runners and the Policing of London, 1750–1840* (Oxford, 2012), passim. See *the Cumberland Pacquet*, 17 April 1792, where it is said runners arrived in London on Monday morning around 8–9 am and Kimber was examined by Sir Sampson Wright around 1 pm.

5   Richardson, BRS 47, p. 224; BA, SMV/9/3/1/10, 1792/3, no. 226; *Northampton Mercury*, 14 April 1792.

6   *Cumberland Pacquet*, 17 April 1792.

7   *Bath Journal*, 16 April 1792; *Bath Herald*, 14 April 1792; *London Chronicle*, 7–10 April 1792; *Evening Mail*, 9–11 April 1792; *Star*, 10 April 1792; *World*, 10 April 1792. The *World* has a detailed account of Dowling's deposition, which shows he addressed both episodes.

8   *Cumberland Pacquet*, 17 April 1792.

9   *St James's Chronicle*, 21–4 April 1792; *Morning Herald*, 24 April 1792.

10   *World*, 7 April 1792; *Star*, 9 April 1792; *Diary, or Woodfall's Register*, 12 April 1792.

11   *Eastern Herald* [Portland, Maine], 4 June 1792; *Connecticut Courant* [Hartford], 8 June 1792; *Maryland Journal*, 12 June 1792, *Salem Gazette*, 3 July 1792.

12   The trial was also reported in the periodical press. See *Annual Register*, 34 (1972), 24 and *Gentleman's Magazine*, 62 part 1 (1792), 571, 62 part 2 (1792), 741. For the supplement, see the *Newcastle Courant*, 7 April 1792.

13   *World*, 10 April 1792; *Public Advertiser*, 11 April 1792; *Diary, or Woodfall's Register*, 11 April 1792; *London Chronicle*, 7–10 April, 1792. The *Cumberland Pacquet*, 17 April 1792, also declined to report the proceedings at Bow Street.

14   *Diary, or Woodfall's Register*, 12 April 1792.

15   'National Assembly', a newspaper clipping in the Gale collection of Slavery and Anti-Slavery. The Kimber story is the third item. In the margin the source is written as *St James's Chronicle*, 10–12 April, 1792, which is incorrect.

16   *Norfolk Chronicle*, 9 June 1792; *Kentish Gazette*, 12 June 1792.

17   *Lloyd's Evening Post*, 6 June 1792.

18   See Stephen Fuller's letter to Jamaican authorities, 7 April 1790, in the *Diary, or Woodfall's Register*, 12 August 1790.

19   *The trial of Captain John Kimber for the murder of two female slaves* (London, 1792), p. vi.

20   *The Trial of Captain John Kimber for the murder of a Negro girl* (London, 1792), pp. 14–15.

21   Brycchan Carey, *British Abolitionism and the Rhetoric of Sensibility*, p. 144.

22   Only one of these accounts is to be found on ECSTC. One other is in common circulation through https://archive.org/trialofcaptainjohnkimber, and is available in the Library of Congress and the British Library. Two others are *only* to be found in the libraries in the United States. See Appendix. The MS version of the trial is to be found in TNA, HCA 1/61, ff. 166–172. Most scholars use only the two easily accessible versions.

23   John Sugden, *Nelson. A Dream of Glory* (London, 2004), pp. 399–400; *Cobbett's Political Register*, 21 Feb. 1807, p. 296.

24   A Robert Harrison backed the *Lady Harrison*, a former French prize, on a slave voyage in 1802. See SV 82210.

25   *Diary, or Woodfall's Register*, 24 April 1792.

26   SV 17149, *Two Brothers*, 1746; TNA, HCA 26/55, f. 30, 3 Jan. 1781.

27   Dresser, *Slavery Obscured*, pp. 139, 148, tables 7 and 8.

28 Noble appears to have underwritten cargoes to Leghorn and Smyrna as well as Newfoundland. See BA, 44352/9/3/29. He also transported provisions from America's Middle Colonies to the Mediterranean as part of multilateral voyages in the Atlantic. See Kenneth Morgan, 'Shipping Patterns and the Atlantic Trade of Bristol', *William and Mary Quarterly*, 46/3 (1989), 524.

29 Richardson, BRS 47, p. 87, *Hector*, 1783/6, SMV 1785–6, no. 96; SVD, 17921; Damer Powell, *Bristol Privateers*, pp. 252, 259, 265, 283, 294–5, 297–8.

30 Latimer, *Annals of Bristol*, 2:495.

31 *Whole proceedings*, pp. 35–7; *Trial of Captain Kimber for the murder of a Negro girl*, p. 24; *Trial of Kimber for the murder of two female slaves*, p. 31; *Bath Herald*, 9 June 1792.

32 *Whole proceedings*, p. 37.

33 Richardson, BRS 47, no. 1792/33, p. 223: the *Queen Charlotte*, 44 tons, to Annamaboe and Barbados.

34 *Whole proceedings*, p. 17; *The trial of Captain John Kimber for the supposed murder of an African girl*, p. 20.

35 *King v. Devereux*, pp. 10–13.

36 Ibid, p. 38.

37 Ibid, p 54. The pub is sometimes referred to as the Chepstow Boat.

38 Ibid, p. 55.

39 Ibid, p. 53; see also *Diary, or Woodfall's Register*, 7 March 1793.

40 Ibid, p. 18; also in *Derby Mercury*, 28 March 1793.

41 *Trial of Captain Kimber for the murder of a Negro girl*, p. 26.

42 *King v. Devereux*, p. 44.

43 Ibid, p. 44.

44 Richardson, BRS 47, SMV 1792/3, no. 111; *The Bee, or Literary Weekly Intelligencer*, 15 (1793), 111.

45 *FFBJ*, 14 April 1792; *Newcastle Courant*, 14 April 1792. See also *Bath Chronicle*, 19 April 1792, which from being a pro-abolition paper switched sides in the wake of the French Revolution; James Boswell, *Life of Johnson*, ed. Augustine Birrell, 4 vols (Boston, 1902), 4:202.

46 In the Commons both Fenton Cawthorne and Banastre Tarleton had pushed to end the Commons' inquiry as more hostile evidence against the trade from reputable witnesses came to light. See Commons' debate, as reported in *Whitehall Evening Post*, 3–5 Feb. 1791.

47 *Whole Proceedings*, p. 9.

48 *Cobbett's Parliamentary History*, 27 (1788), 587; Clarkson, *An Essay on the Comparative Efficiency of Regulation*, pp. ix–xi. The spelling of Pigott is erratic. In the Ms Trial it is Pigott, see TNA, HCA 1/61, f. 162. See also *Brown's General Law List of 1793*, where Arthur Pigott is listed as a KC and a member of Lincoln's Inn. Because he had a patent

of precedency he could also take cases against the crown, as he did in Kimber's trial.

49   Walvin, *The Zong*, pp. 146–8.

50   Prince Hoare, *Memoirs of Granville Sharp*, 2 vols (London, 1820), 1:132n. Sharp originally applied the rebuke to John Dunning for representing the slave owner in the Somerset case, 1772.

51   TNA, HCA 1/61, f. 171. Kimber had promised Dowling an extra slave, although Jacks the owner claimed Dowling was only entitled to one.

52   TNA, HCA 1/61, ff. 167–169.

53   *Trial of Kimber for the murder of two female slaves*, p. 17; *Trial of Kimber for the supposed murder of an African girl*, p. 26. On the Dolben Act, see 28 George III, c. 54, clauses 3 and 4. These accounts, the captain's register and the surgeon's journal, had to be sworn before the customs commissioner where the slaves were delivered, and copies were then sent on to London.

54   TNA, HCA 1/61, ff. 167v–168.

55   TNA, HCA 1/61, f. 171.

56   *Trial of Kimber for the murder of two female slaves*, p. 15.

57   Riddle and Laughter [Laugher] are real people, not fictions; cf. Carey, *British Abolitionism*, pp. 183–4.

58   *Trial of Kimber for the supposed murder of an African girl*, pp. 39–40. Thomas Laugher is likely the son mentioned in *The distant traders guide and residents local directory for the mercantile town of Birmingham* (Birmingham, 1788?), p. 10. The father, John Laugher, is noted in the 1775 Birmingham directory. The surgeon is probably Billingsby Riddle, but it could be William Pitts, the surgeon of the *Wasp*; see *Whole Proceedings*, pp. 23, 31. Other pamphlets jumble their names and affiliations. See first cited and *Trial of Kimber for the murder of two female slaves*, p. 29.

59   *Trial of Kimber for the murder of two female slaves*, p. 23; TNA 1/61, f. 170v.

60   *King v. Devereux*, pp. 30–1.

61   Slave mortality on Hutcheson's previous two voyages on the *Wasp* ran at 33 and 9 per cent. The insurrection occurred under Captain Bowen in 1785. See SVD, 17945, 18058, 18088.

62   Ibid, p. 31.

63   *Trial of Kimber for the murder of two female slaves*, p. 25.

64   *Trial of Captain Kimber for the murder of a Negro girl*, p. 25.

65   Ibid, p. 24; TNA, HCA 1/61, ff. 170v–171.

66   *Trial of Captain Kimber for the murder of a Negro girl*, p. 24.

67   *Cobbett's Parliament History*, 27 (1788), 579. For Sir John and William Scott, see biographies by Brian Murphy and R. G. Thorne, in *The History of Parliament: The House of Commons, 1790–1820*, ed. R. G.

Thorne (London, 1986), accessed through www.historyofparliament. org, 9 April 2018.

68   TNA, Adm 2/1063, p. 256. The admiralty solicitor did have plenty of time to organise the case against George Hindmarsh, who was accused of murdering a mate on the slave coast, because some of the witnesses had been held in custody for 18 months to give evidence. See TNA, Adm 2/1063, pp. 261–2.

69   Rose was a member of the Goldsmiths' Company and possibly a commissioner of the land tax. Information on the jurymen is derived from trade directories and a printed list of the London liverymen for 1796. The *Bath Herald*, 27 July 1793, claimed one of the jurymen was a West India planter, or more probably, someone with a stake in a plantation.

70   *Bristol Mercury*, 11 June 1792.

71   *Life of Wilberforce*, 1:360.

72   Srividhya Swaminathan, 'Reporting Atrocities: A Comparison of the *Zong* and the Trial of Captain John Kimber', *Slavery and Abolition*, 31/4 (Dec. 2010), 484, 490.

73   Under 39 George III, c. 27. See Gregory Durston, *The Admiralty Sessions, 1536–1834. Maritime Crime and the Silver Oar* (Cambridge, 2017), pp. 29–30, 171.

74   TNA, HCA 1/61, f. 166v.

75   *Genuine Statement of Facts*, appendix, p. 3.

76   TNA, C 107/5, Box No. 2, no. 25. William Dineley to James Rogers, Bananoes Islands, 3 March 1791. This vessel was Rogers' other *Recovery*, sailing to Cape Mount via Boston. See Richardson, BRS 47, *Recovery* 1791/28, p. 194.

77   *Trial of Kimber for the supposed murder of an African girl*, pp. 28, 30. Dowling said he did not dispense mercury for the gonorrhoea.

78   John Woodall, *The Surgions Mate* (London, 1617), p. 275; James Lind, *An essay on diseases incidental to Europeans in hot climes* (London, 1792), p. 278.

79   TNA, HCA 1/61, ff. 172–172v. Steven Bivens speculates that No-name might have had yaws, for which there is no evidence. He also claims No-name had syphilis, but various accounts very explicitly state Dowling thought it was gonorrhoea, as his testimony at the trial and at Bow Street illustrates. See Steven Bivens, *Living Cargo. How Black Britain Performs Its Past* (Minneapolis, London, 2016), p. 42. Saidiya Hartman disputes the girl had dysentery. See Saidiya Hartman, *Lose Your Mother* (New York, 2007), pp. 140–1.

80   *Trial of Kimber for the murder of a Negro girl*, p. 24; TNA, HCA 1/61, f. 170v.

81 *Stamford Mercury*, 15 June 1792. The contested nature of the trial is played down by Srividhya Swaminathan and ignored by Katrina Thompson, who misleadingly writes that the trial was published so that the public could judge for themselves 'the humanity of the trade'. She claims that the malevolent treatment of slaves on board the Recovery went 'unrecognized', which is untrue. Thompson, *Ring Shout, Wheel About*, p. 45.

82 *Public Advertiser*, 3 April 1792.

83 Niel Douglas, *The African Slave Trade* (Edinburgh, 1792), pp. 197–8.

84 BM 2007, 7058.3. The print appeared around the middle of May 1792, either the 10th or 14th of the month. See also the *World*, 18 Sept. 1792. For comments, see Paula E. Dumas, *Proslavery Britain: Fighting for Slavery in an Era of Abolition* (Basingstoke, 2016), p. 99; David Alexander, *Richard Newton and English Caricature in the 1790s* (Manchester, 1998), pp. 24–41, 161; Raphael Hörmann, 'Black Jacobin: Towards a Genealogy of a Transatlantic Trope', in *Transatlantic Revolutionary Cultures 1789–1861*, eds Charlotte Lerg and Heléna Tóth (Leiden and Boston, 2018), p. 34.

85 The print echoes Banastre Tarleton's negative comments on the pro-abolition petitioners, see *Parliamentary Register*, 32 (1792), 208.

86 The phrase 'beyond dispute a fact' crops up in virtually every account of Wilberforce's speech of 2 April 1792 in the Commons. See *Parliamentary Register*, 32 (1792), 171; see *FFBJ*, 7 April 1792, for one provincial version.

87 BM Satires 8419; see *Bath Chronicle*, 14 June 1792, citing Lord Camden's perorations on the virtues of the jury in the context of the Libel Act.

88 *Universal Magazine* (April, 1792), p. 292; *London Chronicle*, 31 March–2 April 1792; *Pugh's Hereford Journal*, 11 April 1792. The charge that Kimber's crew was greatly depleted does not appear on all accounts. See *The debate on a motion for the abolition of the slave trade*, but one wonders whether it was edited out of this pamphlet version of the Commons debate.

89 BA, SMV/9/3/1/10, Muster rolls, *Recovery* 1791–2, no. 246; SMV/9/3/1/11, *Levant*, 1793–4, no. 203.

90 *Substance of a speech intended to have been made on Mr. Wilberforce's motion*, p. 50.

91 TNA, HCA 1/61, f. 169.

92 TNA, HCA 1/61, f. 171. For a public acknowledgement of the circumstantial way in which the accusation against Kimber was launched, see *Norfolk Chronicle*, 9 June 1792.

93 *St James's Chronicle*, 21–4 April 1792; *The Senator, or Parliamentary Chronicle* (1792), 641; *The Times*, 24 April 1792; *Sussex Weekly Advertiser*, 30 April 1792.

94 *St James's Chronicle*, 9–12 June 1792; *London Chronicle*, 12 June 1792.

95 Most historical accounts only mention one or two. See Carey, *British Abolitionism*, p. 183; Finkelman, *Slavery in the Court Room*, p. 279; Swaminathan, 'Reporting Atrocities', 494. In fact, four survive, although not the official version printed by Rivington. I have found no extant copy of this, although one is noted in Stephen B. Griswold, ed., *Catalogue of the New York State Library. Subject Index of the Law Library* (Albany, 1883), p. 197. The *Kentish Gazette*, 22 June 1792, also mentioned one 'with the real, true and particular substance of the depositions' before John Noble, the Bristol Lord Mayor. This might be the *Genuine State of Facts*, cited in note 75.

96 *FFBJ*, 16 June 1792.

97 See Appendix.

98 *Trial of Kimber for the supposed murder of an African girl*, introductory address, np.

99 Ibid, pp. 30, 37.

100 *The trial of Kimber for the murder of two female slaves*, pp. v–vii, 35–6.

101 *Public Advertiser*, 15 June 1792.

102 Walvin, *The Zong*, p. 153. Bivens thinks there were no legal grounds for the trial, but offers no evidence for this. He also wrongly claims that Wilberforce took up the case *after* the trial. See Bivens, *Living Cargo*, pp. 44–5.

103 *Trial of Kimber for the murder of two female slaves*, p. 20.

104 Ibid, p. 24.

105 *Derby Mercury*, 14 June 1792; see *Bath Chronicle*, 14 June 1792, *Pugh's Hereford Journal*, 13 June 1792, for the Solicitor General's remark that the defence did not address the material charge against Kimber.

106 *Star*, 23 June 1792. The pamphlet was entitled *Observations in the particular case of Captain John Kimber*. Extracts were printed in *FFBJ*, 16 June 1792.

107 *Genuine State of Facts*, appendix, p. 1.

108 *The Times*, 11 June 1792.

109 *Genuine State of Facts*, appendix, p. 4.

110 *Life of Wilberforce*, 1:357.

111 Ibid, 1:358–9.

112 See Reginald Coupland, *Wilberforce* (Oxford, 1923), p. 218; SV 8066; on possible legal action, see *Manchester Mercury*, 14 August 1792; *Bury and Norwich Post*, 8 August, 1792; *Northampton Mercury*, 11 Aug. 1792.

113 *Life of Wilberforce*, 2:51, 169.

114 BL, Add. Ms. 41262 A, f. 114.

115 *St James's Chronicle*, 14–16 June 1792; *Leeds Mercury*, 23 June 1792; *Derby Mercury*, 21 June 1792.

116 *Evening Mail*, 15–18 June 1792.

117 *Diary, or Loudon's Register*, 22 Sept. 1792; *Claypoole's Daily Advertiser*, 25 Sept. 1792.

118 *Federal Gazette* [Philadelphia], 6 Oct. 1792. News of Wilberforce's accusations in the Commons was carried in newspapers from Portland Maine to Maryland, although curiously not in Boston.

119 *The Whole of the Proceedings and Trial of Captain John Kimber for the wilful murder of a Negro Girl*, price 6d. The only copy of this pamphlet is to be found in New York Public Library.

120 *Whole Proceedings*, pp. 32–7. In the petitioning campaign, Edinburgh mustered 9,000 signatories, and Glasgow 13,000. See Wilson, *Clarkson*, pp. 75–6.

121 *Leeds Mercury*, 21 April 1792; *St James's Chronicle*, 12–14 June 1792.

122 *St James's Chronicle*, 23–6, 28–30 June 1792.

123 *Derby Mercury*, 28 March 1793. In the *Cumberland Pacquet*, 2 April 1793 and the *Sheffield Register*, 19 April 1793, Devereux's trial ran for over a column of print.

124 Thomas Peake, *Cases determined at Nisi Prius, in the court of King's Bench from Easter term, 30 Geo. III to Michaelmas term, 35 Geo III* (London, 3rd ed., 1820) pp. 227–8; *London Packet*, 13–20 Feb. 1793; *Evening Post*, 18–20 Feb. 1793; *FFBJ*, 23 Feb. 1793; *Bonner and Middleton's Bristol Journal*, 23 Feb. 1793.

125 See *Brown's General Law List of 1793* and www.historyofparliament. org. for Aldborough and Boroughbridge.

126 Lincoln's Inn Library, Catalogue of Dampier MSS, Buller Paper Books, no. 688, http://www.lincolnsinnlibrary.org.uk, retrieved 16 April 2018; *General Evening Post*, 6–8 June 1793; *St James's Chronicle*, 6–8 June 1793.

127 Wilson, *Clarkson*, p. 85; *Bath Journal*, 28 July 1793; *Bath Herald*, 27 July 1793. The last newspaper claimed only one juryman refused to sign the petition for a pardon, the 'West Indian planter'.

128 *Lloyd's Evening Post*, 17–19 June 1793, *Evening Post*, 19–21 June 1793; *Morning Post*, 5 July 1793; *London Packet*, 17–19 July 1793.

129 *Lloyds Evening Post*, 5–7 Nov. 1792; Robert Watson, *The Life of Lord George Gordon* (London, 1795), p. 126; *Kentish Gazette*, 9 Nov. 1792; *Hampshire Chronicle*, 12 Nov. 1792; *Newcastle Chronicle*, 10 Nov. 1792; *Norfolk Chronicle*, 10 Nov. 1792.

130 *King v. Devereux*, pp. 1–2.

131 Ibid, pp. 3–4.

132 Ibid, p. 9.

133 See Oxford DNB entry on Lord Kenyon by C. Douglas Hay; Neil
     Douglas, *Thoughts on modern politics* (London, 1793), pp. 19-20; At
     the conclusion of a 'crim. con.' trial in 1791, that is, one in which a
     husband sued another man for a 'trespass' on his wife's body, Lord
     Kenyon declared it was 'lamentable' that judges and juries were
     called upon to decide such cases, but 'they were the guardians of the
     morals of the people and ought never to relax in their exertions to
     prevent the commission of crimes that struck at the root of private
     happiness, religion, morality, and the well-being of society.' *Derby
     Mercury*, 23 June 1791.

134 *King v. Devereux*, p. 17.

135 Ibid, pp. 19, 27; *The Bee*, 15 (1793), 110.

136 Ibid, p. 30.

137 Ibid, pp. 32–4. In 'her own language' said the *Derby Mercury*, 28
     March 1793.

138 Ibid, p. 39; *Trial of Kimber for the murder of two female slaves*, p. 22.

139 A British TV series in which Garrow, among other things, prosecutes
     the captain of the *Zong* for throwing over 130 slaves overboard on the
     grounds that he was jettisoning 'cargo' to save other passengers on
     the ship. Garrow was never part of the Zong case, and Collingwood
     died in Jamaica, before the trial began.

140 Ibid, p. 49.

141 Ibid, p. 58; *Bath Herald*, 23 Feb. 1793.

142 *True Briton*, 26 Feb. 1793; Douglas, *Thoughts on modern politics*, pp.
     19–20.

143 Ibid, p. 20.

144 *Life of Wilberforce*, 2:305. Wilberforce contributed £200 and he was
     asked to pay another £500 in 1796. The final bill was around £1,700–
     1,800, much of it raised by subscription. See Griggs, *Thomas Clark-
     son, The Friend of Slaves*, p. 71 and Wilson, *Clarkson*, p. 85. On the
     suggestion Wilberforce was humiliated by the verdict, see Emma
     Christopher, '"The Slave Trade is Merciful Compared to [This]":
     Slave Traders, Convict Transportation, and the Abolitionists', in
     *Many Middle Passages. Forced Migration and the Making of the Mod-
     ern World*, eds Emma Christopher, Cassandra Phybus and Marcus
     Rediker (Berkeley and Los Angeles, 2007), p. 122.

145 *Evening Mail*, 25–7 Feb. 1793; *Lloyd's Evening Post*, 25–7 Feb. 1793,
     22–4 May 1793; *Diary, or Woodfall's Register*, 27 Feb. 1793; *Gazetteer*,
     27 Feb. 1793. The issue of Kimber's acquittal re-emerged on 22 May
     1793 when Wilberforce moved the House consider in committee a
     bill to prevent British subjects supplying foreign settlements with
     slaves. On this occasion Sir William Smith's remarks were blunter,

claiming Kimber's 'innocence' was 'strongly refuted in the trial of Mr. Devereux'. *Lloyd's Evening Post*, 22–4 May 1793.

146 *Northampton Mercury*, 23 Feb. 1793.

Chapter 5: Abolition and revolution

1 For the importance of revolution in pushing the notion of intrinsic natural rights, see Lynn Hunt, 'The Paradoxical Origins of Human Rights', in *Human Rights and Revolutions*, eds Jeffrey N. Wasserstrom et al. (Lanham, MD, 2007), pp. 3–21.

2 *Arminian Magazine*, 22 (1799), 366.

3 John Newton, Thoughts upon the African Slave Trade (London, 1788). Marcus Wood, *Slavery, Empathy and Pornography* (Oxford, 2002), pp. 30–7.

4 Gloucester Record Office, Granville Sharp papers, D 3549 13/1/L 1. Sharp subsequently became disillusioned by its violent course. In a letter to the Marquis of Bellgarde, 21 Nov. 1789, he wrote: 'If there was less Deism and Infidelity in France and less of Superstition and Ignorance of the Scriptures in Flanders, I should entertain better hopes of the Stability of their late very wonderful successes, but I fear a dreadful reverse in both these States.' D 3549 13/1/B 18.

5 Schama, *Rough Crossings*, p. 263. Griggs, *Clarkson. Friend of Slaves*, pp. 57–8.

6 Clarence J. Munford and Michael Zeuske, 'Black Slavery, Class Struggle, Fear and Revolution in St. Domingue and Cuba, 1785–1795', *Journal of Negro Slavery*, 73/1 (Winter–Autumn 1988), 15; Robert Stein, 'The Free Men of Colour and the Revolution in St Domingue, 1789–1792', *Histoire sociale/Social History*, 14 (1981), 14; David P. Geggus, *Slavery, War and Revolution. The British Occupation of Saint Domingue 1793–1798* (Oxford, 1982), p. 19. In Kingston, Jamaica, the group most likely to own slaves were the free coloureds, confounding the too readily assumed racial divide. See Trevor Burnard, 'Kingston, Jamaica: Crucible of Modernity', in *The Black Urban Atlantic in the Age of the Slave Trade*, eds Jorge Cānzares-Esquera, Matt. D. Childs and James Sidbury (Philadelphia, 2013), p. 141.

7 Hugh Thomas, *The Slave Trade* (London, 1998), p. 521.

8 Vincent Ogé was one of the wealthiest free men of colour in St Domingue. He campaigned for full civic and political rights for men like himself and the gradual abolition of slavery, although he argued in 1790–1 that only the union of white and coloured planters could prevent a massive slave insurrection. See Dubois, *Avengers of the New World*, pp. 80–8; and Jeremy D. Popkin, *You Are All Free. The Haitian Revolution and the Abolition of Slavery* (New York, 2010), pp. 34–6.

9   Huntington Library, CN 32 Box 1, ff. 15–16. The ship is not easily
     identified, but it is either the *Britannia* or the *Cornwall*, captained
     by James Bruce between 1772 and 1776. See Richardson, BRS, 47, nos
     1772/4, 1774/4, 1775/7, 1776/8.

10   Huntington Library, Clarkson papers, Clarkson to Cressé, 1 Dec.
     1789, cited in Davis, *The Problem of Slavery*, p. 400.

11   Cooper, *Considerations on the slave trade*, p. 16.

12   HL, CN 32 Box 1, f. 13.

13   *General Evening Post*, 14 July 1791.

14   *Morning Herald*, 15 June 1791. See also *Public Advertiser*, 29 June 1791.

15   Christina Parolin, *Radical Spaces. Venues of Popular Politics in Lon-
     don, 1790–1845* (Canberra, 2010), pp. 118–21.

16   *Life of Wilberforce*, 1:343–4.

17   Thomas Clarkson, *An essay on the slavery and commerce of the hu-
     man species* (London, 1786), p. 241; Clarkson's pamphlet was also
     published in Dublin and Philadelphia; *Morning Chronicle*, 6 March
     1792.

18   Thomas Clarkson, *The True State of the Case respecting the Insurrec-
     tion at St. Domingo* (Ipswich, 1792), p. 3.

19   *General Evening Post*, 10–12 Sept. 1789; *Diary, or Woodfall's Register*,
     11, 23 Sept. 1789.

20   Charles Mackenzie, *Notes on Haiti*, 2 vols (London 1830) 2:251–7;
     Bryan Edwards, *An historical survey of the French colony in the is-
     land of St Domingo* (London, 1797), pp. 42–3, 82–7; Minutes of the
     Abolition Committee, 29 March 1797, where Edwards' charges about
     abolitionist incitement in the British colonies are addressed.

21   Cited in Ellen Gibson Wilson, *John Clarkson and the African Adven-
     ture* (London, 1980), p. 143.

22   Frank O'Gorman, 'The Paine Burnings of 1792–1793', *Past and Pres-
     ent*, 193/1 (November 2006), 120. O'Gorman suggests 412 known
     burnings, but many were not reported.

23   *Bath Herald*, 12 Jan. 1793; *Bath Chronicle*, 14 Feb. 1793.

24   See Nicholas Rogers, 'Burning Tom Paine: Loyalism and Coun-
     ter-Revolution in Britain, 1792–1793', *Histoire sociale/Social History*,
     32/64 (Nov. 1999), 139–71.

25   The petitions are to be found in JHC, 47 (1792), 9 Feb. –2 April 1792.
     For the Paine-burnings and loyalist associations in the South West,
     see Rogers 'Burning Tom Paine', 155–65, and references in the *Bath
     Chronicle, Exeter Flying Post* and *Hampshire Chronicle*, Nov. 1792–
     March 1793.

26   *Bath Herald*, 12 Jan. 1793.

27   *Derby Mercury*, 14 June 1792.

28   *Bath Chronicle*, 10 Jan. 1793.

29 Robert Dozier, *For King, Constitution and Country* (Lexington, KY, 1983) p. 62; Austin Mitchell, 'The Association Movement of 1792–3', *Historical Journal*, 4 (1961), 62.

30 David Eastwood, 'Patriotism and the English State in the 1790s', in *The French Revolution and British Popular Politics*, ed. Mark Philp (Cambridge, 1991), pp. 146–68.

31 Hannah More, *Thoughts on the importance of the manners of the great to general society* (London, 1799), pp. 113–15.

32 Frank O'Gorman, 'Manchester Loyalism in the 1790s', in *Return to Peterloo*, ed. Robert Poole (Manchester 2014), p. 25.

33 BL, Add. Ms. 27,811, f. 9, cited in James Walvin, 'Abolishing the Slave Trade: Anti-Slavery and Popular Radicalism, 1776–1807', in *Artisans, Peasants & Proletarians 1760–1860*, eds Clive Emsley and James Walvin (London, 1985), p. 45. Note also a toast at the anniversary dinner of the Society for Constitutional Information in April 1792, chaired by Major Cartwright: 'May the sun in his course see none but freemen, and those that deserve to be free.' *Derby Mercury*, 26 April 1792.

34 William Winterbotham, *The commemoration of national deliverances and the dawning day: two sermons preached November 5th and 18th, 1792* (London, 1792), pp. 50–1; James Epstein, 'Sermons of Sedition. The Trials of William Winterbotham', in *Political Trials in the Age of Revolutions*, eds Michael T. Davis et al. (London, 2019), pp. 103–36.

35 Amanda Goodrich, 'Radical "Citizens of the World", 1790–1795. The Early Career of Henry Redhead Yorke', *Journal of British Studies*, 53 (July 2014), 615–17.

36 *Proceedings of the Public Meeting, held at Sheffield in the open air, 7 April 1794* (Sheffield, 1794), pp. 22–5. Cited in Hochschild, *Bury the Chains*, p. 245.

37 *St James's Chronicle*, 3–6 March 1792; *London Chronicle*, 29 Oct.–1 Nov. 1791; *Morning Chronicle*, 23 Feb. 1792; *A particular account of of the insurrection of the Negroes of St. Domingo* (4th ed., London, 1792), pp. 3–5.

38 [William Roscoe], *An Inquiry into the Causes of the Insurrection of the Negroes in the Island of St. Domingo* (London, 1792), pp. 24–5; *Life of Wilberforce*, 1:340–1; Geggus, *Slavery, War and Revolution*, p. 82.

39 [William Roscoe], *An Inquiry*, p. 3; See also David Geggus, 'British Opinion and the Emergence of Haiti, 1791–1805', in *Slavery and British Society 1776–1846*, ed. James Walvin (London, 1982), p. 127. The debating society at Coachmakers' Hall considered whether the St Domingue insurrection was caused by abolitionist agitation or the cruelties of the slave trade. See *Morning Chronicle*, 24 Nov. 1791.

40 Clarkson, *True State of the Case*, p. 8. Clarkson's previous remark in his *Essay on the slavery and commerce of the human species* (London, 1786), p. 241, that Africans had the 'right to resist' their slavery, was reiterated in *A particular Account of the Insurrection*, p. 31. Slave trade advocates used it to expose abolitionists as mischief makers.

41 *Morning Chronicle*, 12 March 1792; Edwards, *An historical survey of St Domingo*, pp. 84–5.

42 *Morning Chronicle*, 12 May 1792; *Whitehall Evening Post*, 10 Dec. 1791.

43 *Cobbett's Parliamentary History*, 30 (1793), 654–7; see also earlier iterations of abolitionist incitement in St Domingue in the *Public Advertiser*, 9 Dec. 1791 and the *Whitehall Evening Post*, 8–10 Dec. 1791.

44 *Life of Wilberforce*, 2:18. Robespierre's comment was translated into English, and disseminated. See *A particular account of the insurrection*, p. 14n.

45 Ibid, 1:369; Griggs, *Clarkson. Friend of Slaves*, p. 58; Roger Anstey, *The Atlantic Slave Trade and British Abolition 1760–1810* (London, 1975), p. 276.

46 Seymour Drescher, 'People and Parliament: the Rhetoric of the British Slave Trade', *Journal of Interdisciplinary History*, 20/4 (1990), 568–9. My view concurs with that of Robin Blackburn, *The Overthrow of Colonial Slavery 1776–1848* (London, 1988), p. 150.

47 *Cobbett's Parliamentary History*, 32 (1796), 752–3.

48 On Hugues and his invasions, see David Barry Gaspar, 'La Guerre des Bois: Revolution, War and Slavery in Saint Lucia, 1793–1838', in *A Turbulent Time. The French Revolution and the Great Caribbean*, eds D. B. Gaspar and David Patrick Geggus (Bloomington, IN, 1997), 102–30.

49 David Geggus, 'The British Government and the Saint Domingue Slave Revolt, 1791–1793', *English Historical Review*, 96/376 (April, 1981), 285–305.

50 Davis, *The Problem of Slavery*, pp. 364–5 and chapter 9. Seymour Drescher acknowledges that the French and St Domingue revolutions arrested the British abolitionist movement but contradictorily continues to argue that it followed 'its own stable trajectory'. He also claims 'British abolition advances after 1787', and he would include the 1792 motion for gradual abolition as an advance, did not occur in moments of military, economic or political crisis. It is difficult to cast 1792 as not part of a domestic and international political crisis. See Drescher, 'History's Engines', 737–48.

51 Duke University, William Smith Papers, Wyvill to Smith, 1 Dec. 1795, in the *Abolition and Emancipation* archive, reel 89.

52   BL, Add MS. 21256, ff. 74–75, Rough Minutes of the Abolition Committee, 25 June 1795.

53   Figures from Richardson, BRS 47. On the Jamaican trade, see Latimer, 2:519. See also Marshall, 'The Anti-Slave Trade Movement in Bristol', pp. 212–14.

54   Gloucester RO, Granville Sharp papers, D 3549 13/1/G2, Gandy to Sharp, 4 August 1796; Dresser, *Slavery Obscured*, pp. 178–9.

55   Mary Wollstonecraft, *A Vindication of the Rights of Men* (London, 1790), p. 145; Samuel Taylor Coleridge, *The Watchman* (Bristol, 1796), pp. 100–9. The essay was published on 26 March 1796.

56   See especially Drescher, *Econocide* and Joseph E. Inikori, *Africans and the Industrial Revolution in England: A Study in International Trade and Development* (Cambridge, 2002).

57   Joan Baum, *Mind-Forg'd Manacles. Slavery and the English Romantic Poets* (New Haven, 1994), p. 33.

58   Robert Southey, *Poems* (Bristol, 1797), pp. 33, 37.

59   Ibid, p. 38.

60   Robert Southey, *Poems*, 2 vols (Bristol, 1799), 2:107–14.

61   Robert Southey, *Poetical Works*, 15 vols (London 1812–21), 11:53.

62   Carol Bolton, *Writing the Empire. Robert Southey and the Romantic Imagination* (London, 2014), pp. 42–6.

63   Southey, *Poetical Works*, 11:49–51.

64   Coleridge, *The Watchman* (1796), p. 87. On Southey's knowledge of the Kimber affair, see Bolton, *Writing the Empire*, p. 47.

65   Bragge was the first son of Charles Bragge, of Cleve Hill, Mangotsfield, just outside of Bristol. He was a lawyer on the Western Circuit who inherited the estate of his maternal uncle in Gloucestershire, Poole Bathurst, and eventually became known as Bragge Bathurst. See http://historyofparliament.org/members.

66   *Telegraph*, 31 May 1796.

67   The final poll was Sheffield, 715, Bragge 679, Hobhouse 102, and the eccentric David Lewis, 4. It is likely that approximately 1,500 voters of the eligible 5,500 cast their vote. Somewhat ironically, Hobhouse entered parliament in a by-election the following year, buying the seat at Bletchingley from the local patron, Sir Robert Clayton, for £4,000.

68   Wilson, *Thomas Clarkson*, p. 86; *Norfolk Chronicle*, 14 Sept. 1793.

69   BA, SMV/9/3/1/11, Muster roll, *Levant*, 1793–4, no. 203.

70   *King v. Devereux*, pp. 6–8.

71   SV 18148.

72   The ink is very faint on the muster roll but it appears that the surgeon died. It's conceivable he was discharged. Kimber was forced to find

another surgeon in Jamaica, Robert Scott, who entered on 20 September 1793 for the homeward run.

73 SV 80975; HL, mssMY box 18, Zachary Macaulay's journal, 30 Jan. 1797.

74 London Metropolitan Archive, MS. 11936/409/665732 and 670051; SVD, 80974, 80975.

75 TNA, PROB 11/1390/145. The addresses and occupations of his legatee and trustees are reconstructed from Bristol directories and Alfred Beaven's, *Bristol lists: municipal and miscellaneous* (Bristol, 1899).

76 Stephen Behrendt has made some calculations of wealth from probate inventories, although they are necessarily very approximate. This Kimber's will talks of giving £500 to cousin Samuel Brown of London, gentlemen, in the event of death of the prime beneficiary, John Tozer, and the remainder to his sister Patience Brownlow. See Behrendt, 'The Captains in the British Slave Trade', 108–9 and TNA, PROB 11/1390/145.

77 Richardson, BRS 47, *Hope* 1802–4, p. 260. Curiously, not in the slave voyages database.

78 *Royal Cornwall Gazette*, 3 Jan. 1807; *Salisbury and Winchester Journal*, 5 Jan. 1807; *Exeter Flying Post*, 8 Jan. 1807; *Morning Chronicle*, 5 Jan. 1807.

79 Cornwall Record Office, CY/7158, 15 Dec. 1767.

80 Cornwall Record Office, TF/1830/1-11, TF/1852.

81 There is a reference to Kimber 'and family' in one pamphlet, *An Appeal to the Candour of both Houses of Parliament* (London 1793), p. 23, but it may be purely rhetorical.

82 *Public Ledger*, 9 April 1807.

Chapter 6: Afterthoughts

1 Keith Wrightson, *Ralph Taylor's Summer. A Scrivener, His City and the Plague* (New Haven, 2011), xi. For a broad approach to the topic, see John Brewer, 'Microhistory and the Histories of Everyday Life', *Cultural and Social History*, 7/1 (2010), 87–109.

2 Giovanni Levi, 'On Microhistory', in *New Perspectives in Historical Writing*, ed. Peter Burke (University Park, PA, 1997), p. 94. Early references to micro-history were not necessarily linked to the narrative mode but could encompass collective biography. See Sivert Langholm, 'On the Scope of Micro-history', *Scandinavian Journal of History*, 1/1 (1976), 3–24.

3 Edward Muir, 'Introduction: Observing Trifles', in *Microhistory and the Lost Peoples of Europe*, ed. Edward Muir and Guido Ruggerio

(Baltimore, 1991), xii–xiii. Carl Ginzburg, *The Cheese and the Worms. The Cosmos of a Sixteenth-Century Miller*, trans John and Anne C. Tedeschi (Baltimore, 1982).

4   David Levine and Keith Wrightson, *Poverty and Piety in an English Village: Terling, 1525–1700* (Oxford and New York, 1979).

5   Muir, 'Observing Trifles', pp. xiv–xv.

6   Pierre Nora, 'The Return of the Event', in *Histories, French Constructions of the Past*, eds Jacques Revel and Lynn Hunt (New York, 1995), pp. 427–36.

7   *Calendar State Papers Colonial, America and the West Indies 1677–1680* (London, 1896), p. 120.

8   5 Geo II c 7 [1732]; 23 Geo II c 31, clause 29 [1750]; 25 Geo II c 40 clause 9 [1752] where the former Royal Africa Company was to be compensated for its castle slaves.

9   Blevins, *Living Cargo*, p. 45.

10   Jenny S. Martinez, *The Slave Trade and the Origins of International Human Rights Law* (Oxford, 2012), p. 18; Hunt, 'The Paradoxical Origins of Human Rights', pp. 4–5; see also Francis Hargrave, *An Argument in the Case of James Somersett* (London, 1772), pp. 15, 19–20.

11   Joseph Davy's notes Michaelmas 1705–Trinity 1706, f. 22. In *Smith v. Gould* [KB 1705–6] reported in *English Reports*, v. 91, Salkeld 2:666. Cited by James Oldham, 'New Light on Mansfield and Slavery', *Journal of British Studies*, 27/1 (1988), 49.

12   Glover, 'Witnessing African War', 504, 509–10.

13   SV 36032; TNA, SP 36/39/2, f. 97. For a full account of the case, see Madeline Joy Wood, 'Captain Cupit's Boy: Slavery, Crime and the Courts in the 18th century British Atlantic' (unpublished PhD Dissertation, University of Calgary, 2014).

14   TNA, SP 36/40/2, f. 99. Warrant for pardon, April 1737.

15   *Gregson v. Gilbert*, 1783, 3 Douglas, 234.

16   Jane Webster, 'The *Zong* in the Context of the Eighteenth-century Slave Trade', *Journal of Legal History*, 28/3 (Dec. 2007), 285–98.

17   Padraic X. Scanlan, *Freedom's Debtors. British Antislavery in Sierra Leone in the Age of Revolution* (New Haven, 2017), p. 99.

18   Granville Sharp, *An appendix to the Representation of the injustice and dangerous tendency of tolerating slavery* (London, 1772), pp. 7–9; Hoare, *Memoirs of Granville Sharp*, 2:xx–xxi, appendix 8.

19   Hunt, 'The Paradoxical Origins of Human Rights', pp. 9–12, where personal autonomy is seen as an essential characteristic and precondition of human rights. For the indictment v Captain Lugen, see HCA 1/21, f. 14; for the voyage, SV 17391.

20   27 Henry VIII, c. 4, 5.

21   Newton, *Thoughts Upon the African slave trade*, pp. 12, 14–16; David Richardson, 'Shipboard Revolts, African Authority and the Slave Trade', *William and Mary Quarterly*, 58/1 (2001), 69–92. Slave revolts were most frequent in the period 1750–1794, although, proportionate to the number of ships that sailed, they occurred principally in the Upper Guinea regions such as Senegambia and the Windward Coast, not in the Bight of Biafra where Bristol ships were most active in the 1790s. See Eltis, *Rise of African Slavery*, pp. 181, 232. For the suggestion that British ships experienced a revolt every two years, see Jay Coughtry, *The Notorious Triangle: Rhode Island and the African Slave Trade, 1700–1807* (Philadelphia, 1981), pp. 151–2.

22   TNA, HCA 1/61, ff. 37–39; SP 37/7, ff. 293c–298. There is an entry in one of the Newgate Calendars online, https://www.exclassics.com/newgate/ng444.htm. There is some disparity in the accounts as to whether Jack or Caesar was the cabin boy, and some newspapers imply he was executed for the murder of the latter. The evidence, especially the manuscript evidence, suggests not.

23   TNA, CO 5/1375, ff. 52, 55, 145–146; CO 5/1378, f. 127.

24   TNA, HCA 1/61, f. 38. The notes on the proceedings make it clear that the Ferguson's trial centred on Jack, not on the other seamen, Peter and Thomas. For evidence of their beatings, see TNA, CO 5/1375, ff. 147–148.

25   TNA, HCA 1/61, f. 38; SP 37/7, ff. 295–298. Murphy pointed to the fact that Jack had not complained of his beating, and that he had fallen into a hold of stone ballast and remained there undiscovered for five hours. The judge, Baron Parker, was more impressed by the fact that Jack had a black spot of his chest, a sign of internal haemorrhaging.

26   The chair of the High Court of Admiralty, Sir Thomas Salusbury, had recommended dissection for Ferguson, but the Admiralty, perhaps feeling the heat of public dissatisfaction over impressment for the Falklands War, wanted a more dramatic example. See *London Evening Post*, 18 Dec. 1770; *Middlesex Journal*, 18–20 Dec., 31 Dec.–Jan. 1, 1771; *Bingsley's Weekly Journal*, 22 Dec., 5 Jan. 1771; *Connecticut Courant*, 2–9 April 1771.

27   Donnan, ed. *Documents Illustrative of the Slave Trade*, 4:527–9; SVD, 80854.

28   The case was reported in the *Charleston Courier*, 16, 17 Jan., 28 May 1807.

29   Christopher Brown, *Moral Capital. Foundations of British Abolitionism* (Williamsburg, 2006), passim.

30   On the Mansfield decision, see William M. Wiecek, 'Somerset: Lords Mansfield and the Legitimacy of Slavery in the Anglo-American

World', *University of Chicago Law Review*, 42/1 (1974), 86–146 and
James Oldham,'New Light on Mansfield and Slavery', 45–68. On its
reception, Carey, *British Abolitionism*, pp. 178–9. In fact, runaway
slaves in France stood a better chance of winning their freedom
because the Parlement of Paris defied the royal edicts allowing
French colonists to bring domestic slaves to France. In the 154 cases
brought before the Admiralty Court in Paris between 1730 and 1790,
257 enslaved men and women were freed, every case finding for the
plaintiff. See Blackburn, *American Crucible*, p. 126.

31 William Roberts, *Memoirs of the life and correspondence of Mrs. Hannah More*, 2 vols (New York, 1834), 1:354; Horace Walpole, *The Yale
Edition of Horace Walpole's Correspondence*, ed. C. S. Lewis et al.,
42 vols (New Haven, 1961), 31:350; Paul Edwards and James Walvin,
Black Personalities in the Era of the Slave Trade (Baton Rouge, 1983),
pp. 33–4. Eliga Gould helpful article on the legal pluralism of the
British empire makes too hard a distinction between a 'legal' metro-
pole and a 'violent' periphery. See Gould, 'Zones of Law, Zones of
Violence', 471–510.

32 *Bonner and Middleton's Bristol Journal*, 8 Dec. 1792, cited by Latimer,
Annals of Bristol, 2:492.

33 *Bristol Gazette*, 25 June, 2 July 1772; *General Evening Post*, 25–7 June
1772; *Morning Chronicle*, 24 June 1772; Alexander Jackman, 'Judging a
Judge: A Reappraisal of Lord Mansfield and the Somerset Case', *Journal of Legal History*, 39/2 (2018), 152–5; F. O. Shyllon, *Black Slaves in
Britain* (London, 1974), pp. 110, 173.

34 Brown, *Moral Capital*, pp. 97–101; Clarkson, *History*, 1:78–9.

35 William R. Cotter, 'The Somerset Case and the Abolition of Slavery
in England', *History*, 79/255 (1994), 52; Gomer Williams, *History of the
Liverpool Privateers* (Liverpool, 1897), p. 563.

36 Brown, *Moral Capital*, p. 100.

37 *London Courant*, 9 March 1792; see also *FFBJ*, 16 March 1792.

38 *Morning Chronicle*, 18 March 1783; Ramsay, *An essay on the treat-
ment and conversion of African slaves*, p. 35 n; Cooper, *Letters on the
Slave Trade*, pp. 14–16; George Gregory, *Essays Historical and Moral*
(London, 1788), pp. 355–7; Cugoano, *Thoughts and Sentiments on the
Evil of Slavery*, ed. Carretta, p. 85; Anita Rupprecht, '"A Very Uncom-
mon Case": Representations of the *Zong* and the British Campaign to
Abolish the Slave Trade', *Journal of Legal History*, 28/3 (Dec. 2007)
329–46; Baucom, *Specters of the Atlantic*, pp. 31, 220.

39 National Maritime Musuem, REC/19, cited in Walvin, *The Zong*, pp.
146–7.

40 *A New Act of Assembly of the Island of Jamaica ... being the present Code Noir of the Island* (London, 1789), clauses 13, 15, 42, pp. 5,

6, 11. The act also tightened the vigilance surrounding the festivities and mobility of slaves. See also McCahill, *Correspondence of Stephen Fuller*, p. 66.

41 Andrew T. Fede, *Homicide Justified. The Legality of Killing Slaves in the United States and the Atlantic World* (Athens, GA, 2017), pp. 58–9. See also Claudius K. Fergus, *Revolutionary Emancipation. Slavery and Abolition in the British West Indies* (Baton Rouge, 2013), pp. 44–5, who focuses on the ameliorist tendencies in the Grenada Guardian Act of 1784 as a model for other islands.

42 See testimony of Judge Adair, of Antigua, in James M. Adair, *Unanswerable arguments against the abolition of the slave trade* (London, 1790?), p. 151.

43 Gordon Turnbull, *An Apology for Negro Slavery, or the West-India Planters Vindicated* (2nd ed., London 1786), pp. 36–7.

44 *Bath Journal*, 16 April 1792; Elsa V. Goveia, *Slave Society in the British Leeward Islands at the End of the Eighteenth Century* (New Haven and London, 1965), p. 191.

45 Paul Finkelman, *The Law of Freedom and Bondage: A Case Book* (New York 1986), pp. 200–1; Andrew T. Fede, *People Without Rights* (New York and London, 1992), pp. 66–7.

46 For a good account of white unity, see Trevor Burnard, *Mastery, Tyranny, & Desire. Thomas Thistlewood and his Slaves in the Anglo-Jamaican World* (Chapel Hill and London, 2004), ch. 3.

47 Lambert, 82:159.

48 Lambert, 82:171–2.

49 Ramsay, *An essay on the treatment and conversion of African slaves*, p. 15.

50 Lambert, 71:278–9, 290–1.

51 Lambert, 71:102; see also Turnbull, *Apology for Negro Slavery*, p. 37.

52 See, for example, Turnbull, *Apology for Negro Slavery*, p. 54.

53 The Dolben Act also tightened up the conditions for insuring slave 'cargoes' and in response to the Zong case, refused insurance for live slaves thrown overboard. In practice marine insurance did not move in line with the Dolben Act until 1794. See James Oldham, 'Insurance Litigation Involving the *Zong* and Other British Slave Ships, 1780–1807', *Journal of Legal History*, 28/3 (Dec. 2007), 299–318.

54 Jesse Foot, *A defence of the planters in the West Indies* (London, 1792), p. 66; *Substance of a speech intended to have been made on Mr. Wilberforce's motion*, pp. 48, 50–1.

55 Lambert, 82:308.

57 *Connecticut Courant*, 18 July 1791.

58 Klein thought smallpox was more serious threat than dysentery. See Klein, *Middle Passage*, p. 234. On the *Prince Henry* in 1762 a

combination of smallpox and dysentery killed many slaves on the coast and on board, perhaps half of the total. *Public Advertiser*, 1 March 1763; SV 90803.

59 Ibid.

60 Rediker, *The Slave Ship*, pp. 343–6; *American Mercury*, 6 June 1791.

61 The *Derby Mercury*, 1 Sept. 1791, carried an account of a shipwreck in which 230 slaves drowned. The correspondent sardonically said they had been 'found guilty of having been born on the coast of Guinea – of black parents'.

62 *World*, 22 July 1791; *Star*, 28 July 1791.

63 J. M. Beattie, *Crime and the Courts in England 1660–1800* (Princeton, 1986), p. 612, table 10.14.

64 Hortense J. Spillers, 'Mama's Baby, Papa's Maybe: An American Grammar Book', *Diacritics*, 17/2 (1987), 67, cited in Martha Cutter, *The Illustrated Slave* (Athens, GA, 2017), p. 41. See also Diana Paton, 'Decency, Dependency and the Lash: Gender and the British Debate over Slave Emancipation, 1830–34', *Slavery and Abolition*, 17 (1996), 162–84.

65 Kathleen Wilson, *The Island Race. Englishness, Empire and Gender in the Eighteenth Century* (London and New York, 2003), p. 179.

66 Houlbrooke, *A short address to the people of Scotland*, p. 23. It is noteworthy that a plantation mistress superintends the flogging of a male and female slave, the former quite naked, in Richard Newton's print *A Forcible Appeal for the Abolition of the Slave Trade*, which appeared the day Wilberforce addressed parliament in April 1792. See Alexander, *Richard Newton*, plate 3, pp. 31 and 143.

67 On this theme, see Karen Halttunen, 'Humanitarianism and the Pornography of Pain in Anglo-American Culture', *American Historical Review*, 100/2 (1995), 303–34. For an example of a pregnant woman whipped on the back and buttocks, a pit having been dug to accommodate her belly, see William Bell Crafton, *A short sketch of the evidence delivered before a Committee of the House of Commons for the abolition of the slave trade* (London, 1792), p. 10 n. For the importance of gender ideology in the 1830s emancipation debate, see Diana Paton, 'Decency, Dependency and the Lash', 163–84.

68 Mary Wollstonecraft, *Vindication of the Rights of Men*, p. 145.

69 Lambert, 82:25.

70 Lambert, 82:179–80; 200–1; for further examples of gross brutality, see Marisa Fuentes, *Dispossessed Lives: Enslaved Women, Violence and the Archive* (Philadelphia, 2006), pp. 124–6.

71 Lambert, 82:190.

72 Old Bailey online, t17670909; Kristina Straub, 'The Tortured Apprentice: Sexual Monstrosity and the Suffering of Poor Children in the

Brownrigg Murder Case', in *Monstrous Dreams of Reason*, eds Laura Rosenthal and Mita Choudhury (London, 2002), pp. 66–81. The frontispiece to one account, *God's Revenge Against Murder! Or, the Tragical Histories and Horrid Cruelties of Elizabeth Brownrigg* (London, 1767) shows a naked Mary Clifford hoisted up and whipped by Brownrigg, rather like Kimber's flogging of No-name, save that Kimber flogged the slave in more salacious postures. I thank Steve Poole for this reference. For another flagrant abuse of an apprentice, this time at the hands of the captain of an oyster dredger, see the case of William Allen, which came up at the Portsmouth Quarter Sessions a few months after the Kimber trial. The pauper apprentice, William Allen, did not die at the hands of the Captain Aldridge because two women rescued the boy from his 'care'. Aldridge was sent to prison for three and a half months and fined £15 for refusing his ward 'the common necessaries of life' and beating him with 'boat-hooks, mop-sticks' and 'rope-ends'. The boy could scarcely breathe when he entered the poorhouse. See *Hampshire Chronicle*, 23 July 1792.

73   Returns of 'People sentenced and suffered to be whipped, 1816–1823', *House of Commons Parliamentary Papers*, 15 (1823), 280.

74   Fred Anderson, *Crucible of War: The Seven Years' War and the Fate of Empire in British North America, 1754–1766* (New York, 2000), pp. 287, 781–2, cited in Burnard, *Mastery, Tyranny, and Desire*, p. 105; Douglas Hay and Nicholas Rogers, *Eighteenth-Century English Society. Shuttles and Swords* (Oxford, 1997), p. 150. For Wilson, see *Ordinary of Newgate's Account*, 24 Sept. 1722, Old Bailey online, OA17220924.

75   *Parliamentary Register*, 32 (1792), 183–5; *Cobbett's Parliamentary History*, 29 (1791–2), 1077; Lambert, 71:87.

76   Samuel Leech, *Thirty Years from Home, or a Voice from the Lower Deck* (Boston, 1843), pp. 29, 50.

77   Alexander Somerville, *Autobiography of a working man* (London, 1848), pp. 288–9.

78   Steven Baule and Don Hagist, 'The Regimental Punishment Book of the Boston Detachments of the Royal Irish Regiment and 65th Regiment 1774–5', *Journal of the Society for Army Research*, 88 (2010), 5–18; Huntington Library, San Marino, CA, Militia Stowe 23.

79   Militia Stowe 23, pp. 15–19.

80   *Hansard*, vol. 16, 26 Feb. 1827, col. 679 cited in Brigitte Mitchell, 'The Debate in Parliament about the Abolition of Flogging during the Early Nineteenth Century, with References to the Windsor Garrison', *Journal Society of Army Research*, 88 (2010) 19–28.

81   Baule and Hagist, 'The Regimental Punishment Book of the Boston Detachments', 5–18.

82   John D. Byrn, Jr, *Crime and Punishment in the Royal Navy: Discipline on the Leeward Islands Station 1784–1812* (Aldershot, 1989), p. 75.

83   Greg Dening, *Mr Bligh's Bad Language. Passion, Power and Theatre on the Bounty* (Cambridge, 1992), pp. 114–15, 383.

84   Patrick Underwood, Steven Pfaff and Michael Hechter, 'Threat, Deterrence, and Penal Severity: An Analysis of Flogging in the Royal Navy 1740–1820', *Social Science History*, 42 (Fall, 2018), 411–39; Thomas Malcomson, *Order and Disorder in the British Navy* (Woodbridge, 2016), p. 190.

85   *Five Naval Journals 1789–1817*, ed. Rear-Admiral H. G. Thursfield (London: Navy Record Society, 1951), p. 36.

86   William Spavens, *The Narrative of William Spavens, a Chelsea Pensioner, By Himself* (1796: London ed., 1998) p. 65.

87   Charles Pemberton, *Pel Verjuice*, cited in Henry Baynham, *From the Lower Deck. The Navy 1700–1840* (London, 1969), p. 129; Jacob Nagle, *The Nagle Journal. A Diary of the Life of Jacob Nagle, sailor, from the year 1775 to 1841*, ed. John C. Dann (New York, 1988), p. 62.

88   [William Robinson] Jack Nastyface, *Nautical Economy, of Forecastle Recollections of Events during the Last War* (London, 1836), p. 148.

89   Jeffrey Duane Glasco, '"We are a Neglected Set": Masculinity, Mutiny and Revolution in the Royal Navy of 1797' (unpublished PhD dissertation, University of Arizona, 2001), pp. 242–5, 256–60; Rogers, *The Press Gang*, pp. 107–8.

90   For some general reflections on the whipping of slaves, see James Walvin, *Black Ivory. Slavery in the British Empire* (New York, 2001), pp. 238–42. For the importance of strategies of rule in understanding punishment, see Douglas Hay, 'Property, Authority and the Criminal Law', in Douglas Hay et al., *Albion's Fatal Tree. Crime and Society in Eighteenth-Century England* (London, 1975), pp. 17–64.

91   Lambert, 82:43.

92   *Arminian Magazine*, 21 (1798), 106–7.

93   TNA, Adm 1/3675, ff. 396–401.

94   TNA, Adm 1/3675, ff. 218, 233.

95   *General Evening Post*, 6-8 Oct. 1748.

96   The phrase 'try it on' is mentioned twice in the depositions. The plantation had previously belonged to the Pinney family of Bristol.

97   TNA, CO 152/33, minutes of trial, 1 May 1810; CO 152/96, Elliot to Liverpool no. 14, 20 Nov. 1810. See also Lambert, 82:152, and Lauren Benton, '"This Melancholy Labyrinth": The Trial of Arthur Hodge And The Boundaries of Imperial Law', *Alabama Law Review*, 64 (2012), 99–100.

98   *Case in Nevis, 1817* (London, 1818?), p. 16. Huggins ran into trouble
     in 1817 for ordering the whipping of slaves on an estate under his
     charge.

99   Thomas Thistlewood gave his runaway slaves 100–150 lashes, brand-
     ed them on the face or cut off an ear. He was the consummate planter
     sadist, although not alone. See Walvin, *Black Ivory*, 239–40, and Bur-
     nard, *Mastery, Tyranny and Desire*, pp. 96–7. James Towne thought
     40–50 lashes were quite typical on the plantations he had visited.
     Lambert, 82:25.

100 Lambert, 71:85. Franklyn had resided in Antigua and Tobago.

101 Burnard, *Mastery, Tyranny and Desire*, p. 104; Ward, *British West
     Indian Slavery*, p. 199; Herbert G. Gutman, *Slavery and the Numbers
     Game* (Urbana and Chicago, 1975), pp. 17–41. Gutman showed that
     slaves were whipped on average every fourth or fifth day, although
     there were whipping 'frolics' in which whole teams of cotton pickers
     were punished. See also Fogel and Engerman, *Time on the Cross*, pp.
     144–7, who misread the evidence and 'averaged out' the realities.

102 Lambert, 82:48; William Fox, *An address to the people of Great Brit-
     ain on the propriety of abstaining from West Indian sugar and rum*
     (London, 1791); and *An Abridgment of the Minutes of Evidence, 1791*,
     p. 27.

103 Clarkson, *Substance of Evidence*, p. 55; Lambert, 82:48.

104 Lambert, 82: 25, 205.

105 Lambert, 82: 25–6.

106 *An abstract of the evidence delivered before a select committee of the
     House of Commons*, p. 66. See also Falconbridge's testimony in Lam-
     bert, 72:309, 340.

107 See Hunt, 'The Paradoxical Origins of Human Rights', pp. 12–15. John
     Gabriel Stedman, *Narrative of a five years' expedition against the re-
     volted Negroes of Surinam*, 2 vols (London, 1796), 1:110. For a popular
     pamphlet that detailed grotesque punishments, see Cooper, *Letters
     on the slave trade*, pp. 19–20, 23–4.

108 Benton, '"This Melancholy Labyrinth"', 102; Benton, 'Abolition and
     Imperial Law 1790–1820', 367.

109 TNA, CO 152/97, no. 39, G. Elliot to Lord Liverpool, 9 May 1811. See
     also Benton, '"This Melancholy Labyrinth"', 91–122.

110 Hartman, *Lose Your Mother*, p. 138.

111 Saidiya Hartman, 'Venus in Two Acts', *Small Axe*, 12/2 (June 2008),
     11.

112 Ibid, 12.

113 Orlando Patterson, *Slavery and Social Death: A Comparative Study*
     (Cambridge, MA, 1982).

114 Hartman, *Lose Your Mother*, pp. 143–4.

115 Ibid, p. 144.
116 Ibid, p. 141.
117 Ibid, p. 143.
118 Ibid, p. 145.
119 Ibid, p. 149. For the original indictment, see TNA, HCA 1/25, part 1.
120 Ibid, p. 142.
121 Marcus Wood, *Blind Memory. Visual Representations of Slavery in England and America 1780–1865* (Manchester, 2000), pp. 9–10.
122 Ann Laura Stoler, *Along the Archival Grain. Epistemic Anxieties and Colonial Common Sense* (Princeton, 2010).
123 Fuentes, *Dispossessed Lives*, pp. 126–7, 142. For the notion of the 'punctum', see Roland Barthes, *Camera Lucida: Reflections on Photography*, trans. Richard Howard (New York, 1981), pp. 25ff.
124 Lambert, 69:125–6, 72:276–7; *Abridgement of Evidence* (1790), p. 232.
125 *Derby Mercury*, 15 Sept. 1791.
126 Lambert, 72:275, 277, 279–80; Clarkson, *History*, 2:363–4.
127 On the importance of the electronic archive, see Arjun Appadurai, 'Archive and Aspiration', in *Information is Alive*, eds Joke Brouwer and Arjun Mulder (Rotterdam 2003), pp. 14–25. The ethnic clusters project has been conducted by researchers at the Harriet Tubman Institute at York University, Toronto.
128 Antoinette Burton, 'Introduction', in *Archive Stories: Facts, Fictions, and the Writing of History*, eds Antoinette Burton et al. (Durham, NC, 2006), p. 14.
129 Cugoano speaks succinctly of his enslavement on board the ship and the plan to blow it up, but he clearly identifies with the 'thousands' that suffered in similar circumstances. See Cugoano, *Thoughts and Sentiments*, pp. 15–16. Equiano offers the fullest account of the Middle Passage among the nine Africans who left life histories of their ordeal, but his account is complicated by the fact that he may have been born in Carolina. On this question see Vincent Carretta, 'Olaudah Equiano or Gustavus Vasa? New Light on an Eighteenth-Century Question of Identity', *Slavery and Abolition*, 20/3 (1999) 95–105; Paul E. Lovejoy, 'Autobiography and Memory: Gustavus Vasa alias Olaudah Equiano, the African', *Slavery and Abolition*, 27/3 (2006), 317–47; and their subsequent debate of the matter in *Slavery and Abolition*, 28/1 (2007), 115–19, 121–5. For an argument that stresses the shifting, situational identity of Equiano, see James H. Sweet, 'Mistaken Identities? Olaudah Equiano, Domingos Álavres, and the Methodological Challenges of Studying the African Diaspora', *American Historical Review*, 114/2 (April 2009), 279–306. For a summary of the extant life histories of the Middle Passage, see J. S. Handler, 'Survivors of the Middle Passage: Life Histories of Enslaved Africans

in British America', *Slavery and Abolition*, 23/1 (2002), 25–56. See also Stephanie Smallwood, *Saltwater Slavery* (Cambridge, MA, 2007), pp. 202–7, who compares the disjointed account of the Barbadian slave, 'Sibell', to the linear trajectory of Equiano's narrative.

130 *Trial of Kimber for the supposed murder of an African girl*, p. 11; *Whole of the Proceedings and Trial of Captain John Kimber*, p. 11. This does not appear in *Trial of Kimber for the murder of two female slaves*, where it is suggested that her condition simply prevented her from dancing with the others.

131 See Rosalind Morris "Introduction", in *Can the Subaltern Speak? Reflections on the History of an Idea*, ed. Rosalind Morris (New York, 2010), p. 13. The collection begins with Gayatri Spivak's essay 'Can the Subaltern Speak?' first published in G. Spivak, *A Critique of Postcolonial Reason: Towards a History of the Vanishing Present* (Cambridge, 1999), pp. 241–311.

132 BA, 45933/4, logbook of the *Black Prince*, 8 March 1763.

133 Richardson, 'Shipboard Revolts', 76; Rediker, *Slave Ship*, pp. 293–8.

134 John Atkins, *A Voyage to Guinea, Brasil and the West Indies* (London, 1735), pp. 71–3.

135 *The Times*, 1 July 1785; Rediker, *Slave Ship*, p. 288.

136 Greg Dening, *History's Anthropology. The Death of William Gooch* (Lanham, MD, 1988); *Mr. Bligh's Bad Language: Passion, Power and Theatre on the Bounty* (Cambridge, 1994) and *Performances* (Chicago, 1996).

137 See, for example, Inga Clendinnen, *Dancing with Strangers: Europeans and Australians at First Contact* (Cambridge, 2005) and Stephen Greenblatt, *Marvelous Possessions* (Chicago. 1991), ch. 4.

138 Robert Bisset, *The History of the Negro Slave Trade*, 2 vols (London 1805) 2:167–8.

139 James McQueen, *The West India Colonies* (London 1824), pp. 134–5 n; *A General History of Negro Slavery* (Cambridge 1826), p. 55.

140 Clarkson, *History*, 2:355–73. The bombardment is cited, p. 361.

141 Duke University, Wilberforce letters box 1, folder 3, letter from William Rathbone, July 1793, Liverpool.

142 *The enormity of the slave trade* (New York, 1861), p. 25.

143 J. M. W. Turner, *Slavers Throwing Overboard the Dead and Dying, Typhoon Coming On*, exhibited 1840, now located in the Museum of Fine Arts, Boston.

Bibliography

———◆———

MS sources and internet databases

BA, 45933/4, logbook of the *Black Prince*, 1762–4

BA, 45933/8, Articles of agreement on the *Hornet*, 13 April 1780

BA, DC EP/J/4/18, probate inventories, 1721

BA, SMV/9/3/1, Ships' muster rolls, 1748–95

BL, Add. Ms. 21 255, minutes of the Abolition Committee, London [in AE collection]

Duke University, Thomas Leyland's *Christopher* logbook, 1791–2 [in AE collection]

Duke University, William Smith papers [in AE collection]

Gloucester Record Office, Granville Sharp papers, D 3549 13/1 [in AE collection]

Huntington Library, San Marino, CA, Thomas Clarkson Papers, CN 32 Box 1

Huntington Library, Zachary Macaulay's journal, 1797, mssMY box 18 [in AE collection]

Huntington Library, Court martial book of the Royal Berkshire Militia, 1798–9, Militia Stowe 23.

Lincoln's Inn Library, Catalogue of Dampier MSS, Buller Paper Books, no. 688, retrieved from http://www.lincolnsinnlibrary.org.uk

LMA, Sunfire Insurance Registers, MS 11936/409

MMM, D/EARLE/1/1, 4, papers of the Earle family [in AE collection]

PortCities Bristol, www.discoveringbristol.org.uk

UCL, Legacies of Slave Ownership, http://www.ucl.ac.uk/lbs

SV, Slave voyages database, www.slavevoyages.org

TNA, Adm 1/314, letters from commanders-in-chief, Leeward Islands, 1781–8

TNA, Adm 1/1709, 2289, Captain's in-letters to Admiralty

TNA, Adm 1/3671-83, Admiralty Solicitor papers, 1721–93

TNA, Adm 36/9365, muster book, August–September 1780.

TNA, BT 6/3, Board of Trade reports, 1776

TNA. CO 5/1375, 1378, Colonial Office papers, David Ferguson case, 1770

TNA, CO 111/1, Colonial Office papers, Berbice, Demerara, Essequibo, 1781–3

TNA, CO 152/96, Colonial Office, Leeward Islands, 1810–11

TNA, HCA 1/21, Calendar of prisoners, indictments, 1759

TNA, HCA 1/25, Indictments 1790–7

TNA, HCA 1/58, Examinations of pirates and other criminals, 1750–66

TNA, HCA 1/61, Proceedings of the High Court of Admiralty, 1759–1824

TNA, HCA 26/39, 48, 55, Letters of marque, 1780–1

TNA, HO 26/1, Home Office, Criminal Register, 1792

TNA, PROB 11/1390/145, will of John Kimber, gentleman, of Winterbourne, Gloucestershire.

Newspapers and periodicals

American Mercury
Annual Register
Arminian Magazine
Bath Chronicle
Bath Herald
Bath Journal
Berrow's Worcester Journal
Bingsley's Weekly Journal
Bonner and Middleton's Bristol Journal
Bristol Gazette
Bristol Mercury
Bury and Norwich Post
Caledonian Mercury
Charleston Courier
Claypoole's Daily Advertiser
Cobbett's Political Register
Connecticut Courant
Cumberland Pacquet
Derby Mercury
Diary, or Loudon's Register [New York]
Diary, or Woodfall's Register
Eastern Herald [Portland, Maine]
Evening Mail
Evening Post

Exeter Flying Post
Federal Gazette [Philadelphia]
Felix Farley's Bristol Journal
Gazetteer
General Evening Post
Gentleman's Magazine
Hampshire Chronicle
Ipswich Journal
Kentish Gazette
Kingston Daily Advertiser
Leeds Mercury
Lloyd's Evening Post
London Chronicle
London Gazette
London Evening Post
London Packet
Manchester Mercury
Maryland Journal
Middlesex Journal
Morning Chronicle
Morning Herald
Morning Post
Morning Star
Newcastle Chronicle
Newcastle Courant
Norfolk Chronicle
Northampton Mercury
Oracle
Parliamentary Register
Pennsylvania Gazette
Public Advertiser
Public Ledger
Pugh's Hereford Journal
Royal Cornwall Gazette
St James's Chronicle
Salem Gazette
Salisbury and Winchester Journal
Senator, or Parliamentary Chronicle
Sheffield Register
Stamford Mercury
Star

Sussex Weekly Advertiser
Telegraph
The Bee, or Literary Weekly Intelligencer
The Times
True Briton
Universal Magazine
Whitehall Evening Post
World

Primary printed sources

Adair, James M. *Unanswerable arguments against the abolition of the slave trade* (London, 1790?).

A New Act of Assembly of the Island of Jamaica ... being the present Code Noir of the Island (London, 1789).

Anon. *Abridgment of the minutes of evidence, 1791* (London, 1791).

Anon. *An abstract of the evidence delivered before a Select Committee of the House of Commons ... 1790 and 1791* (London, 1791).

Anon. *An accurate account of that horrible and inhuman traffic, the Slave Trade* (London, 1816).

Anon. *An alphabetical list of the freeholders and burgesses ... of the city and county of Bristol who polled at the election in the year 1734* (London, 1734).

Anon. An Appeal to the Candour of both Houses of Parliament *with a recapitulation of the facts respecting the abolition of the slave trade* (London 1793).

Anon. *Case in Nevis, 1817* (London, 1818?)

Anon. *The committee appointed to enquire into the state of the trade to Newfoundland* (London, 1793).

Anon. *A country gentleman's reasons for voting against Mr. Wilberforce's motion for a bill to prohibit the importation of African negroes into the colonies* (London, 1792).

Anon. *The debate on a motion for the abolition of the slave trade ... the second of April 1792, reported in detail* (London, 1792).

Anon. *The enormity of the slave trade* (New York, 1861).

Anon. *A General History of Negro Slavery* (Cambridge 1826).

Anon. *Genuine State of Facts. The trial ... for the supposed murder of an African Girl* (2nd ed., London, 1792).

Anon. *God's Revenge Against Murder! Or, the Tragical Histories and Horrid Cruelties of Elizabeth Brownrigg* (London, 1767).

Anon. *A particular account of the insurrection of the Negroes of St. Domingo* (4th ed., London, 1792).

Anon. *Substance of a speech intended to have been made on Mr. Wilberforce's motion* (2nd ed., London, 1792).

Anon. *The Trial of Captain John Kimber for the murder of a Negro girl* (London, 1792).

Anon. *The Trial of Captain John Kimber for the murder of two female slaves* (London, 1792).

Anon. *The Trial of Captain John Kimber for the supposed murder of an African girl* (2nd ed., London, 1792).

Anon. *The Whole of the Proceedings and Trial of Captain John Kimber for the wilful murder of a negro girl* (10th ed., Edinburgh, 1792).

Armistead, Wilson. *A Cloud of witnesses against slavery and oppression* (London, 1853).

Atkins, John. *A Voyage to Guinea, Brasil and the West Indies* (London, 1735).

Baynham, Henry. *From the Lower Deck. The Navy 1700–1840* (London, 1969).

Beatson, Robert. *Naval and Military Memoirs of Great Britain from 1727 to 1783,* 6 vols (London, 1790).

Benezet, Anthony. *Some historical account of Guinea* (London, 1772).

Bisset Robert, *The History of the Negro Slave Trade*, 2 vols (London 1805).

Calendar State Papers Colonial, America and the West Indies 1677–1680 (London, 1896).

Chatterton, Thomas. *The Squire in his Chariot* (London, 1775).

Clarke, Edward Daniel. *A tour through the south of England* (London, 1793).

Clarkson, Thomas. *An essay on the slavery and commerce of the human species* (London, 1786).

Clarkson, Thomas. *An essay on the comparative efficiency of regulation or abolition, as applied to the slave trade* (London, 1788).

Clarkson, Thomas. *An essay on the impolicy of the African slave trade* (London, 1789).

Clarkson, Thomas. *Letters on the slave trade ... written at Paris in December 1789 and January 1790* (London, 1791).

Clarkson, Thomas. *The history of the rise, progress and accomplishment of the abolition of the slave trade by the British Parliament*, 2 vols (London, 1808).

Clarkson, Thomas. *The Substance of the Evidence of Sundry Persons on the Slave Trade* (London, 1789).

Clarkson, Thomas. *The True State of the Case respecting the Insurrection at St. Domingo* (Ipswich, 1792).

Crafton, William Bell. *A short sketch of the evidence delivered before a Committee of the House of Commons for the abolition of the slave trade* (London, 1792).

Cobbett's Parliamentary History, vols 27–9 (1788–92).

Coleridge, Samuel Taylor. *The Watchman* (Bristol, 1796).

Cooper, Thomas. *Considerations on the slave trade and the consumption of West Indian Produce* (London, 1791).

Cooper, Thomas. *Letters on the Slave Trade* (Manchester, 1787).

Cugoano, Ottobah. *Thoughts and Sentiments on the Evil of Slavery*, ed. Vincent Carretta (London, 1787).

Davenant, Charles. *Reflections upon the constitution and management of the trade to Africa* (London, 1709).

Donnan, Elizabeth, ed. *Documents Illustrative of the slave trade to America*, 4 vols (Washington, 1931).

Douglas, Niel. *The African Slave Trade* (Edinburgh, 1792).

Douglas, Niel. *Thoughts on modern politics* (London, 1793).

Edwards, Bryan. *An historical survey of the French colony in the island of St Domingo* (London, 1797).

Equiano, Olaudah. *The Interesting Narrative*, ed. Vincent Carretta (New York, 1995).

Falconbridge, Alexander. *An account of the slave trade on the coast of Africa* (London, 1788).

Finkelman, Paul. *Slavery in the Court Room. An annotated bibliography of American Cases* (Washington DC, 1985).

Foot, Jesse. *A defence of the planters in the West Indies* (London, 1792).

Fox, William. *An address to the people of Great Britain on the propriety of abstaining from West Indian sugar and rum* (London, 1791).

Gregory, George. *Essays Historical and Moral* (London, 1788).

Hargrave. Francis. *An Argument in the Case of James Somersett* (London, 1772).

Holroyd, John Baker, Lord Sheffield. *Observations on the project for abolishing the slave trade* (London, 1790).

[Houlbrooke, Theophilus]. A short address to the people of Scotland on the subject of the slave trade (Edinburgh, 1792).

Houlbrooke, Theophilus. *A short address originally written to the people of Scotland* (Shrewsbury, 1792).

Journals of the House of Commons.

Lambert, Sheila. ed. *House of Commons Sessional Papers of the Eighteenth Century*, 175 vols (Wilmington, DE, 1975).

Leech, Samuel. *Thirty Years from Home, or a Voice from the Lower Deck* (Boston, 1843).

Lewis, David. *A letter to the Reverend Edward Barry, MD* (Bristol 1790).

Lind, James. *An essay on diseases incidental to Europeans in hot climes* (London, 1792).

Mackenzie, Charles. *Notes on Haiti*, 2 vols (London 1830).

Marsom, J. and Ramsay, W. *Trials at Law and Pleadings of Counsel: The King v. Stephen Devereux* (London, 1793).

Marx, Karl. *Manifesto of the Communist Party*, in David Fernbach, ed. *The Revolutions of 1848. Political Writings I*, (Harmondsworth, 1973).

McQueen, James. *The West India Colonies* (London, 1824).

Minchinton, Walter. *Letters of Marque Declarations against America, 1777–1782* (Bristol, 1980).

Hannah More, *Slavery, a Poem* (London, 1788).

More, Hannah. *Thoughts on the importance of the manners of the great to general society* (London, 1799).

Morgan, Kenneth, ed. *The Bright-Meyler Papers: A Bristol-West Indian Connection, 1732–1837* (New York, 2007).

Nagle, Jacob. *The Nagle Journal. A Diary of the Life of Jacob Nagle, sailor, from the year 1775 to 1841*, ed. John C. Dann (New York, 1988).

Newton, John. *Thoughts Upon the African Slave Trade* (London, 1788).

Peake, Thomas. *Cases determined at Nisi Prius, in the court of King's Bench from Easter term, 30 Geo. III to Michaelmas term, 35 Geo III* (3rd ed., London, 1820).

Pope, Alexander. *Works*. 10 vols (London, 1806).

Proceedings of the Hon. House of Assembly of Jamaica on the sugar and slave-trade (London, 1793).

Ramsay, James. *An essay on the treatment and conversion of African slaves* (London, 1785).

Ranby, John. *Observations on the evidence given before the committee of the Privy Council and the House of Commons* (London, 1791).

Report of the Jamaican House of Assembly (London, 1792).

Richardson, David. *Bristol, Africa and the Eighteenth-Century Slave Trade to America. Volume 3, The Years of Decline, 1746–1769* (BRS, 42; Bristol, 1991).

Richardson, David. *Bristol, Africa and the Eighteenth-Century Slave Trade to America. Volume 4, The Final Years, 1770–1807* (BRS, 47; Bristol, 1996).

[Robinson, William.] Jack Nastyface. *Nautical Economy, of Forecastle Recollections of Events during the Last War* (London, 1836).

[Roscoe, William]. *An Inquiry into the Causes of the Insurrection of the Negroes in the Island of St. Domingo* (London, 1792).

Sharp, Granville. *An appendix to the Representation of the injustice and dangerous tendency of tolerating slavery* (London, 1772).

Somerville, Alexander. *Autobiography of a working man* (London, 1848).

Southey, Robert. *Poems* (Bristol, 1797).

Southey, Robert. *Poems*, 2 vols (Bristol, 1799).

Southey, Robert. *Poetical Works*, 15 vols (London 1812–21).

Spavens, William. *The Narrative of William Spavens, a Chelsea Pensioner, By Himself* (1796: London ed., 1998).

Stedman, John Gabriel. *Narrative of a five years' expedition against the revolted Negroes of Surinam*, 2 vols (London, 1796).

The Proceedings on His Majesty's Commission of Oyer and Terminer and Gaol Delivery for the High Court of Admiralty, 9 March 1759 (London 1759).

Thursfield, Rear-Admiral H. G. *Five Naval Journals 1789–1817* (Navy Record Society: London, 1951).

Turnbull, Gordon. *An Apology for Negro Slavery, or the West-India Planters Vindicated* (2nd ed., London, 1786).

Two reports of the Committee of the Assembly in Jamaica on the Slave Trade (London, 1789).

Walpole, Horace. *The Yale Edition of Horace Walpole's Correspondence*, eds C. S. Lewis et al., 42 vols (New Haven, 1961)

Watson, Robert. *The Life of Lord George Gordon* (London, 1795).

Wilberforce, William. *A letter on the abolition of the slave trade* (London, 1807).

Wilberforce, R. I. and S. *The Life of William Wilberforce*, 2 vols (London, 1838).

Winterbotham, William. *The commemoration of national deliverances and the dawning day: two sermons preached November 5th and 18th, 1792* (London, 1792).

Wollstonecraft, Mary. *A Vindication of the Rights of Men* (London, 1790).

Woodall, John. *The Surgions Mate* (London, 1617).

Secondary sources

Books and chapters in books

Alexander, David. *Richard Newton and English Caricature in the 1790s* (Manchester, 1998).

Anderson, Fred. *Crucible of War: The Seven Years' War and the Fate of Empire in British North America, 1754–1766* (New York, 2000).

Anstey, Roger. *The Atlantic Slave Trade and British Abolition 1760–1810* (London, 1975).

Appadurai, Arjun. 'Archive and Aspiration', in *Information is Alive*, eds Joke Brouwer and Arjun Mulder (Rotterdam, 2003), pp. 14–25.

Bannister, Jerry. *The Rule of the Admirals: Law, Custom and Naval Government in Newfoundland, 1699–1832* (Toronto, 2003).

Barthes, Roland. *Camera Lucida: Reflections on Photography*, trans. Richard Howard (New York, 1981).

Baucom, Ian. *Specters of the Atlantic. Finance Capital, Slavery and the Philosophy of History* (Durham, NC and London, 2005).

Baum, Joan. *Mind-Forg'd Manacles. Slavery and the English Romantic Poets* (New Haven, 1994).

Beattie, J. M. *Crime and the Courts in England 1660–1800* (Princeton, 1986).

Beattie, J. M. *The First English Detectives. The Bow Street Runners and the Policing of London, 1750–1840* (Oxford, 2012).

Behrendt, Stephen D. 'Human Capital in the British Slave Trade', in *Liverpool and Transatlantic Slavery*, eds David Richardson et al. (Liverpool, 2007), pp. 66–97.

Behrendt, Stephen D., Latham, J. H. and Northup, David, eds. *The Diary of Antera Duke* (Oxford, 2010).

Bender, Thomas. *The Antislavery Debate. The Antislavery Debate. Capitalism and Abolitionism as a Problem of Historical Interpretation* (Berkeley and Los Angeles, 1992).

Bivens, Stevens. *Living Cargo. How Black Britain Performs Its Past* (Minneapolis and London, 2016).

Blackburn, Robin. *The Overthrow of Colonial Slavery 1776–1848* (London, 1988).

Blackburn, Robin. *The American Crucible. Slavery, Emancipation and Human Rights* (London, 2011).

Bolton, Carol. *Writing the Empire. Robert Southey and the Romantic Imagination* (London, 2014).

Boswell, James. *Life of Johnson*, ed. Augustine Birrell, 4 vols (Boston, 1902).

Breward, Mike. 'Crewing the Slave Trade: The Bristol Ships' Muster Rolls, 1790–1795', in *A City Built Upon the Water, Maritime Bristol*, ed. Steve Poole (Bristol, 2013), pp. 94–113.

Brown, Christopher Leslie. *Moral Capital. Foundations of British Abolitionism* (Williamsburg, 2006).

Burnard, Trevor. *Mastery, Tyranny, & Desire. Thomas Thistlewood and his Slaves in the Anglo-Jamaican World* (Chapel Hill and London, 2004).

Burnard, Trevor. 'Kingston, Jamaica: Crucible of Modernity', in *The Black Urban Atlantic in the Age of the Slave Trade*, eds Jorge Cãnzares-Esquera, Matt D. Childs and James Sidbury (Philadelphia, 2013), pp. 122–46.

Burton, Antoinette et al., eds. *Archive Stories: Facts, Fictions, and the Writing of History* (Durham, NC, 2006).

Byrn, John D., Jr. *Crime and Punishment in the Royal Navy: Discipline on the Leeward Islands Station 1784–1812* (Aldershot,1989).

Byrne, Paula. *Belle. The Slave Daughter and the Lord Chief Justice* (New York, 2014).

Bush, Barbara. *Slave Women in Caribbean Society 1650–1838* (Kingston, Jamaica, 1990).

Carey, Brycchan. *British Abolitionism and the Rhetoric of Sensibility. Writing, Sentiment and Slavery, 1760–1807* (London, 2005).

Christopher, Emma. *Slave Ship Sailors and their Captive Cargoes 1730–1807* (Cambridge, 2006).

Christopher, Emma. '"The Slave Trade is Merciful Compared to [This]": Slave Traders, Convict Transportation, and the Abolitionists', in *Many Middle Passages. Forced Migration and the Making of the Modern World*, eds Emma Christopher, Cassandra Phybus and Marcus Rediker (Berkeley and Los Angeles, 2007), pp. 120–39.

Clendinnen, Inga. *Dancing with Strangers: Europeans and Australians at First Contact* (Cambridge, 2005).

Clowes, Sir William Laird. *The Royal Navy*, 6 vols (London, 1897–1903).

Coughtry Jay. *The Notorious Triangle: Rhode Island and the African Slave Trade, 1700–1807* (Philadelphia, 1981).

Coupland, Reginald. *Wilberforce* (Oxford, 1923).

Craton, Michael and Walvin, James. *A Jamaican Plantation. The History of Worthy Park 1670–1970* (Toronto, 1970).

Craton, Michael. *Testing the Chains: Resistance to Slavery in the British West Indies* (Ithaca, NY, 1982).

Cutter, Martha. *The Illustrated Slave* (Athens, GA, 2017).

Davis, David Brion. *The Problem of Slavery in the Age of Revolution, 1770–1823* (Ithaca and London, 1975).

Dening, Greg. *History's Anthropology. The Death of William Gooch* (Lanham, MD, 1988).

Dening, Greg. *Mr Bligh's Bad Language. Passion, Power and Theatre on the Bounty* (Cambridge, 1992).

Dening, Greg. *Performances* (Chicago, 1996).

Dow, George F. *Slave Ships and Slaving* (New York, 2002).

Dozier, Robert. *For King, Constitution and Country* (Lexington, KY, 1983).

Drescher, Seymour. 'The Atlantic Slave Trade and the Holocaust: A Comparative Analysis', in I*s the Holocaust Unique? Perspectives on Comparative Genocide*, ed. Alan S. Rosenbaum (New York, 1969), pp. 65–85.

Drescher, Seymour. *Capitalism and Anti-slavery* (London, 1986).

Drescher, Seymour. *Econocide. British Slavery in the Era of Abolition* (Durham, NC, 2010).

Dresser, Madge. *Slavery Obscured. The Social History of the Slave Trade in an English Provincial Port* (London and New York, 2001).

Dubois, Laurent. *Avengers of the New World. The Story of the Haitian Revolution* (Cambridge, MA, 2004).

Duffy, Michael. 'The French Revolution and British Attitudes to the West Indian Colonies', in *A Turbulent Time. The French Revolution and the Greater Caribbean*, eds D. B. Gaspar and D.P. Geggus (Bloomington, IN, 1997), pp. 78–101.

Dumas, Paula E. *Proslavery Britain: Fighting for Slavery in an Era of Abolition* (Basingstoke, 2016).

Durston, Gregory. *The Admiralty Sessions, 1536–1834. Maritime Crime and the Silver Oar* (Cambridge, 2017).

Eastwood, David. 'Patriotism and the English State in the 1790s', in *The French Revolution and British Popular Politics*, ed. Mark Philp (Cambridge, 1991), pp. 146–68.

Edwards, Paul and Walvin, James. *Black Personalities in the Era of the Slave Trade* (Baton Rouge, 1983).

Eltis, David. *The Rise of African Slavery in the Americas* (Cambridge, 2000).

Epstein, James. 'Sermons of Sedition. The Trials of William Winterbotham', in *Political Trials in the Age of Revolutions*, eds Michael T. Davis et al. (London, 2019), pp. 103–36.

Favret, Mary. 'Flogging: The Anti-Slavery Movement Writes Pornography', in *Essays and Studies 1998: Romanticism and Gender*, ed. Anne Janowitz (Cambridge, 1998), pp. 19–43.

Fede, Andrew T. *People Without Rights* (New York and London, 1992).

Fede, Andrew T. *Homicide Justified. The Legality of Killing Slaves in the United States and the Atlantic World* (Athens, GA, 2017).

Fergus, Claudius K. *Revolutionary Emancipation. Slavery and Abolition in the British West Indies* (Baton Rouge, 2013).

Finkelman, Paul. *The Law of Freedom and Bondage: A Case Book* (New York, 1986).

Fogel, Robert William and Engerman, Stanley L. *Time on the Cross. The Economics of American Negro Slavery* (Boston, 1974).

Fryer, Peter. *Staying Power. The History of Black People in Britain* (London, 1985).

Fuentes, Marisa. *Dispossessed Lives: Enslaved Women, Violence and the Archive* (Philadelphia, 2006).

Gaspar, David Barry. 'La Guerre des Bois: Revolution, War and Slavery in Saint Lucia, 1793–1838', in *A Turbulent Time. The French Revolution and the Great Caribbean*, eds D. B. Gaspar and David Patrick Geggus (Bloomington, IN, 1997), pp. 102–30.

Geggus, David P. *Slavery, War and Revolution. The British Occupation of Saint Domingue 1793–1798* (Oxford, 1982).

Geggus, David P. 'British Opinion and the Emergence of Haiti, 1791–1805', in *Slavery and British Society 1776–1846*, ed. James Walvin (London, 1982), pp. 123–49.

Geggus, David P. 'Sugar and Coffee in Saint Domingue', in *Cultivation and Culture. Labor and the Shaping of Slave Life in the Americas*, eds Ira Berlin and Philip D. Morgan (Charlottesville, VA and London, 1993), pp. 73–98.

Geggus, David. P. 'Slavery, War, and Revolution in the Great Caribbean, 1789–1815', in *A Turbulent Time. The French Revolution and the Greater Caribbean* (Bloomington, IN, 1997), pp. 1–50.

Geggus, David P. *Haitian Revolutionary Studies* (Bloomington and Indianapolis, IN, 2002).

Ginzburg, Carlo. *The Cheese and the Worms. The Cosmos of a Sixteenth-Century Miller*, trans. John and Anne C. Tedeschi (Baltimore, 1982).

Goveia, Elsa V. *Slave Society in the British Leeward Islands at the End of the Eighteenth Century* (New Haven, CT and London, 1965).

Greenblatt, Stephen. *Marvelous Possessions* (Chicago, 1991).

Greenhill, Basil and Nix, Michael. 'North Devon Shipping, Trade and Ports 1786–1939', in *The New Maritime History of Devon*, 2 vols, ed. Michael Duffy et al. (London, 1994), 2:48–59.

Griggs, Earl Leslie. *Thomas Clarkson. The Friend of Slaves* (London, 1936).

Gutman, Herbert G. *Slavery and the Numbers Game* (Urbana and Chicago, 1975).

Hamilton, Douglas and Blyth, Robert J., eds. *Representing Slavery* (London, 2007).

Harrison, Mark. *Crowds and History* (Cambridge, 1988).

Hartman, Saidiya. *Lose Your Mother* (New York, 2007).

Hay, Douglas. 'Property, Authority and the Criminal Law', in Douglas Hay et al., *Albion's Fatal Tree. Crime and Society in Eighteenth-Century England* (London, 1975), p. 17–64.

Hay, Douglas, and Rogers, Nicholas. *Eighteenth-Century English Society. Shuttles and Swords* (Oxford, 1997).

Hempton, David. 'Popular Evangelicalism and the Shaping of British Moral Sensibilities, 1770–1840', in *British Abolitionism and the Question of Moral Progress in History*, ed. Donald A. Yerxa (Columbia, SC, 2012), pp. 50–80.

Hoare, Prince. *Memoirs of Granville Sharp*, 2 vols (London, 1820).

Hochschild, Adam. *Bury the Chains* (Boston, 2005).

Honychurch, Lennox. *In the Forests of Freedom. The Fighting Maroons of Dominica* (London, 2017).

Hörmann, Raphael. 'Black Jacobin: Towards a Genealogy of a Transatlantic Trope', in *Transatlantic Revolutionary Cultures 1789–1861*, eds Charlotte Lerg and Heléna Tóth (Leiden and Boston, 2018), pp. 19–49.

Hulme, Peter. *Colonial Encounters. Europe and the Native Caribbean 1492–1797* (London and New York, 1986).

Hunt, Lynn. 'The Paradoxical Origins of Human Rights', in *Human Rights and Revolutions*, eds Jeffrey N. Wasserstrom et al. (Lanham, MD, 2007), 3–21.

Inikori, Joseph E. *Africans and the Industrial Revolution in England: A Study in International Trade and Development* (Cambridge, 2002).

Klein, Herbert S. *The Middle Passage. Comparative Studies in the Atlantic Slave Trade* (Princeton, 1969).

Latimer, John. *Annals of Bristol*, 3 vols (Bristol 1893, Bath reprint 1970).

Levi, Giovanni. 'On Microhistory', in *New Perspectives in Historical Writing*, ed. Peter Burke (University Park, PA, 1997), pp. 97–119.

Levine, David and Wrightson, Keith. *Poverty and Piety in an English Village: Terling, 1525–1700* (Oxford and New York, 1979).

Linebaugh, Peter and Rediker, Marcus. *The Many Headed Hydra* (Boston, MA, 2001).

Lovejoy Paul E. and Richardson, David. 'African Agency and the Liverpool Slave Trade', in *Liverpool and Transatlantic Slavery*, eds David Richardson et al. (Liverpool, 2007), pp. 43–65.

Malcomson, Thomas, *Order and Disorder in the British Navy* (Woodbridge, 2016).

Mannix, Daniel P. with Cowley, Malcolm. *Black Cargoes. A History of the Atlantic Slave Trade 1518–1865* (New York, 1962).

Marshall, Peter. 'The Anti-Slave Trade Movement in Bristol', in *Bristol in the Eighteenth Century*, ed. Patrick McGrath (Newton Abbot, 1972), pp. 185–215.

Martinez, Jenny S. *The Slave Trade and the Origins of International Human Rights Law* (Oxford, 2012).

McCahill, M. W. *The Correspondence of Stephen Fuller 1788-1795: Jamaica, the West India Interest at Westminster and the Campaign to Preserve the Slave Trade* (London, 2014).

Midgley, Clare. *Women Against Slavery. The British Campaigns 1780–1870* (London and New York, 1992).

Morgan, Kenneth. *A Short History of Transatlantic Slavery* (London, 2016).

Morris, Rosalind, ed. *Can the Subaltern Speak? Reflections on the History of an Idea* (New York, 2010).

Muir, Edward. 'Introduction: Observing Trifles', in *Microhistory and the Lost Peoples of Europe*, eds Edward Muir and Guido Ruggerio (Baltimore, 1991), pp. vii–xxviii.

Neale, R. S. *Bath, 1660–1850: A Social History* (London, 1981).

Nora, Pierre. 'The Return of the Event', in *Histories, French Constructions of the Past*, eds Jacques Revel and Lynn Hunt (New York, 1995), pp. 427–36.

O'Gorman, Frank. 'Manchester Loyalism in the 1790s', in *Return to Peterloo*, ed. Robert Poole (Manchester 2014), pp. 19–32.

Oldfield, J. R. *Popular Politics and British Anti-Slavery* (London, 1998).

Paley, Ruth 'After Somerset: Mansfield, Slavery and the Law in England, 1772–1830', in *Law, Crime and English Society 1660–1830*, ed. Norma Landau (Cambridge, 2002), pp. 165–84.

Parolin, Christina. *Radical Spaces. Venues of Popular Politics in London, 1790–1845* (Canberra, 2010).

Patterson, Orlando. *Slavery and Social Death: A Comparative Study* (Cambridge, MA, 1982).

Pinfold, John, ed. *The Slave Trade Debate. Contemporary Writings For and Against* (Oxford, 2007).

Poole, Steve and Rogers, Nicholas. *Bristol From Below* (Woodbridge, 2016).

Popkin, Jeremy D. *You Are All Free. The Haitian Revolution and the Abolition of Slavery* (New York, 2010).

Porter, Dale H. *The Abolition of the Slave Trade in England 1784–1807* (Ann Arbor, MI, 1970).

Powell, J. W. Damer. *Bristol Privateers and Ships of War* (Bristol, 1930).

Price, Jacob. 'Credit in the Slave Trade and Plantation Economies', in *Slavery and the Rise of the Atlantic System*, ed. Barbara L. Soltow (Cambridge, 1991), pp. 293–339.

Randall, Adrian. *Before the Luddites* (Cambridge, 1991).

Rawley James A. [with Behrendt, Stephen D.] *The Transatlantic Slave Trade* (Lincoln, NE and London, 2005).

Rediker, Marcus. *The Slave Ship. A Human History* (New York, 2007).

Richardson, David. 'Consuming Goods, Consuming People. Reflections on the Transatlantic Slave Trade', in *The Rise and Demise of Slavery and the Slave Trade in the Atlantic World*, eds Philip Misevich and Kristin Mann (Rochester, NY, 2016), pp. 31–63.

Roberts William. *Memoirs of the Life and Correspondence of Mrs. Hannah More*, 2 vols (New York, 1834).

Rodger, N. A. M. *The Wooden World* (London, 1988).

Rodger, N. A. M. 'Devon and the Royal Navy, 1689–1815' in *New Maritime History of Devon*, eds Michael Duffy et al., 2 vols (London, 1994), 1:209–15.

Rogers, Nicholas. *The Press Gang* (London, 2007).

Sam, Genuine Dicky. *Liverpool and Slavery. An Historical Account of the Liverpool-African Slave Trade* (Liverpool, 1884).

Scanlan, Padraic X. *Freedom's Debtors. British Antislavery in Sierra Leone in the Age of Revolution* (New Haven, 2017).

Schama, Simon. *Rough Crossings. Britain, the Slaves and the American Revolution* (London, 2005).

Schwarz, Suzanne. 'Commerce, Civilization and Christianity: The Development of the Sierra Leone Company', in *Liverpool and Transatlantic Slavery*, eds David Richardson et al. (Liverpool, 2007), pp. 252–76.

Sheridan, Richard. 'Slave Demography in the British West Indies and the Abolition of the Slave Trade', in *The Abolition of the Atlantic Slave Trade*, eds David Eltis and James Walvin (Madison, WI, 1981), pp. 259–85.

Sheridan, Richard. *Doctors and Slaves. A Medical and Demographic History of Slavery in the British West Indies, 1680–1834* (London and New York, 1985).

Shyllon F. O. *Black Slaves in Britain* (London, 1974).

Smallwood, Stephanie. *Saltwater Slavery* (Cambridge, MA, 2007).

Sparks, Randy J. *The Two Princes of Calabar: An Eighteenth-Century Atlantic Odyssey* (Cambridge, MA, 2004).

Spivak, Gayatri. 'Can the Subaltern Speak?' in G. Spivak, *A Critique of Postcolonial Reason: Towards a History of the Vanishing Present* (Cambridge, 1999), pp. 241–311.

Starkey, David J. *British Privateering Enterprise in the Eighteenth Century* (Exeter, 1990).

Stoler, Ann Laura. *Along the Archival Grain. Epistemic Anxieties and Colonial Common Sense* (Princeton, 2010).

Straub Kristina. 'The Tortured Apprentice: Sexual Monstrosity and the Suffering of Poor Children in the Brownrigg Murder Case', in *Monstrous Dreams of Reason*, eds Laura Rosenthal and Mita Choudhury (London, 2002), pp. 66–81.

Sugden, John. Nelson. *A Dream of Glory* (London, 2004).

Thomas, Hugh. *The Slave Trade* (London, 1998).

Thompson, E. P. *The Making of the English Working Class* (London, 1963).

Thompson, E. P. *Customs in Common* (London and New York, 1991).

Thompson, Katrina Dyonne. *Ring Shout, Wheel About. The Racial Politics of Music and Dance in North American Slavery* (Urbana, Chicago, Springfield, 2014).

Thorne, R. G. ed. *The History of Parliament: The House of Commons, 1790–1820* (London, 1986).

Tibbles, Anthony. *Liverpool and the Slave Trade* (Liverpool, 2018).

Walvin, James. 'Abolishing the Slave Trade: Anti-Slavery and Popular Radicalism, 1776-1807', in *Artisans, Peasants & Proletarians 1760–1860*, eds Clive Emsley and James Walvin (London, 1985), pp. 32–56.

Walvin, James, *Black Ivory. Slavery in the British Empire* (New York, 2001).

Walvin, James. *The Zong. A Massacre, the Law and the End of Slavery* (New Haven, 2011).

Ward, J. R. *British West Indian Slavery 1750–1834* (Oxford, 1988).
Williams, Gomer. *History of the Liverpool Privateers* (Liverpool, 1897),
Wilson, Ellen Gibson. *John Clarkson and the African Adventure* (London, 1980).
Wilson, Ellen Gibson. *Thomas Clarkson: A Biography* (Basingstoke, 1989).
Wilson, Kathleen. *The Island Race. Englishness, Empire and Gender in the Eighteenth Century* (London and New York, 2003).
Wood, Marcus. *Blind Memory. Visual Representations of Slavery in England and America 1780–1865* (Manchester, 2000).
Wood, Marcus. *Slavery, Empathy and Pornography* (Oxford, 2002).
Wrightson, Keith. *Ralph Taylor's Summer. A Scrivener, His City and the Plague* (New Haven, 2011).

Articles

Baule, Steven and Hagist, Don. 'The Regimental Punishment Book of the Boston Detachments of the Royal Irish Regiment and 65th regiment 1774–5', *Journal of the Society for Army Research*, 88 (2010), 5–18.
Behrendt, Stephen D. 'The Captains in the British Slave Trade from 1785 to 1807', *Trans. Historical Society of Lancashire and Cheshire*, 140 (1991), 79–140.
Behrendt, Stephen D. 'The Annual Volume and Regional Distribution of the British Slave Trade, 1780–1807', *Journal of African History*, 38 (1997), 187–211.
Benton, Lauren. 'Abolition and Imperial Law, 1790–1820', *Journal of Imperial and Commonwealth History*, 39/3 (Sept. 2011), 355–74.
Benton, Lauren. '"This Melancholy Labyrinth": The Trial of Arthur Hodge and the Boundaries of Imperial Law', *Alabama Law Review*, 64 (2012), 91–122.
Brewer, John. 'Microhistory and the Histories of Everyday Life', *Cultural and Social History*, 7/1 (2010), 87–109.
Carretta, Vincent. 'Olaudah Equiano or Gustavus Vasa? New Light on an Eighteenth-Century Question of Identity', *Slavery and Abolition*, 20/3 (1999), 95–105.
Cohen, Raymond. 'Deaths of Slaves in the Middle Passage', *Journal of Economic History*, 45/3 (1985), 685–92.
Cotter, William R. 'The Somerset Case and the Abolition of Slavery in England', *History*, 79/255 (1994), 31–56.

Drescher, Seymour. 'People and Parliament: the Rhetoric of the British Slave Trade', *Journal of Interdisciplinary History*, 20/4 (1990), 561–80.

Drescher, Seymour. 'Public Opinion and Parliament in the Abolition of the British Slave Trade', *Parliamentary History*, 26 supplement (2007), 42–65.

Drescher, Seymour. 'History's Engines: British Mobilization in the Age of Revolution', *William and Mary Quarterly*, 66/4 (Oct. 2009), 737–56.

Eltis, David. 'Mortality and Voyage in the Middle Passage: New Evidence from the Nineteenth Century', *Journal of Economic History*, 44/2 (1984), 301–8.

Eltis, David and Engerman, Stanley L. 'Was the Slave Trade Dominated by Men?' *Journal of Interdisciplinary History*, 23/2 (1992), 237–57.

Eltis, David, and Richardson, David, 'Productivity in the Transatlantic Slave Trade', *Explorations in Economic History*, 32/4 (1995), 465–84.

Engerman, Stanley. 'The Slave Trade and British Capital Formation in the Eighteenth Century', *Business History Review*, 46 (1972), 430–43.

Fissell, Mary E. 'The "Sick and Drooping Poor" in Eighteenth-Century Bristol and Its Region', *Social History of Medicine*, 2/1 (1989), 35–58.

Geggus, David. 'The British Government and the Saint Domingue Slave Revolt, 1791–1793', *English Historical Review*, 96/376 (April, 1981), 285–305.

Geggus, David. 'The French and Haitian Revolutions and Resistance to Slavery in the New World: An Overview', *Revue Française d'Histoire d'Outre-Mer*, 282/3 (1989) 102–24.

Glover, Jeffrey. 'Witnessing African War: Slavery, the Laws of War and Anglo-American Abolitionism', *William and Mary Quarterly*, 74/3 (2017), 503–32.

Goodrich, Amanda. 'Radical "Citizens of the World", 1790–1795. The Early Career of Henry Redhead Yorke', *Journal of British Studies*, 53 (July 2014), 611–35.

Gould, Eliga H. 'Zones of Law, Zones of Violence: The Legal Geography of the British Atlantic, circa 1772', *William and Mary Quarterly*, 60/3 (2003), 471–510.

Hall, Douglas. 'Absentee Proprietorship in the West Indies, to about 1850', *Jamaican Historical Review*, 4 (1964), 15–35.

Haltttunen, Karen. 'Humanitarianism and the Pornography of Pain in Anglo-American Culture', *American Historical Review*, 100/2 (1995), 303–34.

Handler, J. S. 'Survivors of the Middle Passage: Life Histories of Enslaved Africans in British America', *Slavery and Abolition*, 23/1 (2002), 25–56.

Hartman, Saidiya. 'Venus in Two Acts', *Small Axe*, 12/2 (June 2008), 1–14.

Holman, J. R. 'Orphans in Pre-Industrial Towns – The Case of Bristol in the Late Seventeenth Century', *Local Population Studies*, 15 (Autumn 1975), 40–4.

Jackman, Alexander. 'Judging a Judge: A Reappraisal of Lord Mansfield and the Somerset Case', *Journal of Legal History*, 39/2 (2018), 140–56.

Langholm, Sivert. 'On the Scope of Micro-history', *Scandinavian Journal of History*, 1/1 (1976), 3–24.

LoGerfo, James W. 'Sir William Dolben and "The Cause of Humanity": The Passage of the Slave Trade Regulation Act of 1788', *Eighteenth-Century Studies*, 6/4 (Summer, 1973), 431–51.

Lovejoy, Paul E. 'Autobiography and Memory: Gustavus Vasa alias Olaudah Equiano, the African', *Slavery and Abolition*, 27/3 (2006), 317–47.

Lovejoy, Paul E. 'Pawnship, Debt and "Freedom" in Atlantic Africa During the Era of the Slave Trade: A Re-assessment', *Journal of African History*, 55 (2014), 55–78.

Lovejoy, Paul E. and Richardson, David. 'Trust, Pawnship and Atlantic History: The Institutional Foundations of the Old Calabar Slave Trade', *American Historical Review*, 104/2 (1999), 333–55.

Lovejoy, Paul E. and Richardson, David. '"This Horrid Hole": Royal Authority, Commerce and Credit at Bonny, 1690–1840', *Journal of African History*, 45 (2004), 363–92.

Marshall, Bernard A. 'Maronage in Slave Plantation Societies: A Case Study of Dominica 1785–815', *Caribbean Quarterly*, 54/4 (2008), 103–10.

Mitchell, Austin. 'The Association Movement of 1792–3', *Historical Journal*, 4/1 (1961), 56–77.

Mitchell, Brigitte. 'The Debate in Parliament about the Abolition of Flogging During the Early Nineteenth century, with References to the Windsor Garrison', *Journal Society of Army Research*, 88 (2010) 19–28.

Morgan, Sir Clifford N. 'Surgery and Surgeons in Eighteenth-Century London', *Annals of the Royal College of Surgeons of England* (1967), 1–37.

Morgan, Kenneth. 'Shipping Patterns and the Atlantic Trade of Bristol', *William and Mary Quarterly*, 46/3 (1989), 506–38.

Morgan, Kenneth. 'Bristol West India Merchants in the Eighteenth Century', *Trans. Royal Historical Society*, 3 (1993), 183–208.

Munford Clarence J. and Zeuske, Michael. 'Black Slavery, Class Struggle, Fear and Revolution in St. Domingue and Cuba, 1785–1795', *Journal of Negro Slavery*, 73/1 (Winter–Autumn 1988), 12–32.

O'Gorman, Frank. 'The Paine Burnings of 1792–1793', *Past and Present*, 193/1 (November 2006), 111–55.

Oldham, James. 'New Light on Mansfield and Slavery', *Journal of British Studies*, 27/1 (1988), 45–68.

Oldham, James. 'Insurance Litigation Involving the *Zong* and Other British Slave Ships, 1780–1807', *Journal of Legal History*, 28/3 (Dec. 2007), 299–318.

Paton, Diana. 'Decency, Dependency and the Lash: Gender and the British Debate over Slave Emancipation, 1830–34', *Slavery and Abolition*, 17 (1996) 162–84.

Richardson, David. 'Shipboard Revolts, African Authority and the Slave Trade', *William and Mary Quarterly*, 58/1 (2001), 69–92.

Richardson, David. 'Slavery and Bristol's "Golden Age"', *Slavery and Abolition*, 26/1 (April 2005), 35–54.

Rogers, Nicholas. 'Burning Tom Paine: Loyalism and Counter-Revolution in Britain, 1792–1793', *Histoire sociale/Social History*, 32/64 (Nov. 1999), 139–71.

Rupprecht, Anita. '"A Very Uncommon Case": Representations of the *Zong* and the British Campaign to Abolish the Slave Trade', *Journal of Legal History*, 28/3 (Dec. 2007) 329–46.

Schofield, R. S. 'Dimensions of Illiteracy, 1750–1850', *Explorations in Economic History*, 10 (1973), 437–54.

Sheridan, Richard. 'The Commercial and Financial Organization of the British Slave Trade, 1750–1807', *Economic History Review*, 11 (1958–9), 249–63.

Sparks, Randy J. 'Two Princes of Calabar: An Atlantic Odyssey from Slavery to Freedom', *William and Mary Quarterly*, 59/3 (2002), 555–84.

Stein, Robert. 'The Free Men of Colour and the Revolution in St. Domingue, 1789–1792', *Histoire sociale/Social History*, 14 (1981), 7–28.

Swaminathan, Srividhya. 'Reporting Atrocities: A Comparison of the *Zong* and the Trial of Captain John Kimber', *Slavery and Abolition*, 31/4 (Dec. 2010), 483–99.

Sweet, James H. 'Mistaken Identities? Olaudah Equiano, Domingos Álavres, and the Methodological Challenges of Studying the African Diaspora', *American Historical Review*, 114/2 (April 2009), 279–306.

Thompson, E. P. 'Time, Work-Discipline and Industrial Capitalism', *Past and Present*, 50 (1971), 56–97.

Underwood, Patrick, Pfaff, Steven and Hechter, Michael. 'Threat, Deterrence, and Penal Severity: An Analysis of Flogging in the Royal Navy 1740–1820', *Social Science History*, 42 (Fall, 2018), 411–39.

Wahrman, Dror. 'Virtual Representation: Parliamentary Reporting and the Language of Class in the 1790s', *Past and Present*, 136 (1992), 83–113.

Webster, Jane. 'The *Zong* in the Context of the Eighteenth-century Slave Trade', *Journal of Legal History*, 28/3 (Dec. 2007), 285–98.

Wiecek, William M. 'Somerset: Lords Mansfield and the Legitimacy of Slavery in the Anglo-American World', *University of Chicago Law Review*, 42/1 (1974), 86–146.

Unpublished dissertations

Glasco, Jeffrey Duane. '"We are a Neglected Set": Masculinity, Mutiny and Revolution in the Royal Navy of 1797' (unpublished PhD dissertation, University of Arizona, 2001).

Lorentz, Gerald Francis. 'Bristol Fashion: The Maritime Culture of Bristol 1650–1700' (unpublished PhD dissertation, University of Toronto, 1997).

Nix, Michael. 'The Maritime History of the Ports of Bideford and Barnstaple, 1786–1841' (unpublished PhD thesis, University of Leicester, 1991).

Wood, Madeline Joy. 'Captain Cupit's Boy: Slavery, Crime and the Courts in the 18th century British Atlantic' (unpublished PhD Dissertation, University of Calgary, 2014).

Index